Mattie C's Boy

ALSO BY DON KEITH

The Forever Season

Wizard of the Wind

The Rolling Thunder Stockcar Racing Series (with Kent Wright)

Final Bearing (with George Wallace)

Gallant Lady (with Ken Henry)

In the Course of Duty

The Bear: the Legendary Life of Coach Paul "Bear" Bryant

Final Patrol

The Ice Diaries (with Captain William R. Anderson)

War Beneath the Waves

We Be Big (with Rick Burgess and Bill "Bubba" Bussey)

Undersea Warrior

Firing Point (with George Wallace)

Riding the Shortwaves: Exploring the Magic of Amateur Radio

The Last Christmas Ride (with Edie Hand)

The Soldier's Ride (with Edie Hand)

The Christmas Ride: the Miracle of the Lights (with Edie Hand)

The Spin

On the Road to Kingdom Come

MATTIE C's BOY—

the SHELLEY STEWART story

BY

DON KEITH

AS TOLD BY SHELLEY STEWART

NewSouth Books

Montgomery

NewSouth Books
105 S. Court Street
Montgomery, AL 36104

Copyright © 2013 by Don Keith and Shelley Stewart.
All rights reserved under International and Pan-American Copyright Conventions.
Published in the United States by NewSouth Books, a division of NewSouth, Inc.,
Montgomery, Alabama.

Library of Congress Cataloging-in-Publication Data

Keith, Don.
Mattie C.'s boy : the Shelley Stewart story /
by Don Keith as told by Shelley Stewart.
pages cm
Includes index.

ISBN: 978-1-60306-313-5 (hardcover)
ISBN: 978-1-60306-314-2 (ebook)

1. Stewart, Shelley, 1934– 2. Radio broadcasters—United States—Biography.
3. African American radio broadcasters—Biography.
I. Stewart, Shelley, 1934– II. Title.
PN1991.4.S84K36 2013
791.4402′8092—dc23
[B]

2013023738

Book design by Randall Williams
Title page and chapter titles typography illustrations by Rob Hardison

Printed in the United States of America

Contents

One by one their seats were emptied.
One by one they went away.
Now the family is parted.
Will it be complete one day?

Will the circle be unbroken
By and by, by and by?
Is a better home awaiting
In the sky, in the sky?

— FROM "WILL THE CIRCLE BE UNBROKEN?"

~~~~~~~~~~~~~~

The real estate agent was having a difficult time keeping up with his client, a tall, well-dressed black man.

"Mr. Stewart! Mr. Stewart! I wanted to first show you . . ."

But Mr. Stewart was already at the far end of the huge, wall-less office space. Straight off the elevator he had made a beeline for the northwest corner of the swank building's second floor. He stopped there, hands resting on the dusty windowsill. He stared through the smudged window past his own reflection, gazing down at the parking lot below, the ornate landscaped entranceway coming from the street, and a stand of trees.

When the agent caught up, he was surprised to see that his client was crying. Big tears rolled down each cheek. The agent paused, cleared his throat, and finally spoke.

"I am so sorry, Mr. Stewart. Did I do something wrong?"

Stewart touched the glass, pointing.

"There used to be a lake down there way before you were born, right below where we are standing," the tall man said, speaking so quietly the agent had to strain to hear the words. "Edgewood Lake. There was a cable somebody had hung in a big tree over yonder and you could swing across the lake to get to the other side if you wanted to. Bubba and I, we used to catch catfish right down there. Not for fun, mind you. We caught them because we were hungry and we didn't have anything else to eat. We fried those fish up and ate them, sitting right over yonder next to the highway. Took some back for our younger brothers, Sam and David, too. They were hungry as we were. See, I was born just over that hill there in a white family's house where my momma worked."

The agent did not know what to say. He stood, uncomfortably rocking from heel to toe.

"I'll take it!" Stewart said, so firmly and suddenly it startled the real estate man.

"But Mr. Stewart, we haven't even talked about build-out or . . ."

"I'll take it!" Stewart turned to face the agent, unashamed of the tears that still fell from his eyes. "And my office will be right here, this corner, where the lake bank used to be."

Most potential lessees—especially big and powerful ones, like Mr. Stewart—haggled over every nuance of a deal, and the bigger the space, the larger the deal, the more detailed the negotiation. This was the first time the agent's client had been to this property. There had been little discussion of terms.

"Then we'll firm up the details and get the agreement drawn up, sir," the man told Stewart. "Thank you, sir. Thank you very much."

Stewart stood there a few moments, dabbing at his eyes with a well-used tissue he had retrieved from his jacket pocket. He again surveyed the view below.

"No, I want to thank you, young man," he finally said. "Now I have to go over to Grace Hill. I got to tell Mattie C. something. You know what I got to tell her?"

"No, Mr. Stewart. I don't."

The tall man smiled.

"Momma, the circle is finally complete."

MATTIE C.'S BOY

PRologue

Wide-eyed and helpless, the boy watched his daddy murder his momma with an ax.

The boy and his older brother cried, begging their daddy not to hurt her. Slim Stewart was drunk, though. He paid no attention to his boys' pleas. He did not care that they were watching. It happened so quickly, and he was so strong and mad and mean, it was over in only a few minutes.

At first, the fight between their parents seemed no different from all the others the boys had witnessed. It was a regular thing. They were outside playing when they saw their daddy striding purposefully up the hill toward them. As usual, he was weaving a bit, talking out loud to himself. They knew he was most likely coming from Miss Martha's shot house down on the corner. The joint sold untaxed and illegal homebrew whiskey by the drink. That was Huell "Slim" Stewart's beverage of choice. The boys had seen their daddy down there plenty of times, usually as they walked alongside their mother on her way to her maid's job at the white folks' house. Other times, too, when the brothers wandered the neighborhood seeking adventure. If Slim ever noticed his wife and sons passing by the joint or his other two baby boys tucked into the carriage she pushed, he gave no sign.

The boys knew, though, that if he was coming from Miss Martha's, he would be in his usual foul mood. That also meant he was dangerously, violently drunk.

Shurley, the younger boy, looked at his brother. Bubba was seven and often took charge in such situations.

"Shurley, we better go tell Momma Daddy's coming," the older brother said. They ran to the house as quickly as they could.

Mattie C. was inside the airless little shack, cooking Sunday dinner, ironing clothes, working as usual. Also as usual, as she worked she loudly and proudly sang her favorite gospel songs—"Precious Lord, Take my Hand." "Were You There when They Crucified My Lord?" "Will the Circle Be Unbroken?"—in a clear, pretty voice.

She hushed her singing when her boys burst through the door.

"Daddy's coming up the street," Bubba told her. "He's drunk."

A cloud passed over her face as she set her jaw. Slim Stewart did not often show up at their home anymore. He usually hung around the alleys and streets within a few blocks of where his wife and kids lived. Even so, days would pass without him coming home. When he did, it was typically a Sunday, after he had drunk up or gambled away his odd-job wages.

Mattie C. braced herself. She knew exactly what to expect. Slim would be mad, half-crazy from the rot-gut whiskey, the only kind he could afford to buy. She knew exactly what he wanted from her as well. He had certainly been gambling. He had lost what little money he earned from the meager jobs he took when he got hungry. Or, more likely, thirsty.

Sure enough, "Mattie, give me some money," was the first thing he said when he burst through the screen door. The words were slurred and irate. The slam of the door punctuated his command.

"Huell, you know I ain't got no money," she told him. Mattie C. stood behind the ironing board and the stack of freshly pressed clothes, starched and still warm from her iron. The aroma of frying chicken and boiling greens filled the house. Bluster was all the protection she had from him and his drunken rages. That usually worked. "What little money I got I need for food for me and the boys. And for the insurance policy."

Shurley and Bubba stood there, watching, scared. Their younger brothers, Sam and David, thankfully were asleep in their bed on the other side of the shack.

Mattie C. had only one strategy. Maybe she could bluff her way through, convince him she was not going to give him any money this time. Then he would storm out of the house, back out into the August heat to sober up, to find some dice money somewhere else and leave them alone for a while. Then again, he usually slapped her around some first.

"I done told you woman, give me some goddamn money."

"And Huell, I done told you . . ."

Slim slapped her hard across the face with the back of his big hand. She stumbled backward, hand pressed to her lower lip that instantly spurted blood. He shoved away the ironing board, sending the clothes flying all over the cramped room. He grabbed her in his strong arms.

Somehow, she broke away and darted down the hallway. There was something different in her eyes this time. Usually it was a blow or two and he was gone at the first sight of blood. Now she was afraid of Slim.

The passage led toward the tiny place's back bedroom. That was the only direction away from his fists. Her flight also drew her crazy husband away from her boys. She might even be able to get out the lone window in the room, but the back of the house sat on the side of a steep hill, almost in the treetops. It was a long way down to the ground back there.

"Daddy, don't hurt her!" Shurley and Bubba both pleaded, still crying. "Don't hurt Momma!"

For a moment, Shurley thought their appeals might be working. Slim did not immediately follow Mattie C. down the hallway. Instead, he took two steps into what passed for a kitchen. There he picked up the ax Mattie C. kept to break up whatever wood they could scrounge for cooking and for heat in the winter. Slim knew it would be leaning against the wall behind the wood-burning stove where the greens still boiled and the chicken sizzled in hot grease.

"Don't hit Momma!" the boys yelled in unison. They followed him down the hallway. Even they sensed their father's rage had hit a new plateau this time.

Mattie C. stood near the rear window, open to try to capture a stray breeze. She feared Slim would not be satisfied with simply bloodying her nose or busting her lip this time. He probably owed a dice debt to somebody who was meaner than he was.

"Huell, don't hurt me," she told him, trying to conjure up the strength to sound threatening, even as blood streamed down her chin. He glared at her, his eyes wild and hateful. Then he glanced back at Shurley and Bubba, standing there watching him, terror on their young faces.

He raised the ax, trying to scare them away.

"No! Lord," Mattie cried. "Don't take my kids away from me. Please, please don't hurt my children."

Shurley Stewart would never forget the sound of his mother's voice that day, pleading with his father. He would hear it the rest of his life. He would also remember the animal rage on his daddy's face.

Suddenly Slim turned back toward her and, without hesitation, swung the ax hard. He struck Mattie squarely in the chest with the flat side of the blade. The power of that mighty blow to the slender woman's breastbone was likely enough to kill her. The force sent her flying out the open bedroom window, into the clutches of a thick-limbed pecan tree below.

Slim dropped the ax, shoved the boys aside, and rushed past them, headed outside. Shurley raced to the window and stood on tiptoes to look over the sill. For the rest of his life, he would regret it.

The boy hoped to see his momma getting up off the ground, dusting herself off, and running away, looking for help to subdue Slim. But there she was, hanging upside-down in the tree limbs, her bleeding body draped at an odd, improbable angle.

The boy watched from above as his daddy pushed his mother's leg loose from the crook in the tree trunk that held her. She fell hard to the ground in a lump. She did not move. Slim bent over her, kneeled next to her, took her head into his lap.

"Oh, Mattie, I'm sorry. So sorry . . ." he cried pitifully.

Someone must have seen them there. In a few minutes, Shurley heard the wavering howl of an approaching ambulance siren. Neighborhood dogs bayed in harmony.

Shurley reasoned that it was a good sign that the ambulance attendants hurried to get his momma onto a stretcher and into the back of the big vehicle with the flashing red lights. She was still alive, then. The hospital would make her okay. Somebody said that they were taking her to Hillman Hospital on Birmingham's south side. There, in the basement of the hospital, was where Negroes went for emergency treatment.

Shurley and Bubba did not talk much about what they had witnessed, nor did they try to explain to their younger brothers what happened. Sam and David were certainly wide awake from all the screaming and scuffling and the siren but they were too young to know what was going on.

Momma would get fixed up at the hospital and she would be coming home soon, Bubba and Shurley assured each other. Slim would stay away for a good while now. He did not want to end up in jail. At least his absence would give them some peace.

Women from the Rosedale community stopped by with plates and platters of food, cakes and pies, more fare than any of the boys had ever seen in their lives. They ate until their bellies ached and then ate some more. The neighborhood ladies hugged the boys, held them on their knees, and urged them to go on and eat another bite or two. The boys' aunt—their mother's sister—Emily Williams lived just down the street and she stopped in to check on the four boys, too. The scowl on her face did not go away for the next several days.

"She is such a sweet lady, your momma," they all would say, clucking and shaking their heads sadly. "She don't deserve such trash as that for an old man."

"Mattie sure enough works hard. Sees after you boys. And she sings like an angel."

"We prayin' hard for her. We prayin' hard she's going to be all right, if it is God's will."

Still not a one of them updated the boys on how their mother was doing at the hospital or when she would be coming home to them. If their father came back to the house, they did not see him. If he did return, it was likely at night when they were asleep. Then he would just be looking for where Mattie C. might have hidden from him what little money she had.

A day passed. Then another.

The four Stewart boys, ranging in age from the infant David to seven-year-old Huell Jerome—long since dubbed "Bubba" because of the way Shurley pronounced "brother" when he started talking—were mostly by themselves. The neighborhood ladies or their Aunt Emily did stop by and look in on them.

Several days later, Bubba and Shurley were outside, playing on the little house's narrow front porch, escaping the stifling August heat inside. David lay on an old blanket. Sam was hemmed in beneath the porch, playing in the dirt. The bell in the tower at the Bethel African Methodist Episcopal Church down the hill began to peal. The reverberations echoed off all the houses along Rosedale's narrow streets.

It tolled slowly, sadly.

Bubba stopped playing. A solemn look crossed his dirty little face.

"Somebody dead," he reported knowingly.

If the bell rang quickly, someone was ill. It was a call for neighbors to come assist, men helping men, women helping women. The church bell was a simple but effective means of tribal communication for the entire Rosedale community. Nobody had telephones there.

But if the bell's pealing was slow, it meant someone in the neighborhood had passed away. Then people gathered to offer condolences, bring food, and help the grieving.

The boys watched as first one neighbor and then another came out their front doors and walked down to the church. There they would learn who had gone to join Jesus in heaven. Then, a few minutes later, each of the neighbors walked back up the hill. But not to their own houses. They headed instead to the little shotgun shack where Mattie C. Stewart had made as good a home as she could for her children, despite all the obstacles that had been lined up against her.

Sad-eyed, some shedding tears, they hugged the boys and told them things were now better for their momma. She was sitting by the side of Jesus. Her suffering was done.

Shurley and Bubba were not so sure things were better. Certainly not for them. They cried because they already desperately missed their mother. David and Sam just stared wide-eyed at all the strangers coming and going in their little house.

As the neighbors consoled the children, Bubba suddenly stood up and announced to everyone within earshot, "Daddy killed Momma."

"Yes, he did," Shurley added, nodding vigorously.

"What's that?" one of the men asked, and the boys told him again.

"Daddy hit Momma with the ax and knocked her out the window into the tree."

"Yes, he did."

Later that day, two police officers came by and talked to the boys. They told the policemen the story exactly as it happened. The brothers cried softly as they described the argument, the swing of the ax, and their momma tumbling backward out the window into the grasp of the pecan tree.

Of course, Slim Stewart had a different version when the police tracked him down. Yes, there had been a little lovers' spat between them, but Mattie C. jumped out the window of her own will. He never hit her. He tried to catch her as she jumped. The tree did the damage to her frail body that ultimately claimed her life. After all, he stayed with her until the ambulance came, didn't he? A man who had just murdered his wife would have run away, right?

In that place and time, the life of a black person was not worth much. And even if Slim Stewart's story was suspect, as far as the police were concerned this had been just another nigger-killing. Their attitude was that niggers killed niggers all the time; whether it was over a dice game or household money, it did not really amount to much in the grand scheme of things. Had the crime been against a white citizen, the situation would have been different, of course. Besides, the testimony of a couple of colored kids, not-quite-five and a mere seven years old, against their own daddy was hardly enough to mount even a manslaughter case.

Beyond those initial questions from the police, there would be no further investigation into what happened that steamy, hot August day in Rosedale, just over Red Mountain, south of Birmingham, Alabama.

The death certificate on file with the Jefferson County Department of Health would succinctly list the cause of death of "Mattie C. Stewart, female, Negro" as "Self."

Not a day would go by that the younger boy, Shurley, would not think of his mother and the dreadful way he watched her die at his father's hand. That recurring vision included what he saw when he leaned over the window sill and looked out at his momma, hanging in that pecan tree.

Stuck there in the limbs, bleeding, Mattie C. would forevermore be associated in the boy's mind with Jesus hanging from the cross on Mount Calvary. His daddy had crucified her while their sons watched.

There was something else, too. The boy would fervently maintain that his daddy did not actually take his momma from him that hot August morning. She would continue to come to Shurley, to counsel and advise him and tell him the things he needed to do.

She would clearly speak to him in her strong but loving voice. She helped him decide what was right and wrong, and how he could use his talents for good. It was she who advised him to put on whatever mask was necessary to see him through hardships and heartbreaks.

He would not always listen to her, but she never gave up on him.

He is convinced to this day, three-quarters of a century later, that it is the continued guidance from his mother that has shaped the man Shelley that the wide-eyed four-year-old Shurley eventually became. It was Mattie C. who helped the boy through the most unimaginably cruel childhood, the pall of discrimination, the rocky shoals of relationships, and the eventual loss of each of his brothers.

It was his mother who, from the grave, made sure her boy grew up to accomplish so many remarkable things and that he one day became such a strong voice for so many.

She told him she would never leave him. Mattie C. kept that promise to her boy.

J ump forward almost twenty-four years. An imminent showdown was looming, one that would soon give Mattie C.'s boy a powerful opportunity to follow his momma's advice, to employ his talent and will to lift up others and to do his part to help change the unchangeable.

On Monday, January 14, 1963, George Corley Wallace took the oath of office and became governor of the state of Alabama. He won the job by receiving the highest number of votes of any gubernatorial candidate in the state's history. His inaugural speech that day was partially written by Asa Carter, a member of Wallace's election team and a leader in the Ku Klux Klan. Wallace asked Carter to include some lines in the speech that would really get the crowd going on a cold winter day. He also wanted to make it clear that he intended to keep his campaign promise to enforce racial segregation as the law of the land.

Wallace stood on the same spot in front of the state capitol in Montgomery where Jefferson Davis was sworn in a century earlier as president of the Confederate States of America. That point of interest was duly noted in the speech. The new governor delivered the fiery words exactly as Carter wrote them. One line from the speech would define not only his governorship over the next few years but also his ultimate legacy. They would also wrap up in one sentence the defiant attitude at that time of the majority of the white people in the state of Alabama as well as across the South.

"In the name of the greatest people that have ever trod this earth," Wallace intoned, "I draw the line in the dust and toss the gauntlet before the feet of tyranny, and I say segregation now, segregation tomorrow, segregation forever."

Those defiant words, written by a Klansman, were delivered by a former prizefighter who had decided to stake his political future on one primary issue. He promised to maintain a way of life that was already being vigorously challenged mere blocks from where he stood, as well as just ninety miles up U.S. Highway 31 in Birmingham. Amplified and broadcast, his clear vow rang out across a city, a state, and a region that were, in early 1963, poised to be a flashpoint for change.

Those words set the tone for an unprecedented year of brutal confrontation *and ultimate transformation. A year when men and women bravely marched in the streets, went to jail, and died to assure the gauntlet thrown down by the former Klansman and the new governor would be challenged and cast aside. A year in which even children took to the streets, went to jail, and died.*

1963 would become the year when strong voices clashed with closed minds and changed forever the course of human history. Much of it happened just up the road in Birmingham, the Magic City.

SLIM & SNIPE

Huell "Slim" Stewart had quite the reputation around the little African American enclave of Rosedale, just south of Birmingham. He was known as a brutal man who took delight in killing animals just to shock those who watched him do it. In a brief tenure as a butcher back in his hometown of Phenix City, Alabama, he would entertain white people by stalking a hog in its pen, armed only with a big knife. Then he would pounce on the critter, cut its throat, and then lick the hot blood off his hands while they gasped at his savagery.

He often demonstrated for a wide-eyed audience—one that sometimes included his two oldest children—a unique way to kill an opossum. He pulled the snarling, hissing creature from its cage by its tail and danced around the yard with it, all the while carrying on a spiel worthy of a carnival barker.

"I'm gon show y'all how I deal with a varmint that snarls and spits and shows his old ugly yellow teeth at me!" he promised. "Y'all just sit back and watch the show, ladies and gentlemens."

Then he lowered the wriggling possum to the ground and placed his boot heel on its head. With one quick jerk of its tail, he snapped the animal's neck, killing it instantly.

His neighbors in Rosedale, where he had settled with his wife, Mattie, in the midst of the Great Depression, knew what kind of person Slim Stewart was. They knew him to be a rough man with a penchant for drink, a preference for back-alley gambling, and as violently blunt in his dealings with his fellow man as he was with pigs and possums.

Everyone knew the story of Slim's showdown with another neighborhood two-bit gambler named Homer. One owed the other some money, though it

Huell Jerome Stewart Sr.—died 1953.

was never clear who owed whom. When Homer unleashed a switchblade knife to help settle the matter, Slim promptly ran away. Everyone who knew him was amazed at this unexpected development. Slim was not one to run away from confrontation. He usually stood and fought toe-to-toe, though that was often because he was too drunk to do anything else.

However, in this skirmish, each time Slim made a circuit of the gambling joint where the clash had started, he was making a wider and wider orbit, all the while with Homer in hot pursuit with his switchblade. Slim had spied an ax next to a pile of wood at the far corner of the yard. When his circling became wide enough, he grabbed the ax and got ready for Homer to come tearing around the corner of the house in pursuit. Slim was a strong man to be so skinny. He struck Homer a powerful blow to the head with the flat side of the ax blade.

Some of those watching thought Homer was dead. He lay there in the dust as still as a tomb, barely breathing. Slim Stewart did not care if the man was dead or alive. Homer had pulled a knife on him, hissed at him, and showed him his yellow teeth. The matter ended, Stewart went back inside the gambling joint and resumed his interrupted dice game.

Homer was hurt badly but somehow survived. He carried the indentation in his skull from Slim's ax blade for the rest of his days, though.

IT WAS NEVER CLEAR how Huell met Mattie C. She was born to Willis Johnson and Emily Butts Johnson on a farm in Crisp County, Georgia, near Cordele. Somewhere along the way she was blessed with the nickname "Snipe." To this day, nobody knows what the "C" stood for.

The family was relatively small for that time, with only four children, three girls and one boy. Most rural people had as many kids as they could in order to have more help to work the farm. Boys were especially prized. With only one brother, Mattie and her sisters, Mamie and Emily, had to work even harder than most, chopping wood, picking cotton, making a garden, tending to the farm animals, and more.

Willis Johnson was known as an especially hard-working man, one of the few black folks in the area who actually owned the property he farmed. He managed to squeeze a living from his land despite the odds against him.

Mattie C. Stewart—died
August 8, 1939.

That is until one crop year turned sour and that was all it took. He lost everything. He and his family had no choice. They became sharecroppers, working even harder for much less on some white man's property, all just to stay alive.

Sometime later, around 1925, Mattie left home seeking a better life than sharecropping could ever provide. She lived for a short time in Columbus, Georgia, a city that hugged the state border with Alabama. That is likely where she first met and kindled a romance with Huell "Slim" Stewart.

UNLIKE HIS FUTURE WIFE, Huell came from a huge family. He had a dozen brothers and sisters. His father, Alonzo Stewart, held down a better than average job as foreman at the Southeastern Compress cotton gin and warehouse across the Chattahoochee River from Columbus, in Phenix City, Alabama. Alonzo Stewart was apparently the first in his family to spell his last name "Stewart." His father, Huell's paternal grandfather, had taken the last name of "Steward" from an area plantation owner and former slave holder.

Huell's mother, Rosa Lee, worked as a housekeeper and maid for white folks. Interestingly, for most of her working life, she worked for the family of Albert Patterson, a prominent local lawyer. Patterson would eventually run for and win the Democratic nomination—tantamount to election in those days—to become Alabama's attorney general in 1954. However, before Albert Patterson ever took office, he was assassinated by gangsters. They took issue with his pledge to clean up the vice and organized crime and corruption then rampant in Phenix City.

As part of her job, Rosa Lee Stewart had changed the diapers of and cared for Patterson's son, John. He had grown up to serve in the Army during World War II and then to become a lawyer like his father. After his father was murdered, John won a special election to replace him as the Democratic nominee and took office as the attorney general. Four years later, he ran for governor as a self-proclaimed segregationist.

In his campaign for the state's highest office, white voters saw John Patterson as more rigid against racial integration and the emerging civil rights movement than his strongest opponent. That opposing candidate, the one whom Attorney General John Patterson beat with fifty-five percent of the

Shelley's maternal grandparents, Willis & Emily Johnson.

vote, was a young circuit judge named George Corley Wallace. After losing that racially charged election, Judge Wallace vowed that he would run again in four years, but he would never again allow himself to be "out-segged"—to be portrayed as any less vigorous in his defense of racial segregation—in a political fight.

SOMETIME IN LATE 1925 or early 1926, Mattie Johnson decided, as many African Americans of the time did, that her greatest opportunity to settle down and make a living lay in a bigger town than Columbus or Phenix City. For many blacks (and even poor whites), that meant traveling far north, to Chicago, St. Louis, Detroit, or New York City. For Mattie, the choice was between Birmingham and Atlanta, though neither town was really all that large at the time. However, they offered more promise for a better life than did the cotton-mill towns and sharecropper farms along the Chattahoochee River.

Birmingham was something of a boom town, a newcomer, its prosperity stoked by its red-smoke steel mills. It was the only place on the planet where all the materials needed to make steel were located within one hundred miles. In the Roaring '20s, the demand for Birmingham-made steel had led to riches for those absentee owners who operated the mills. The city had grown so fast it acquired the nickname "the Magic City."

The managers and supervisors who moved to Birmingham to run the mills, as well as those who sold those newcomers their homes, furniture, fashions, fancy meals, automobiles, and other trappings of wealth did very well. Spectacular homes of the wealthy rimmed Red Mountain south of the city's downtown, a ridge so named because of the rich veins of blood-red ore that lay just beneath the surface. Many steel executives moved to other suburban towns "over the mountain," such as Mountain Brook and Vestavia Hills.

Mattie Johnson got word that all those rich white folks up there in Birmingham needed maids, housekeepers, and nannies—women who were dependable and were willing to work hard for minimal but steady pay. If you found the right job, you could work there for the rest of your life.

But Mattie had no money, not even enough for a bus ticket, unless she used what little she had saved to live on once she got there until she received her first wages. The typical way for Negroes and down-on-their-luck poor white folks to get to Birmingham or any other destination was to catch a ride on a freight train. That was exactly what Mattie Johnson did.

She found a place to stay at a rough, cheap boardinghouse on 10th Avenue North in the city's eastern section, a gritty industrial area near the airport where many blacks had settled. And she found work almost immediately as a maid for the Felton family, on the other side of Red Mountain in Mountain Brook. The job was hard but still far easier than what she had done on the farm back in Georgia. The pay was meager, just enough to feed herself, pay the rent at the boardinghouse, and keep the holes patched in her shoes. She rarely even had bus money and walked the ten miles or so each day to and from work.

It was during this time that Slim Stewart followed Mattie to Birmingham and they married. Slim and Snipe were a legal couple, but the mating never seemed to gel. The two were different in so many ways.

Mattie C. was a hard worker. Slim avoided steady employment. Mattie C. was a teetotaler. Slim drank anything with alcohol in it. Mattie C. saved all the money she could. Slim let it dribble through his fingers at a dice game or juke joint.

Mattie's sisters Mamie and Emily eventually migrated up to Birmingham, too. Mamie met and married Henry Pickens, a hard-working man who made a half-way decent living in one of the city's factories. The two settled in the Collegeville neighborhood, an African American area just north of downtown. It may as well have been Detroit or Chicago as far as Mattie was concerned because the two sisters rarely saw each other.

Emily first lived "on the place"—in the white home where she worked as a housekeeper—then married a man named Williams and used her maid's wages—and a brutally frugal lifestyle—to enable her to rent a shotgun house in Rosedale.

That small neighborhood—consisting of a pocket of black families, all struggling—had been carved out along the south slope of Red Mountain. It lay in the midst of surrounding all-white neighborhoods. Just to the east of Rosedale was Mountain Brook, one of the wealthiest towns in America and where Mattie had found work with the Feltons. To the north, along the ridge and mostly within the city limits of Birmingham, were the impressive homes of the steel barons and wealthier merchants. From their lofty mansions, they could look out to the north and see the working class neighborhoods of their employees stretched up and down Jones Valley from northeast to southwest. They could also see their mills and blast furnaces in action along the valley floor below. While that gaze northward may have elicited a few feelings of homesickness, they could also watch money being made at the mills without their own families having to hear the rumble, feel the hellish heat, or breathe the red-tinged smoke.

On the other two sides of Rosedale was the community of Homewood, a far less ritzy working-class town, primarily made up of second- and third-generation immigrants—Greeks, Italians, and others—most of whom had moved to the area to find jobs in those very same steel mills. They found plenty of work all right, three shifts a day, six and seven days a week, as the hunger for steel during World War I and the booming 1920s grew to be insatiable.

African Americans enjoyed only a very small part of that prosperity. Only sixty years had passed since the Civil War and many of the blacks in the area had parents and grandparents who had been slaves. The mills required men with strong backs so blacks had job opportunities there, but the work they were given was always the dirtiest and most dangerous and paid the lowest wages.

But it was steady work. And those white people who prospered most from the city's industrial boom needed maids and housekeepers. At a time when most white families had a father who worked and a mother who did not, black families required two breadwinners to merely survive. A few black women could work as teachers or nurses but most were domestics, like Mattie C. Johnson Stewart and her sisters.

SOON AFTER THEY MARRIED, Huell and Mattie moved "on the place" with a new employer, the Morgan family, on Edgehill Road in Homewood. That room in the basement was where both Jerome and Shurley were born. With the growing family, they soon relocated to a house on 18th Place in Rosedale. It was a small shotgun house almost directly across the street from Mattie's sister, Emily. But aside from exchanging a few shouted words from their respective front porches, Mattie and Emily rarely visited with each other. Part of the reason was that Emily was afraid of Slim Stewart.

The Morgan residence, where Mattie continued to work, was located in a more upscale section of Homewood very near Mountain Brook. But it was only a mile or two on the other side of U.S. Highway 31 from Rosedale, so Mattie's commute was not so hard. Rosedale was also near the street car line so Huell had a convenient way to get to the odd jobs he sometimes picked up, initially to get money to live on as his little family quickly grew, but eventually more to scrounge up liquor and gambling money.

And the family was growing. Huell Jerome Stewart Jr. was born in 1932. Next came Alonzo, named for Slim's father, but the baby lived only a short time. Mattie was heartbroken but almost immediately she was pregnant with another boy. This one would be called Shurley by all who knew him. That was 1934. Sam came along in '37, after the move to Rosedale, followed by David in 1939.

Even with four lively boys, Mattie C. continued to go each weekday to the Morgan house to work. Jerome—by then labeled "Bubba"—and Shurley walked along beside her, down the hill, across Highway 31. Then they strolled along the busy street to where they made the left turn and followed the sidewalk to the big brick house perched on the side of a hill amid tall shade trees. After the two youngest boys came along, Mattie pushed Sam and David the whole way, crammed together in a stroller intended for a single baby.

While their mother worked all day, Bubba and Shurley entertained themselves as best they could in the backyard, playing games, making up adventures, watching the scudding clouds overhead through the pine branches. They also cared for their younger brothers, who were placed on a blanket in the shade or, if the weather was bad, kept in the stroller on the back porch. The two older boys fed their brothers, changed their diapers, and ran to fetch their mother if the babies needed her attention.

Shurley would never forget the sound of his mother's voice drifting out the open windows as she sang the old spirituals she loved so much. "In the sweet bye and bye, we shall meet on that glorious shore," she sang. "There's a better home a'waiting, in the sky, Lord, in the sky." From the backyard where he and Bubba played, he could hear Mattie C. singing her gospel songs as she scrubbed floors, cleaned, and cared for the Morgan children inside the big house.

Shurley had other memories of his mother. He rarely saw her smile, even more rarely heard her laugh. She was so sad and solemn most of the time.

Sometimes, though, a colored lady friend who worked for a family down the street stopped by the Morgan house to visit with Mattie. Then, as he and Bubba played tag or gouged out roads in the dirt, Shurley could finally hear the magical sound of his mother's happy laughter. It was a deep, hearty laugh, and it always made him feel good.

So did her frequent hugs. Shurley and his brothers never questioned their mother's love for them. Her devotion to them was total, never in doubt, and her hugs were the best part of it.

As THEY GREW OLDER, Bubba and Shurley played with other neighborhood boys when they were not at the Morgans. They also roved by themselves throughout Rosedale without too much worry. People there tended to watch over their neighbors' kids, discipline them, and send them home if they misbehaved, skinned a knee, or were in any danger.

The boys soon learned their borders. They could wander over the top of Red Mountain, past the massive iron statue of Vulcan, the Greek god of the forge, which watched over the city from his high pedestal. They could even venture near the abandoned ore mines on the north side of the mountain and traverse some of what was left of the old L&N Birmingham Mineral Railroad right-of-way. It ran all the way to Bessemer, ten miles to the west, and to Irondale, about the same distance to the east.

In the other direction, they sometimes meandered as far as Edgewood Lake, a skinny body of water that angled along the valley between Red Mountain to the north and Shades Mountain to the south. They had heard that the lake held some nice, big catfish and they vowed to come back sometime and try to catch a mess of them.

There was one line of demarcation the youngsters dared not cross. Just to the other side of Dunn's Drugstore was the dividing line between "Pecktown," the white section in that part of Homewood, and "Niggertown," which was made up of the 150 or so houses and 500 people who comprised Rosedale. Along that border were black restaurants like Fess's Place and Waterboy's Grill and what looked to be simple, rundown residences. Some of the latter were actually shot houses, places where bootleg or illegal homemade liquor was dispensed to a thirsty clientele. Others of those houses were the locations for continual games of chance, from dice to cards.

Those were the places where the boys often saw their father hanging out. They did not acknowledge him and, if Slim noticed his boys passing by, he ignored them.

Those Niggertown joints were within Homewood's police jurisdiction. Still, their proprietors either paid off the right people or kept down violence within their establishments so it would not create any obvious problems for the city fathers. So long as their activities did not spill over into the white neighborhoods, the illicit business continued with little problems from the law.

Just across the dividing street, there were restaurants that, of course, did not allow blacks inside. But black families would often show up at the back doors of those establishments carrying metal pans. They could collect for their own tables such delicacies as chicken necks, heads and feet, beef and pork bones, pig snouts, tails, brains, and feet, and the wasted bits of fat and gristle trimmed from steaks and pork chops. Black kitchen help at those restaurants saw that what was bound for the garbage went instead to their neighbors.

That was likely where Mattie Stewart had obtained the main course she was preparing for Sunday dinner for her boys the day she and Slim had their final clash.

There was little room for joy in the Stewart home. Slim was rarely there and certainly spent little time with or took much interest in the four boys he had fathered. Days would pass without him coming home. He preferred the company of others like him, the ones who frequented the little houses along Highway 31 at the edge of Niggertown.

There was no observable affection between the boys' parents either. Instead, when Slim was there, he and Mattie argued fiercely and loudly, even in front of their sons. Mattie could hold her own as long as the conflict was verbal. But it often escalated to the frighteningly physical. When her husband slapped or punched her, as he inevitably did, she was not nearly big or strong enough to fight back. He was six-foot-three and strong.

She knew instinctively it was best to not even try. Mattie had long since learned to take his blows, allow him to make his point and vent his drunken anger, and then he would leave again until the next weekend. No matter how drunk or enraged he might be, Slim still knew his wife was like a good plow mule. He never wanted to beat her so badly that she would not be able to go to work. Then she could not earn the money that he would try to confiscate for gambling or whiskey.

That is, until that hot August Sunday in 1939 when Bubba and Shurley Stewart watched wide-eyed as their daddy robbed them of the only anchor they had ever had in their young lives.

If there was a wall in front of the Stewart boys before, it was now a mile high and a hundred miles wide.

2

Root Hog or Die Poor

They were all returning together from the funeral of Mattie Stewart at Bethel A.M.E. church and her burial at Grace Hill Cemetery. Henry Pickens's old hand-cranked Model-T Ford was packed as it strained, wheezed, and sputtered its way back toward Rosedale. All four Stewart boys were crowded into what passed for a back seat. Next to them was Mattie's sister, Mamie Pickens, whose bulk occupied most of the seat. Slim Stewart sat up front beside Henry, slumped low in the seat so his head did not hit the roof when they hit a bump in the rough road.

Mamie asked the question that was likely on all their minds: "What the hell you going to do with these boys, Slim Stewart?" Henry kept driving and was smart enough to keep his mouth closed.

"Hell, I don't know," Slim finally replied. No one actually expected the boys' father to stay home and raise his sons, but obviously they were too young to live by themselves. "Mamie, why don't y'all just take 'em?"

Mamie snorted and they rode on in silence. When they finally got back home—to a house that now seemed so very empty and even more sad than before—the boys remained on the porch while the grown-ups went inside, almost certainly to hash out the brothers' immediate future.

Bubba and Shurley tried to play, as if nothing had changed in their young lives, to not think about what was going to happen to them. Their existence had hardly been idyllic so far, but they still had some sense of home, thanks to their mother. They had enjoyed wandering around Rosedale, playing, and going to the Morgans' house with Mattie. School was coming up soon for Bubba, too. Why couldn't Momma just call out to them, tell Bubba to get the babies in the stroller so they could head on over to the Morgans' for the day?

They hardly knew their Aunt Mamie and Uncle Henry. Neither boy could remember seeing them more than a time or two before the funeral. After all, the couple lived way over Red Mountain on the other side of Birmingham, in the Collegeville neighborhood. But it was not just the distance. The three Johnson sisters had all come up to Birmingham to seek different lives and they had little in common. Mattie rarely saw her sisters, not even Emily, who lived on the same street.

But likely the main reason the sisters never came to see Mattie was Slim Stewart. Mamie and Emily had little use for the man and were openly afraid of him. They did not want to visit their sister if that sorry so-and-so might come around, drunk and mad, and beat on them the way he did their sister.

Shortly, the adults emerged from inside the house. Slim carried a couple of brown grocery sacks that held what few clothes the boys possessed.

"Boys, y'all go on and get in the car with your aunt and uncle," he told Bubba and Shurley. "Help your brothers. Y'all going to stay with Aunt Mamie."

The older boys tried to be brave, to fight off the tears as they climbed back into the old Ford. Shurley Stewart did just what he always did when faced with the frightening unknown or the terrifying reality. He mentally put on a mask, one that hid his true emotions from anyone else.

Uncle Henry gave the hand crank a vigorous spin and the motor came to life with a loud backfire and a cloud of black oil smoke. Then, without even the opportunity to look back at the only home they had ever really known, the Stewart boys were off to Collegeville with relatives who were little more than strangers.

Henry Pickens was a common laborer at the Louisville & Nashville Railroad car wheel shop. The house he and Aunt Mamie shared was small and simple, sitting on a large city block of similar homes that were constantly bathed in a fog of smoke from the plants all around them. The boys were not used to the odd-smelling smoke and the rumbles and squeaks day and night from the heavy industry nearby.

There was one bright spot, though. Even in the middle of the city, Henry and Mamie maintained a decent garden and raised hogs and chickens right on their lot. The food was much better than the chicken feet and necks and pigs' ears they usually had to eat back home.

The boys did not see much of Uncle Henry. He was either at work or out back taking care of the garden and livestock. Aunt Mamie seemed to always be in a foul mood and had few kind words for the quartet of boys she had taken in out of sheer necessity. She mostly ignored them, mumbling and grumbling under her breath all the time about the burden Jesus had placed on her. Meanwhile, the Stewart brothers fended mostly for themselves.

At least, as winter approached, the house was usually warm, Mamie and Henry rarely argued or fought, and they were not hungry. There was no talk of Bubba starting first grade that year so he and Shurley stayed busy as they always had, playing with each other in the back yard with their baby brothers nearby on a blanket, and doing the chores their aunt assigned. They also took on the task of teaching Sam how to use the outhouse that sat at the far back corner of the lot. Except for a few messy accidents that seemed to especially infuriate their aunt, the boys were proudly making progress with that job. David, of course, was still in diapers, still crawling, and was pretty much being cared for by his seven- and now-five-year-old brothers.

Life with Mamie and Henry had settled into an uneasy routine. Christmas lights began to appear on some of the front porches of the houses around Collegeville. A few wreaths hung on front doors and some families brought home small, scraggly cedar Christmas trees. Santa Claus had never seemed to find the Stewarts' house back in Rosedale but now, based on the few conversations Bubba and Shurley had with Collegeville kids their own age, it appeared he usually did make an appearance over on this end of town. Nothing fancy, of course. No bicycles or doll houses or coaster wagons. But he did bring kids some new church shoes sometimes, or a spinning top, candy, a cap pistol, or a bag of sparklers. The boys tried hard to imagine what it would be like to have such playthings show up on Christmas morning.

Aunt Mamie never mentioned the holidays or Santa but the boys began to anticipate Christmas morning anyway. They hardly noticed that their aunt seemed even more irritable than ever. Their uncle appeared to not even notice they were there most of the time.

Then, a few days before Christmas, Mamie and Henry woke the boys up one morning and told them to put their clothes in paper sacks. And to be damn quick about it.

"We taking y'all back to your daddy," their aunt told them as the boys squinted and rubbed the sleep from their eyes. "I'll be damned if I am taking on the raisin' of somebody else's brood. I'll be damned if I'm going to be cleaning up the shit of some baby don't even belong to me."

For the second time since their mother's death, the Stewart boys were riding through the streets of Birmingham in their uncle's Model-T Ford. This time, though, they were headed the opposite direction, back toward the house on 18th Place in Rosedale.

The old Ford shuddered as Henry set the brake as they stopped in front. He and Mamie argued about who was going to face Slim Stewart and give him word that they had brought his four sons back to him. As usual, Mamie won the argument.

Henry hopped out and cautiously approached the door of the house to try to rouse his brother-in-law. But it was an older man who came to the door and spoke with Henry for a moment. Then Henry nodded, turned, and came back down the steps to the car.

"Slim ain't lived here since Mattie got killed," he reported with a shrug. "He say Slim shacked up now with some woman over on Central Avenue, closer to the street car line. Say her name is Marie or something."

"Jesus," Mamie said and pursed her lips, thinking over the options. "He tell you which house?" Henry nodded. Mamie motioned for him to put the car in gear and to drive on over toward Central Avenue. "Hurry up. This old car bouncin' around so it makes my kidneys hurt powerful bad."

Pickens stopped the car adjacent to a vacant lot next to the ramshackle old house where he had been told Slim Stewart now stayed. Mamie climbed out of the car, stood, and stretched her back. Henry set the boys' paper sacks of clothes on the ground next to the curb.

"Your daddy lives in that house over yonder," their aunt told them, pointing. "You tell him I ain't about to raise his four little bastards while he whores around and gambles away all his money." She watched Bubba and Shurley climb out of the vehicle. Shurley helped Sam down and Bubba reached back in and took David in his arms.

Mamie squeezed her bulk back into the car's seat and motioned impatiently for Henry to drive on. "I don't give a damn if you root hog or die poor," were the last words Shurley and Bubba heard from their aunt as they drove off.

Blue smoke swallowed up the Model-T as it disappeared down Central Avenue, leaving the four children standing there, Bubba still holding his infant brother in his arms, Shurley gripping Sam's hand so he could not run away.

The two older boys looked at each other and shrugged. There was nothing else to do.

They picked up the paper sacks that held their few rags of clothes and started walking across the broad vacant lot to the house where the daddy who did not want them—the man they had seen murder their mother—was supposed to be.

It was not a homecoming to look forward to.

3

Sunday Dinner

Marie Thompson was irate when she saw the foursome of ragamuffins standing at her front door. She was even madder when Bubba told her their aunt and uncle had dropped them off and then headed on back to Collegeville. She called out, "Slim Stewart, we sure as hell ain't got no room for this bunch of babies!"

What kind of Christmas gift was this? The old house was too damn full of folks already, Marie fumed. No privacy or room enough for any of them as it was. Marie's sister, Louise, and her niece, Nettie, already lived there with her, along with Slim Stewart. The house only had two bedrooms, a postage-stamp dining area and kitchen, and a narrow back porch. Where the hell was she going to put four kids? Two of them old enough to get in the way, one just old enough to walk but without enough sense yet to stay out of the street, and one of them still in a nasty diaper sagging-full of shit.

"What you want me to do, woman? Set them and their sacks out there for the garbage men to pick up?"

"I'm just sayin' we ain't got room for them here. They ain't welcome in my house."

Slim Stewart looked at his boys, forlornly standing there on the steps, holding their paper bags, listening quietly to the debate. The two older boys were expressionless. Sam was trying to crawl through a hole in the screen door to get inside where it was warm. Bubba held the baby in his arms but seemed on the verge of dropping his heavy, squirming load.

"We'll let 'em stay on the back porch until we can figure this thing out," Slim finally said.

Marie scowled but quit objecting. She did tell him, point-blank, "I don't have a child to die and I don't have a child to cry." She would assume no obligation to care for this scrawny bunch, and she made that perfectly clear to Slim—to the boys, too, who stood and listened as the adults loudly debated the issue of their future.

What happened on that back porch over the next half year defies belief, not only for the unfathomable cruelty and neglect that would be visited upon the Stewart brothers but also for the amazing resourcefulness and fortitude the youngsters exhibited. They did what they did because they had to in order to survive. Bubba and Shurley helped their baby brothers through it all because they knew nobody else would. And because they were convinced that Mattie C. would have wanted them to.

One of the girls threw a couple of thin, dirty blankets onto the rough planks of the porch floor. That would be their bed. Slim rigged up a discarded piece of wooden lattice and tacked some cardboard to it to try to keep the blowing rain and wind off the boys. There was a rusty tin roof overhead but they were virtually outside, in the elements, during an Alabama winter. There could be sleet and snow and the temperatures were low enough to cause frost to spew from the ground. Slim rounded up an old spitting, smoking kerosene heater and set it in the middle of where his sons would have to try to sleep.

For a toilet, the residents of the house used a slop jar that was kept on the back porch. Slim tacked up a ratty old bedspread to afford them some privacy from the boys when the adults did their business. He told his kids, though, that they needed to go out in the yard so the slop jar would not fill up and need emptying so often.

The next day, Slim found an old mattress that had been set out with somebody's trash. He tossed it onto the little stoop for a better bed for the boys.

It was dark and freezing cold during the long winter nights and Bubba and Shurley were afraid to venture off the porch. When they could hold it no longer, they peed on the mattress, right where they lay. Sam's potty training now irrelevant, so did he. The older boys ripped up whatever discarded cloth they could find in other folks' garbage cans for makeshift diapers for

David, but they could not hold the load most of the time. The mattress was soon soaked with urine and smeared with worse.

The old kerosene heater did little to keep them warm. Icy winds blew right around the cardboard. Bubba and Shurley began to develop a bit of the resourcefulness that would stand them in good stead over the coming years. They would wait until the babies had dozed off for their afternoon naps and then they walked a few blocks to U.S. 31, to Damon and Sons coal yard. From their previous wanderings around Rosedale, they knew the owner's grandson would eventually come out the store's back door to play. The Stewart boys assembled an arsenal of rocks, dirt clods, and pine cones and, when he appeared, they peppered the boy with a vigorous barrage. Their target, they knew, would retaliate, but the ammunition he had at hand was big chunks of black coal.

When the battle eventually ebbed, Shurley and Bubba gathered up the coal thrown at them in a rusted old bucket they had found, took it back home, and burned it to keep them and their brothers from freezing to death.

MISERABLE AND PRIMITIVE AS it was, the boys' lives on Marie's back stoop soon fell into a routine. There was only one meal a day, and that was supper. Marie worked at the local tuberculosis sanitarium, just down the way near the lake. She usually brought home the leftovers she scraped off the patients' plates. When she, her sister, her niece—and Slim, when he was home—had picked over what they wanted, she handed out the back door what was left, dumped into and scrambled up in a metal pan, like slop for the hogs. The boys had scrounged up an old piece of sewer pipe and that, turned on its end, passed for their dinner table.

Of course, that was not nearly enough food for hungry, growing boys. Bubba and Shurley soon became expert scavengers. They did not worry about leaving Sam and David alone on the back porch while they went off looking for something to eat. David was not yet walking and stayed put on the mattress. And Sam would never leave David alone so there was no danger of him wandering away.

Their first place to try to harvest the necessities of life was Pecktown, the white section, just down the street and on the other side of U.S. 31. There were two grocery stores there, Hill's and the Piggly Wiggly. Food that had molded or rotted or was otherwise unfit to sell was tossed into garbage bins behind the stores. The boys went through that for anything still edible, fighting with monster rats for the best morsels. Bread with some white showing through the green-black mold was pulled from the bin. Apples and oranges that were not all rot, too. An occasional delivery truck driver would take pity on the skinny colored boys and give them an outdated bottle of milk or an "accidentally" opened bag of cinnamon rolls.

On the other hand, store workers would often step outside if they saw them and chase them away as they would a stray dog or the ever-present gopher rats.

"You little niggers get away from here!" they yelled. "Y'all scaring our customers off. Go on, now."

New sources for food were required. The boys found some old cane poles and some string and manufactured basic fishing tackle. Then they followed others from the neighborhood, carrying their own fishing gear down to Edgewood Lake. There they caught catfish and, without regard to whether they were keeper-sized, they either built a fire and cooked them right there or lugged them back to Central Avenue. An old, rusty coat hanger made a rudimentary fish-gutter. A homemade knife helped peel off the skin and chop off the head. They had watched their daddy do it and mimicked his methods. Even with the bones still in and the flesh not always fully cooked, a catfish cooked over the coal fire was a delicacy for four hungry boys.

Someone had strung a cable from a limb in a tree and the boys could swing over the wide creek that served as the lake's spillway. That put them on the path that followed the lakeshore all the way around to the other side. If the fish were not biting on one side of the lake, they could follow the path around to the other. Sometimes they just swung over and back for the fun of it. Fun was a rare commodity. Almost as rare as food. Then the brothers would lie in the grass in the shade and giggle, forgetting what they had to return to before it got dark.

Somehow, Bubba came up with a beat-up but serviceable BB gun—Shurley never knew where he got it or the BBs to go in it—and they used it to kill birds. Once or twice, they even managed to stun a squirrel until they could grab it and finish it off. There was not much meat on the sparrows or squirrels but they still cleaned and cooked them and made the best of what they had.

Not far down the street, a family kept a cow in a small pen behind their house. The boys got up early, before daylight, and sneaked through the barbed-wire fence. While one brother kept watch, the other milked the cow, getting enough warm liquid to fill David's old cracked baby bottle. Otherwise, they had to mash up whatever sanitarium left-overs or catfish or garbage-can bounty that they were eating so David could have some of it, too.

The boys were careful not to let Slim or Marie or Marie's niece Nettie catch them while they were cooking or eating what they harvested from Piggly Wiggly and Hill's, or the bony catfish they pulled from the lake. They shared the food with their brothers and then hid what was left beneath the porch. They could only hope neighborhood dogs and cats, the ubiquitous rats, or the people who lived inside the house would not find their stash and steal it.

ON SUNDAYS, THOUGH, THE routine was broken, and in a delicious way. It actually gave them something to look forward to each long, cold week.

Slim kept a flock of chickens in a coop behind the house. On Sunday mornings, the boys watched as their daddy made a big show of reaching in and pulling out one of the birds. He held the fluttering, squawking critter up in the air for inspection, and, if the choice suited him, he brought it over to a chopping block with feathers flying everywhere as the bird tried to get loose from its executioner. Sometimes he just grabbed the chicken by its head and gave it a practiced jerk, breaking its neck. Other times, he stuck the chicken on the block, neck in just the right place, and cleanly whacked off its head with one blow of his ax. He then tossed the bird down in the dirt and they all watched as the headless fowl flopped around in the yard, blood splattering everywhere, until it finally died. Sometimes, to Slim Stewart's delight and the boys' horror, the headless chicken improbably jumped up and ran wildly around the small yard until it finally collapsed, dead at last.

Having chickens over there that could dash around with their heads cut off was just one reason the boys stayed away from the side of the yard where the coop was. The other reason was that Slim had set big rat traps back there to snag the huge, brazen rodents that might try to get at his Sunday dinner. He sternly ordered Shurley and Bubba to not go back there or to let Sam crawl over there either. They might trigger the traps accidentally and could lose a toe or finger in the process. They obeyed their daddy's strict orders without question.

But once Slim's brutal show was over, he proudly toted the chicken inside to be plucked, cut up, battered, and dropped into the hot oil. The boys' mouths watered as they smelled the wonderful aroma of frying hen. Their stomachs growled in anticipation. The blood-spattered image of the flopping, dying chicken was washed away by hunger.

They knew what was coming. Once Marie, her kin, and their daddy had eaten their fill, Slim would hand out a pan of fried morsels to the boys on the porch. They were not allowed inside to eat, and there were no breasts or drumsticks, but it was delicious compared to their usual cold leftovers, coal-broiled catfish, green oranges, and moldy white bread. They looked forward to Sundays because they knew they would usually be allowed that special treat.

But one Sunday, as the boys gnawed away, claiming the last bits of meat off the bones of their weekly special dinner, they saw the shadow of someone coming around the corner. It was a policeman. Shurley recognized him at once. He was one of the officers who had questioned the boys about their mother's death. Shurley's first thought was that the law had come back to finally get to the bottom of the killing. Or maybe he and Bubba had been spotted by the neighbor, stealing a few squirts of milk from his cow, and he and Bubba were about to be hauled off to jail.

"Boys, give me whatever that is that y'all are eating there," the policeman ordered and gingerly held out a paper sack.

The boys continued chewing as they curiously put what was left of their prized Sunday meal into the sack, as ordered. The officer stomped back around the house and was gone. They licked off their fingers what was left of the fried, spicy batter, wondering why Homewood Police would care about their fried chicken dinner. Was Slim stealing chickens? Were they going to jail because they were eating ill-gotten bird?

A few days later, the officer came back. This time he was accompanied by a lady he introduced as a nurse from the Jefferson County Department of Health. He told Slim and Marie to summon the boys in from the back porch to hear what he and the health nurse had to say.

"Slim, somebody tipped us off to what has been going on here," the cop told them. The nurse stood there with her arms crossed, frowning, sadly shaking her head, an expression on her face as if she smelled something rank. "We got us a sample to confirm it. Slim, we know you have been feeding these boys fried gopher rats. You know them things are full of disease. If we catch you doing that again, we are going to put you both under the jail. You understand me, boy?"

"Yes, sir, boss," Slim promised, nodding animatedly, bowing to the cop. "You bet we will, boss. We just had a rough patch and food is so damn expensive these days, suh."

The mere mention of jail made the usually confrontational Huell Stewart go all meek and agreeable.

One of Slim's drinking buddies had watched one day as Slim skinned the gophers he had pulled from his traps, placed them in a boiler, and carried them inside for Marie to fry up after she had finished cooking their chicken. Slim even bragged to the man about what he was doing and how much the boys enjoyed their "special dish."

"Them boys be glad to get some meat. Any kind of meat," Stewart told his buddy.

However, the man decided that this was well beyond the pale, even for a man of Slim's cruel, inhumane nature. He told the police what was going on there at that little shack on Central Avenue. The police likely would not have cared what those folks in Niggertown were eating, but it would reflect badly on the city as a whole if there was an epidemic of the black plague right there in Homewood.

And that ended once and for all the boys' special Sunday dinner.

SPRINGTIME OF 1940 WAS a mixed blessing. The weather warmed and the icy wind no longer had the boys huddling around the smoking bucket of coal or the hissing old kerosene heater just so they could feel the blood circulate in their hands and toes. But with the warmth came the blowflies and the bugs and the maggots that inhabited the filthy, decaying mattress on which they slept.

When the sun was out, the boys dragged their bedding out into the yard, hoping it would dry out the urine and chase away the bedbugs, roaches, and fly larvae that had taken up residence in their bed. It helped, but not much. The boys had itchy, infected bug bites all over their bodies.

To amuse themselves and pass time, the two older brothers began crafting homemade knives and spears. They rigged a target and hung it from a fence and spent hours throwing their crude weapons at it. They became relatively skillful and plotted what they would do if the dreaded Ku Klux Klan should come after them, or if Slim came home so drunk he might try to kill one of them or their younger siblings the way he had their momma.

A strong bond had developed between Bubba and Shurley. They were cognizant of the fact that they were on their own, effectively without parents. There was no supervision from Slim, Marie, or the others, even though they lived only a wall away from them. And certainly no encouragement or affection. Bubba and Shurley knew that they were responsible for David and Sam, making sure they got something to eat, that their clothes were changed every few days and washed in rainwater.

They were not aware, though, that their situation was evolving in an almost Darwinian way, that they were growing even stronger and more resourceful because they had to. Had to in order to survive. Without even realizing it, they were set to do whatever it took to endure, to make it until things returned in some way to how life was when Mattie C. was alive and they had some foundation in their lives.

They rarely talked about their mother but they thought about her often. They longed to hear her voice or walk along beside her down to the Morgan house. The boys ached to get one of her powerful hugs or hear her singing gospel songs as she labored. Shurley missed her so deeply that he cried silently almost every night while drifting into sleep. He made sure Bubba never heard or saw him weeping, though. He did not want his older brother to feel bad or make him think he had done something wrong to cause Shurley to cry. But the loneliness and loss was even worse than the hunger pangs that twisted his stomach into knots.

There was one time he felt okay in letting Bubba see him cry. That was on those Sundays when the two boys wandered down to Friendship Baptist Church. They sat under a tree outside one of the open windows and listened to the preaching, singing, and testifying going on inside the building. Those songs brought back so many memories of their momma that they both cried. Neither boy worried that the other one saw the big tears rolling down his cheeks.

THOUGH ONLY FIVE YEARS old, Shurley was still perceptive enough to wonder why Slim's relationship with Marie Thompson was so different than it had been with Mattie C. Oh, Marie and Slim argued vigorously, sometimes approaching familiar violence, but it never seemed to go to the extremes it had with their mother. Then Shurley, even at so young an age, figured out what it was.

The pair had one thing in common: whiskey. Marie drank just as much as Slim did. Drunk, they enjoyed each other's company immensely, and soon recovered from their spats.

Mattie Stewart did not drink. Not a drop. The only thing she had in common with Slim was those four boys and their one dead brother.

Being inebriated did not soften Marie's attitude toward Slim's boys, though. She still resented them being there, even if they were little bother to her out there on the back stoop. Bubba speculated that they reminded her of Slim's former woman. She was likely jealous of a dead woman. Shurley figured Marie was just a mean old biddy.

As much to try to get along as anything else, both boys attempted to be nice to her in the beginning, to greet her when she came home from her job at the sanitarium. Maybe she would be more pleasant if they were nice to her. Maybe she would even let them sleep inside and eat more than one sorry meal a day.

"Hey, Miss Marie," Bubba said with a smile that first day. Shurley echoed his brother and matched his grin, "putting on his mask," as his mother had taught him.

Marie glared at them for a moment, her hands on her hips.

"What? Y'all don't want to call me 'momma?' You think I ain't good enough to be your momma? Is that it?" and she turned away in a huff.

The next day, both boys were waiting when she came home. They would try to do it the way she seemed to prefer. It was still difficult, though, to make their mouths say the word "momma" to her.

"Hey, Momma!" they both happily called out as she walked up the sidewalk toward the house.

Storm clouds crossed the woman's face. She scowled and stomped her foot in the thick dust there at the foot of the steps.

"What you mean? I ain't your damn momma!"

The boys gave up after that and simply avoided her as much as possible. Clearly, there was no way to please the woman.

THAT SUMMER, THE BOYS continued their wandering, gleaning food where they could, fishing in Edgewood Lake, practicing their knife and spear skills, and, since nobody else would, caring for their brothers as best they could. There was even talk of the two of them attending school that fall. Apparently Slim did not want to risk trouble with the law by not sending the older two for their compulsory education. That would get them away from the house five days a week, too, and that might keep Marie calm.

The thoughts of actually going to a school, being under a real roof each day in a place where it was warm, and maybe even learning to read and write were especially exciting for Shurley. He had heard other kids in the neighborhood talking about reading and cyphering, of learning about things and places beyond the borders of Rosedale. The thought of being able to do such a thing was appealing to the boy who had never even riffled through the pages of a book. Never even seen one up close except for his momma's ragged old Bible.

One day the boys were sitting in the shade on the stoop, trying to stay cool until the sun was finally eclipsed by thunderstorm clouds heaped up over Red Mountain. They heard Marie screeching angrily at Slim after she got home from her job. The brothers looked at each other. She was a loud woman but they had never heard her this loud or incensed before. She was not jumping Slim for his drinking or gambling or lack of gainful employment, though.

"Them bastard boys of yours stole my gold pieces out of my room," she was screaming at him. She stuttered she was so mad. "Twenty-five dollars in g-g-gold! What you going to d-d-do about it? Let 'em get away with it?"

Well, Bubba and Shurley had never even been inside the tiny bedroom where Marie and their daddy slept. They had no idea she had gold coins hidden in there. Even if they had, it would never even have occurred to them to steal from her.

No, half-drunk one night the woman had probably simply misplaced them, put them someplace else in that pigsty of a house. Or their daddy had "borrowed" them and lost them in some back-alley dice game.

Slim kicked open the back screen door and stomped out onto the stoop, lightning flashing in his eyes. The boys denied even knowing the gold pieces existed, and assured their daddy that they certainly had not taken them.

"You took her money all right," Slim bellowed, his face contorted with rage. "And I'm going to show you what happens to sneak-thieves and damn liars."

He grabbed up the first weapon he could find, an old, splintered piece of two-by-four lumber, and began swinging it ferociously at both of his sons.

Shocked at the violent magnitude of his anger, the boys ducked and dodged and tried to get away from him. Slim was a tall man, his arms and legs were long, and when riled he could cover a lot of ground. Before they could get out of the reach of his makeshift club, Bubba had blood streaming from cuts around his eye. And by the time Slim's rage had withered, Shurley stood at the far end of the yard, sobbing, dully studying the odd angles of the bone between his elbow and wrist. His arm was broken in two places.

"Quit that damn crying and come on," Slim told Shurley when he calmed down enough to recognize the damage he had done. He led his boy down to the street car stop, an arm across the youngster's slender shoulders, as if he was powerfully concerned about his son's well-being. Shurley held his throbbing, fractured arm tightly to his chest. He tried to stifle his moans and weeping and to ignore the raw pain. He averted his eyes, trying not to feel the pitying, curious stares from the other passengers on the street car.

"I done told the boy to stop all that running, that he's going to fall down and break his damn arm," Slim said loudly. "Well, he don't listen to his daddy one bit. He did fall and looks like he done broke that arm."

Slim told the same lie to the doctor at the Hillman Clinic emergency room.

"No, he hit me with a piece of lumber," Shurley calmly corrected his daddy between sobs, pointing at Slim with his good hand.

The elder Stewart just shook his head sadly. What was a daddy to do?

"The boy done taken to lying, too. We been praying for the Lord to stop him from telling lies," Slim said. And right there in the middle of the emergency room, Slim Stewart joined hands with the doctor and a nurse and held prayer, asking God to deliver this sinful boy from his lying ways before he came to a sure enough bad end.

The doctor put a plaster cast on Shurley's busted arm. A couple of weeks later, Slim got tired of looking at it—and of it reminding him what he had done—and cut the cast off. Slim explained it to the boy by telling Shurley that he did not need to get out of the habit of using that arm, that he would one day need it to be able to work hard and make a living. He did not want it to be any weaker than the other one. Somehow the bones managed to mend anyway.

SHURLEY HARDLY PAID ANY attention to the hurting arm, though. Something else had happened. Something that changed Shurley's course dramatically, and initially not for the better.

In the wake of the two-by-four whipping at the hand of their father, Bubba Stewart decided he could no longer stay there on the stoop. Not with the man he despised so much often so close by.

Bubba slipped away in the dark of the night. At seven years old, the boy had hit the road to truly make it on his own. He figured whatever he found out there beyond U.S. 31 was better than life would ever be on Slim's and Marie's back stoop.

Neither Marie nor Slim seemed the least bit concerned about the child's disappearance.

"Damn kid's done probably gone and got hisself killed or kidnapped,"

Slim speculated, and that was that. Nobody went looking for Jerome Stewart. Nobody notified the police about a missing seven-year-old. Life just went on there on Central Avenue, exactly the way it had since two days before Christmas, 1939.

Five-year-old Shurley Stewart simply sat out there on the rickety old stoop each day, his skinny legs dangling off the edge, and watched the sun inch downward. He missed his brother mightily.

How could he stand life there at that place with Daddy and Marie without Bubba to share the load with him? Could he go fish at Edgewood Lake all by himself? Did he dare swing to the other side of the lake on that cable if Bubba was not there to give him a shove off the bank? How could he take care of Samuel and David by himself? How would he be able to take the loneliness that had just gotten several magnitudes worse with his brother's departure?

He made up his mind about what he had to do. He began plotting his own escape. Like his brother, Shurley Stewart figured the vast unknown out there could not be any worse than what he was facing there in that little shanty on Central Avenue.

The boy had no idea how wrong he was. Mere yards from where he had experienced the best days so far in his young life—when his beloved mother was still alive—he was about to suffer some of the worst.

4

Salt in Wounds

Shurley knew where he wanted to go when he left Central Avenue. It was only a half mile away. Leaving the cruel house where Slim and Marie had made life near unbearable was an easy decision, and the escape itself consisted only of wrapping up his few stitches of clothes in a bundle and walking away.

Leaving his younger brothers behind was the thing that ripped the boy apart. He told himself that with only the two babies remaining, and without Bubba and Shurley to care for them, Marie or her sister, Louise, Nettie's mother, would have to take them inside. They would be better off with him and Bubba both gone.

But Shurley suspected he might never see any of his brothers again. They would be just as dead to him as his momma was. That was why he cried huge tears as he walked up the road to his Aunt Emily's house, almost across the street from where Mattie C. was murdered.

In his child's mind, Shurley reasoned that Emily—closest in age to his momma—would have more of Mattie's qualities than his Aunt Mamie did. He hardly knew Emily Williams, had only seen her a few times from any closer than porch-to-porch. He and Bubba had been afraid of her early on because her face was covered with large moles, and she was a big woman, much like Aunt Mamie, not petite like his mother.

Shurley had no backup plan if Aunt Emily told him to get off her porch and get on back to Slim Stewart. He only knew he was not going back there. He would go over the top of the mountain and move into one of those abandoned ore mines and live there if he had to.

But Emily Williams seemed truly happy to see him. "Lord have mercy!

44

Looka here, looka here! Who is this young man at my front door?" she had cried out. Still, she had one question before inviting him inside.

"Huell Stewart ain't coming looking for you, is he?"

"No, ma'am."

"Well, I don't give a damn if he do or he don't. I ain't taking none of Huell's shit. You understand?"

With that, she welcomed the boy into her home, another squat shotgun house much like the one nearby where he had once lived. Shurley stepped inside his aunt's place for the first time in his life. But, as accustomed as he was to rancid odors, he was stunned by the stench inside the house.

He soon learned the source. Emily kept a chicken brooder in the kitchen in the rear of the little shack. She had thrown dirt on the floor of the kitchen and young chickens had the run of the room.

A few other things quickly came clear, too. Aunt Emily's husband was no longer in the picture and his name or whereabouts was not mentioned. At least at first. From all appearances, except for the chickens in the kitchen, his aunt lived by herself.

She also insisted on living much the way she had on the sharecropper farm back in rural Georgia. She did not have electricity in the house. She lighted the place with a dim kerosene lamp and cooked on a wood stove. Heat came from the stove and a small fireplace. Emily chopped her own wood to cook and feed the fireplace.

"My daddy done taught me how work like a man," she boasted. "I can do anything a man can do."

That was how it happened that most of the chores immediately became Shurley's responsibility. Now, while Aunt Emily went to her maid's job at the white folks' house, he was expected to chop up and split the wood for the fireplace and stove, wash the dishes, feed the chickens, and even grab one of the birds and wring its neck when it came time to cook one. Shurley never considered chopping off a bird's head—that trauma remained from watching his daddy do it—but he had learned well from Slim how to break one's neck with just the right jerking motion.

Aunt Emily seemed pleasant enough at first, despite her country ways.

She was abrupt at times when she spoke to him, and even acted a bit strange, talking to herself and silently staring hard at the boy, as if trying to read his soul. At least she let Shurley sleep in a warm place, with a mattress and blanket. And she fed him well from her chicken coop and garden and the leftovers she brought home from the white folks. Still, he kept half-expecting her to suddenly hit him for no reason, like other family members had done. For the first week, though, all seemed to be different from the boy's recent experiences.

Then one day Shurley watched curiously as his aunt mixed up a strange-looking and odd-smelling dry potion. It reeked of what the boy would later identify as sulfur. She placed a dish of it beneath the bed where Shurley slept. Then she hummed an odd song as she put other dishes of the stuff in different places around the house. With a transfixed expression on her face, the red light from the fire giving her the countenance of a witch, she mixed more of the powder with water and sprinkled it under the front and back steps of the house.

"That'll keep them away," she said, with no further explanation. Shurley had no idea what she was talking about or who "them" were.

Then one night she woke the boy up from a deep sleep.

"Pee in this damn jar, boy," she ordered.

Shurley shook his head to clear the fog. She told him again, more impatiently this time, to pee in the fruit jar. He did as he was told.

Emily studied the liquid in the jar, like a scientist observing some experiment, then took it to the next room. Though she did this several times during his stay there, Shurley never knew what his aunt did with his urine or why she asked for it. Later he would deduce that she was conducting some kind of voodoo, conjuring up a spell that required the boy's bodily fluids.

Only a week or so after coming to his aunt's house, Shurley was awakened—again from a deep sleep—by Emily screaming at him. When he did not respond as quickly as she wanted, Emily suddenly tossed back his blanket and brutally whipped him on his bare legs with an old piece of electrical cord.

"Wake up! Dammit, get your ass up, boy!" she screeched at him, and then she whipped him again.

"What is it, Aunt Emily," he asked, sobbing hard, trying to curl up to avoid the sting of the cord.

"Wash them damn dishes again!" she ordered, and thrashed him hard across the back. She pointed to the floor where she had carefully arranged the dishes he had washed earlier.

"I didn't get them clean?" he asked, but she did not answer. She only stood there, the electrical cord at the ready, pointing at the dishes arrayed on the floor, as if set out for a meal for the two of them.

Shurley rubbed his smarting legs but jumped up from the bed as ordered. He went to the corner to get wood to fire up the stove for hot dishwater.

"Uh uh! Don't use that wood. Get out yonder and cut some more."

Shurley did as he was told, though he still did not know why she was making him re-do this chore. He went outside in the dewy darkness and chopped up enough wood to build a fire in the stove and heat enough water to do the job.

Then, with the dishes sparkling clean, he put them away and went back to bed. His legs still smarted and oozed blood from the thrashing.

Later on that night, though, just as he had gotten to sleep, she was back. Again she was shrieking, throwing off his blanket, whipping him with the electrical cord, ordering him to cut more wood, heat more water, and wash the very same dishes yet again.

"But Aunt Emily, why you . . . ?

"Boy, don't you sass me. Them white folks are my boss, but damn it to hell, I am your boss. And you going to do what the boss say to do."

He repeated the chores again, and only then did she allow him to finally sleep through the night.

With that, Emily seemed to move on to a new level of cruelty. For no reason that Shurley could discern, she would slap him so hard and unexpectedly that he would go skating across the floor. Or she would kick him so brutally in the rear end that he would have bruises for a week. The blows came with no warning and no explanation of what he had done to deserve such a thing.

He immediately knew the reason for one especially brutal thumping, though. It came when he asked her a perfectly innocent question. They were sitting there in the cool darkness on the front porch, watching quietly as life went on around them on the streets of Rosedale. Aunt Emily seemed in a rare good mood, spitting tobacco into the dust in the yard, commenting on each neighbor who passed by. Still, Shurley was always braced for a violent response from his aunt. It had become more and more common for her, when he least expected it, to strike him, or, without warning, turn and spit a big wad of tobacco juice in his face. This night, though, she seemed contented and calm. Curiosity got the better of the boy.

"Aunt Emily, how come your last name is Williams but there ain't no husband around here?"

She spun his way, a spark from a light up the street snatched up in her eyes. Shurley knew instantly that he had just crossed a line of some kind, one he had no way of knowing existed. Emily slapped him so hard his chair flipped over and he hit his head hard on the floor.

"You look here, young man!" she hissed. "You don't ask grown folks their business." She kicked him hard in the ribs to emphasize her point. Then again, just in case he did not understand her point.

One time after an especially vicious blow, he summoned up the courage and asked her why. Why did she hit him for no apparent reason, when he was doing nothing wrong?

"Aunt Emily, why you do that? What did I do?"

She grabbed him by his shoulders and pulled his face close to hers. There was a wildness in her eyes that sent a chill up the boy's spine.

"I'm beatin' you down, boy," she told him. "I'm breaking you so the white folks won't have to do it. I'm saving your life, that's what I'm doing, making you tough and putting you in your place. One day you'll thank me. You'll thank me."

By then the boy knew he had not improved his lot in life by coming to his aunt's house. He contemplated going back down to Central Avenue, to Slim's and Marie's. At least he would have his younger brothers with him there. That idea was dashed one day when he crossed paths with his daddy in Pecktown.

Aunt Emily had enrolled Shurley in first grade at Union Baptist School.

The boy took the long way around when walking home, covering some of the same ground he and Bubba had once roamed when they were scrounging for food. He was about to check the trash bin behind the Piggly Wiggly to see if there might be some crusty old cinnamon rolls back there. But when he looked up, he was staring right into the face of Huell Stewart.

The boy turned and ran as fast as he could. He did not know why that was his first instinct, but that was what he did. Slim's long legs made it a very short race. He grabbed his boy by his collar and spun him around to face him.

"You listen to me, boy," he said through clenched teeth. "I'm glad your damn ass is gone. You stay up there with that bitch Emily. I better not see you around my house. You stay away from your brothers, puttin' ideas in their heads. You hear me?"

Shurley nodded, trembling, expecting a blow to the side of his head. But Slim let him go, stood up straight, looked around to make sure nobody else had seen or heard their little father/son talk, and strutted back up the street, back toward Fess's Place or Waterboy's or one of the other places he haunted just over the line in Niggertown.

Shurley hurried home. Since he started to the school, he realized just how imprisoned he had become in his aunt's house. When he got home each day from school, before Emily got home from work, he was forbidden to even go into the front yard. He could only go out back to take care of the chickens, tend the garden, or split wood for the stove.

Emily enlisted neighbors to watch for him violating her rules and Shurley knew if he did, and they reported it, he would get an especially awful beating. So he did exactly as his aunt told him to do. He dared not even go out on the front porch to escape the stifling heat and chicken-shit stench in the house.

But one day, a neighbor told Emily that she had seen her nephew playing with some other boys out next to the street. It was likely some other six-year-old the neighbor had seen, but Emily did not try to investigate or even give Shurley the opportunity to deny it.

Her face hard and fixed, she jerked him up without a word, tied the boy's wrists together with a rope, and threw it over a big nail she had driven above a doorway. She pulled him up until his feet could not touch the floor and tied off the rope to the bedstead. Then she stripped him of all his clothes, underwear and all, leaving him hanging there naked, like a hog about to be slaughtered. Shurley cried and begged and tried to tell her he had done nothing wrong, but she was determined to give him the punishment she was certain he deserved.

She began to whip his back, his buttocks, and his legs with the familiar electrical cord until blood ran down and dripped onto the floor. Then, when she caught her breath, she stepped away, into the kitchen, and soon came back with a box of something. She poured it into her hand and began to rub whatever it was into the oozing wounds.

Salt! She was rubbing salt into the cuts in the boy's back and legs. He screamed and kicked in agony but she ignored it all.

Emily left him hanging there by his wrists all night. She sat nearby in a straight chair and watched him, humming that odd tune of hers. Watched him urinate and defecate, unable to stop himself. Ignored him when he begged her to let him loose, that he would never again do whatever it was that he done.

Hours later, when she fell asleep and almost tumbled out of the chair, she finally loosened the rope and let the boy down. He could only lie there on the floor, moaning quietly. He did not have the strength to cry.

"My daddy taught me how to break a mule," she told Shurley. "That's what I'm doing. I'm breaking you down like a mule, boy. I do it, the white folk won't have to."

Shurley lay on the floor whimpering, still unable to get to his feet. He tried, though.

"I got to get ready and go to school," he told her.

"You ain't going to school today," Emily told him.

"But Miss Foster, she . . ."

"I said you ain't going to school today. See, you don't listen to me. I'll send word up to the school that you got the mumps and you be back in a few days."

Truth was, Emily did not want anyone to see the boy's horrible wounds. The blood would certainly ooze through his shirt if he put one on and he probably could not have sat in a chair, much less stayed there all day long. Not after hanging there, taking the whipping.

As he tried to sit up, to stretch his cramping arms, Aunt Emily's pronouncement that he could not go to school for a few days hurt the boy almost as much as the lashes had. She was denying him the brightest light he had so far in his short life.

And his teacher at the Union Baptist first grade, Mamie Foster, was the brightest light of all.

5

a Spark of Intelligence

Mamie Foster knew some of the Stewart boy's background. She lived in Rosedale herself and on the way to school each day walked right past Shurley's first home and the one he now occupied with his aunt. She likely knew the true story of what had happened to Mattie C. rather than the one Slim told the police. She was one of the neighbor ladies who came to Shurley's house when the Bethel A.M.E. bell told everyone that Mattie C. had gone to be with Jesus.

Somehow, though, the teacher saw something special in this particular boy. She looked past his raggedy clothes. She ignored his complete lack of personal hygiene. He certainly had never even seen a toothbrush, much less used one. His hair was long and dirty and he smelled like chicken manure. He was quiet, too, as if he expected something bad to happen to him if he said anything. There was something raw and primitive about this child, as if he had raised himself in a jungle somewhere, far from the city where he actually was growing up.

Mrs. Foster knew that, like most of the other children who showed up at her school, he had likely never had a parent read to him, never sat on a lap with a loving parent's arms around him while he looked at the pictures in a book, following the words as someone read them to him. No, he likely had not had a book in the house at all.

But Mamie Foster saw beyond all that. She saw a spark of intelligence in his eyes. She noticed the way young Mr. Stewart perked up and listened so very carefully when she read to the class, the way he took the books from the shelf and looked through them hungrily, as if he was trying to figure out what the words meant. He wanted to inhale the pages, not just look at them. She saw how disappointed he was when she took up the books at the end of each day.

Not long after Shurley started school, Mrs. Foster took the boy aside and had a talk with him. He simply stood there, looking at the floor as she spoke, but she knew he was listening.

"There is something different about you, young man," she told him. "And it is a good kind of different. You are going to be somebody. I don't know what life has been like for you so far, but I can tell you this. If you learn to read, you can do anything you want to do. You can be whatever you want to be. You are going to be all right, Shurley."

Shurley was listening and his heart soared. Her words were like a bright beacon to the boy. He told himself he could not disappoint her. He would work hard, learn to read and write, and make her bold prediction come true. He had no idea how, but he vowed to himself to try.

That was not the end of it, though. A few days later, Mrs. Foster brought him two pairs of short pants, two shirts, and a pair of shoes—all store-bought and new. They were the first new clothes the boy had ever worn. A few days later, the teacher stopped by and asked his aunt if it would be all right if she took her nephew to Wiley's Barbershop and got him a haircut. Surprisingly, Emily agreed.

Shurley never knew if the beatings he got later were punishment for going with the teacher to the barbershop or for accepting the new clothes. He never knew why he was being whipped. Why his aunt—a big, strong woman—would pick him up over her head and slam him down hard on the floor. Or stomp him mercilessly in his stomach as he lay there and struggled for breath.

Things were about to take an even sicker turn for Shurley Stewart, though.

As it had with Slim and Marie, life with Aunt Emily had taken on a monotonous routine for the boy. He rose each day before daylight, did his chores, and went to the welcome sanctuary of school. After class, he came home and did homework and read schoolbooks until time for his aunt to come home. He put the books and writing tablet away, out of her sight, before she got there. She resented and ridiculed him if she caught him doing schoolwork or reading.

"Colored don't have no reason to learn to read," she told him. "Don't need to learn to read so you can clean white folks' houses, dig a damn ditch, or work a shift at TCI. Get out yonder and get us some wood cut up for the stove, boy, and put that shit away."

One day, after a trip over the mountain to Birmingham's south side, his aunt returned with a male friend she met there. She and Mr. Houston were still sitting in the dark on the front porch, laughing and talking, when Shurley went on to bed that night.

He was sleeping soundly when Emily awoke him in her usual way, throwing back the covers, loudly telling him to get his ass up. But this night she did not have the electrical cord, nor was she ordering him to pee in a fruit jar.

Instead she stood there in the lamplight empty-handed but totally naked. The boy could also see her new friend standing behind her. He was also nude.

"Wake up, Shurley! Wake up!" she ordered. "Take out your pecker. Take it out!" Embarrassed in front of the total stranger, the boy hesitated. Emily reached and pulled down the boy's underwear, exposing him.

But this night she did not seem angry. She was laughing. So was her male friend.

"You best mind me! Take out your pecker and rub it against Mr. Houston's pecker."

Shurley was crying, confused, ashamed, but he did as he was told.

Aunt Emily laughed even harder. She might have just witnessed the funniest thing she had ever seen. Shurley had never heard her giggling so.

"Now, your dick will grow and be big like Mr. Houston's someday!" she proudly told the boy, as if she had just done him a big favor.

Emily kept company with Mr. Houston for another month or so, and the late-night ritual was repeated many times. Shurley was so humiliated he would never have told anyone what was happening. Emily, though, was concerned he might, and she began spreading the word that her orphaned little nephew was a terrible liar, to not believe anything the little bastard might say.

Pray for him, she told everyone. Pray to the Lord that the boy learns to stop lying before he dies for his sins and goes straight to hell.

Once again it was ingrained in the boy that he was a no-good, rotten liar. That the adults in his life were always right no matter how mean or bizarre they acted toward him.

Meanwhile, Shurley did as instructed and strayed no farther than his aunt's porch when she was not home. Sometimes he glanced up from his schoolbook and gazed longingly past the trees at the distant horizon. The books he was learning to read told of Dick and Jane and a life so very different from the one he had endured so far in his six-and-a-half years. Of families who lived in big houses without chickens inside and potions under the beds, ate meals together around a dining room table, went to church together, played together in yards covered with green grass and swings hung from tree limbs. Of children who went swimming in municipal pools and played in parks built for them with swings and monkey bars and baseball fields. Of kids who went to big schools with hundreds of other kids where they were encouraged to read and learn. Of course, none of the children in those books looked like Shurley Stewart and his few classmates. The kids in those books were all white.

It was a world that was difficult for the boy to imagine. Did it exist out there, beyond his aunt's porch, scruffy petunias, and chicken-wire fence? If it did, would he ever experience it?

It was about ten months after he left Slim and Marie and his younger brothers behind when Shurley finally concluded that he could not stay with Aunt Emily or endure her cruelty any longer. The boy did not know if he could tolerate the beatings, the humiliation, the tobacco juice between the eyes. Yes, he got enough to eat, and he did not have to forage in the garbage cans behind Hill's or catch catfish from Edgewood Lake just to fill his belly. He had a roof over his head. He was no longer living outdoors, and there was another winter of rain, sleet, and wind bearing down on him. He would be leaving school, too, the place he lived to go to each weekday. Would Mamie Foster wonder what happened to him?

Did he dare walk away from Aunt Emily's now? Would he be even worse off if he left this awful place? Was this the life he was destined to lead? Was

Bubba out there somewhere, waiting for Shurley to come find him, or was his big brother long since dead, as Slim had speculated?

Shurley Stewart mulled those questions and finally steeled himself to do the only thing he could. He was convinced Aunt Emily would one day kill him during one of her brutal beatings. If he was to fulfill Mrs. Foster's prediction, he would have to accomplish it somewhere else besides 18th Place in Rosedale.

With no idea of where he was going, how he would eat, where he would find shelter, he disobeyed his aunt's orders for real this time. He boldly walked down the front steps and, without looking back, left Emily Williams's house behind.

He did not even bother to look back.

With nothing more than a few bites of food and the relatively new clothes his first-grade teacher had given him, the boy was on his own, homeless but hopeful. He had no idea what kind of world awaited him out there, but it would certainly be a different one.

And that, the boy reasoned, could not be all bad.

6

Finding Bubba

Something deep inside the boy made him rebel against his aunt's constant physical and emotional beat-downs. But it was also something in what his teacher said to him, about how he was destined for something special, that ultimately pushed him out that door and into the unknown.

Two miles into his journey, Shurley Stewart was starting to have his doubts, though. It was hot and sultry with the morning summer sun beating down on him. He could feel the heat of the pavement through the soles of his shoes. Once over the crest of Red Mountain on U.S. 31, he noticed far more white faces than colored. Not only had he rarely been around any white people, he had not even seen many. Their skin looked odd and milky to him and they talked funny, almost in a foreign language.

Early in his journey, Shurley had stopped under the shade of a big oak tree and gobbled up what food he brought with him. Now he was getting hungry again. And very thirsty.

Then he saw a large gathering of blacks in front of the Birmingham Electric Company building. They were waiting to catch the bus that took them back the way the boy had just come. They were bound for their jobs as maids or gardeners in white folks' homes, orderlies in the nursing homes, and other humble employment. Shurley stood among them for a bit, blending in, hoping none recognized him and would decide to take him back to Aunt Emily's or to Slim Stewart. He stayed alert, ready to dash away if he had to.

Soon he decided to follow an old bus that happened past. It was filled with colored people, too, but it was going the other way, toward the north, opposite the life he had chosen to leave behind. Maybe he would eventually trail after some friendly looking souls when they got off the bus, follow them to a neighborhood where he would feel comfortable, and try to find a porch to sleep under that night. There might be a garbage bin there, too, where he could find supper.

He did not want to venture as far as Collegeville for certain. He had no interest in returning to his aunt who lived there. If she spotted him, he would almost certainly get hauled back to Central Avenue in that old Model-T, too.

The bus stopped and started, taking on and letting off its passengers at each bus stop along the way. That made its progress slow enough that the boy could keep up with it. And despite the way the blue smoke burned his eyes, he stayed with it for several blocks, all the way to 8th Avenue South.

Then he heard a voice in his head. A voice so faint he could not tell where it came from. A voice urging him to turn right at 8th Avenue, then bear right again at an intersection to which he would soon arrive. He did as he was told.

After a while, tired, hot, hungry, and lost, he stopped and sat on the curb for a moment to consider his situation.

You need to keep movin', Shurley.

The voice again, so lost in the whir of the passing traffic that he could not be certain where it came from or whose words they were. Again he obeyed, stood and walked on, into a neighborhood of amazingly big houses, landscaped lawns, and long, winding driveways. It did seem cooler there but he was now unable to ignore his growling stomach.

Beneath his feet, the street abruptly changed from asphalt to cobblestones. Along each side of the roadway were quaint stores that looked as if they had been removed from the pages of some of the magazines and picture books he had seen at Union Baptist School.

Had he walked all the way to a different country?

There was a sign with words on it that he had to sound out, the way Mamie Foster had showed him: Crestline Village.

Even knowing the words on the sign, Shurley still did know where he was. In reality, he had wandered into Mountain Brook, the most affluent city in the South at the time. His attention, though, went right to a busy grocery store on the corner. He knew there would be a garbage bin out back and he could make a meal back there. Sure enough, he was able to gorge himself on rotten apples, brown bananas, and moldy bread.

Reinvigorated, he began looking for some place to hide for the night. The sun was well down and the lightning bugs were already blinking, announcing eminent nightfall. Shurley instinctively knew he would be easily noticed in this neighborhood. If somebody alerted the police, they would likely haul him off to the jailhouse. Daddy and Aunt Emily had both told him in graphic terms what happened to little boys there. Or worse, they would transport him back to Aunt Emily. He could imagine the beating he would get if that happened.

Soon he spied a nice, two-story house, surrounded by a white fence and acres of green grass. Something led him to go over and take a closer look. Behind the house was an outbuilding, obviously some kind of a barn. Warm, fragrant hay would make a good bed and there would be a roof overhead to keep the dew off him. Surely he could hide out there for the night so he could rest up and continue his journey early the next morning, before it got so hot.

Shurley inched around the perimeter of the lot, trying to stay hidden behind the decorative shrubs that grew there. It was almost dark when he approached the barn from the back, across an open area of grazing lot.

A yellow light showed through the doorway of a small attached room. He could see the shadow of someone moving around inside, and then the person was standing at the door, looking directly at the boy. Shurley stopped in his tracks, trying to make himself invisible amid the dusk. Then he decided he had best turn and dash back into the cover of the trees behind him.

Don't run.

The voice was clearer than ever in his head. So clear he was afraid the person coming out the barn door, staring hard at him, could hear it, too.

"Shurley?" the shadowy person suddenly asked. "Shurley, that you?"

Lord! It was Bubba! Jerome "Bubba" Stewart! His big brother!

The brothers had never hugged each other in their lives. No role models had demonstrated for them that kind of behavior. But they did run to each other, grinning and slapping hands.

"Bubba, what you doing here? I thought you was dead."

"I just want to know how you found me, Shurley. You find me, Daddy might can find me."

"I don't know how," the boy answered. He did not want to tell his brother about the voice that had urged him along and guided him all afternoon to end up in this spot. "I just saw the barn and was going to sleep in the hay."

THE BOYS SAT DOWN on a tree stump in the darkness and caught up. Bubba wanted to know about their younger brothers. Shurley explained he had only seen them from a far distance, walking home from school, since he made his own escape from Slim's house. Bubba apologized profusely for leaving them behind. He had just been unable to stand Slim's and Marie's meanness any longer. He was certain either Slim would kill him the next time or he would kill his daddy trying to defend himself.

Soon they went inside and turned off the lamp so it would not disturb the Tennessee Walking Horses that occupied the barn's many stalls. Bubba told Shurley to sleep on his cot in the corner of the tack room while he curled up on some hay. This was where Bubba now lived, and he considered it far superior to the open back porch on Central Avenue. He explained to Shurley that the big house and barn belonged to the Stringfellow family and that he and several other colored boys worked as stable boys and groomsmen. Some lived at the stables while others lived elsewhere and walked to work each day. A few of the horses belonged to the Stringfellows but they also boarded animals for others. Bubba shared the tack room with a boy named Peewee, the eldest of the group at an ancient ten years old. Peewee seemed to take little notice of Bubba's long-lost sibling who had suddenly showed up out of the summer darkness.

Bubba was still talking as Shurley drifted into a marvelously deep sleep. It was as if the weight of all that had happened to him the last year or two had finally caught up with him. Now, finally, he could find some blessed rest there on a cot in a stable tack room.

"Damnation! I go to bed and there's two niggers here. I get up in the morning and there's three niggers."

A tall white man wearing a floppy hat stood there, leaning against the side of the door. There was the glow of first daylight behind him. Bubba sat up groggily and yawned, rubbing the sleep from his eyes, but did not appear to be afraid. For his part, the white man seemed genuinely surprised, but not at all angry.

"Mr. Derryberry, this here's my brother, Shurley," Bubba proudly told the man. Zollie Derryberry was the horse trainer for the stables and lived with his family in a small house on the Stringfellow property.

"Damn, Jerome, you told me you didn't have any kinfolks. How many more of you Stewarts can I expect to show up here like stray dogs or feral cats?"

Shurley cringed. Despite his brother's nonchalant attitude, he was afraid the man was not only going to toss him across the fence into the street but that by coming here, he may have cost Bubba his home and his job, too. But for the moment, Derryberry did not voice any opposition to this unexpected newcomer being there. Instead, he made sure his wife, Wilma, brought extra food for Shurley for breakfast that morning. Then, without even asking if Shurley wanted a job, he put him to work piling up horse manure with a shovel so it could be used as fertilizer. That would become Shurley's primary job, but he would also help Miss Wilma clean her house and do other odd chores.

The Derryberrys had three boys and Miss Wilma made sure that Shurley got some of their hand-me-downs to wear. Somewhere along the way, as he was cleaning house, Shurley noticed that one of the Derryberry boys was having trouble reading his schoolbooks. He stopped mopping and scrubbing long enough to help the white boy pronounce some of the bigger words and figure out what the sentences meant.

"Zollie, this boy can read better than you and me," Miss Wilma told her husband, astonished that a seven-year-old colored child was literate. After that, once they were finished with them, she gave Shurley his choice of the family's subscription magazines. At night, before turning off the oil lamp, he read aloud to Bubba and Peewee the stories from *Life*, *Saturday Evening Post*, and *Reader's Digest*. When he was finished devouring the magazines, he tucked them beneath his cot and soon built up quite the library there.

Huell Jerome Stewart Jr. (Bubba) at horse stable, 1945.

THE FOOD WAS GOOD, sleeping accommodations were fine, and though hard, the work in the Stringfellow stables was not all that bad. No worse than what Aunt Emily made him do, and blessedly free from all the other dark things that went on at her house. Shurley enjoyed the company of not only his brother but also the other stable boys, and even that of the majestic Tennessee Walkers that occupied the stalls and produced an endless supply of fertilizer to shovel. The boys even found time to play horseshoes and other games.

When Bubba and Shurley had the opportunity, they began to hatch a plan to rescue David and Sam from their daddy and Marie. At night, the two dropped to their knees and prayed for the well-being of their baby brothers. At the same time, they began working on their knife- and spear-throwing again, all part of their liberation plan. Or in case Slim or Aunt Emily happened to find out where they were and came for them. Both boys became especially proficient throwing ice picks at a target they rigged on the back of the barn.

However, as the dog days of summer arrived and daylight grew noticeably shorter, Shurley felt a sudden yearning. It was so strong it surprised him. Common sense told him to keep quiet, to work, and keep things on an even keel, to ignore the hankering in his gut.

There was that voice in his head again, though, telling him what he should do. Its counsel for Shurley was once again clear. The end of summer meant school would soon start, and the boy craved to go, to learn more, to work to fulfill the faith Mamie Foster had in him. He determined that the nearest colored school was all the way out in the suburb of Irondale, a good five-mile walk eastward from the Stringfellows' place in Mountain Brook.

Zollie Derryberry had his doubts about his idea, though, when Shurley told him what he wanted to do. "Now, how in hell you going to work, walk all that way out yonder to the colored school and back, and still keep up with your work here, boy?" the horse trainer asked, already shaking his head "no."

"I'll cover for him until he can catch up," Bubba volunteered. Shurley's brother was a favorite of Derryberry's. With no prior training, Bubba had exhibited unusual skill handling the horses, understanding the nuances of training them. He was such a hard worker, too, that there was no doubt he could take up the slack with his brother's chores.

Miss Wilma was on Shurley's side, too.

"Let the boy go to school if he wants to and if he don't mind walking all that way," she urged. "He's a smart one, Zollie. He might turn out all right."

Shurley was up with the sun the morning of the first school day, ready for the long, long walk out to the colored school in Irondale. With directions from Derryberry, he found his way to the typical "separate but equal" Negro elementary school just in time for the opening bell. It was a simple, ugly old building, hot in the summer and early fall when classes started, and drafty and cold in the winter. It was crammed full of ragged kids, most of whom had no interest whatsoever in being there. They had been told often enough it was a waste of time for most colored children to go to school since they were destined to work lowly jobs the rest of their lives.

Not Shurley Stewart. It was school, there were books and maps and teachers, and the boy loved every minute of it.

Soon he was into a regular routine, awakening early, walking to school through rain, sleet, or sunshine, absorbing all the knowledge that he could during the day, walking back home, and then finishing up whatever work Bubba had not been able to get to, going at it until it grew too dark for Shurley to see the manure he was shoveling. Then he did homework by lamplight until the wick had to be snuffed out for the benefit of the horses and their rest.

Weekends were just as busy. Most of the owners came to the Stringfellow place to watch the stable boys exercise their horses they boarded there. The colored boys were virtually invisible to the white folks, who ignored their presence unless they needed one to fetch a saddle or get them a drink of water or bring out and saddle up a particular animal. As a part of their normal conversation, it was common for the men to use the vilest racial slurs, as if the young black boys could not hear them. The men also complained at length about how the "niggers around Birmingham were getting too uppity and don't know their place anymore." Some of the nigger men dared to look right at white women as they passed them on the street. One man reported actually seeing a "buck" look a white man in the eyes when he talked to him.

"Some of them end up with their nuts on a stake, they'll learn. Our white boys are all going off to fight this damn war so it's up to us to keep the niggers in their place until the boys get back from teaching Hitler and the Japs a lesson."

Shurley heard the hateful words and the "in their place" sentiments plenty of times. He had become an accomplished eavesdropper. It was just another way of learning things. However, now that he was older, and now that he spent more time among them, he was even more aware of and attuned to the attitude of most white folks toward people of color.

It did not hurt him to hear such. It did not even make him angry. It simply was the way it was, the way it always had been.

Then something else happened that made the boy come to a powerful realization about how things were.

When he had the opportunity, Shurley sometimes wandered back down to Crestline Village to look about, to watch how people behaved, how they did things in a world as foreign to him as the architecture in the shopping area. Though he now had plenty of food to eat, out of habit he still sometimes checked the garbage bins behind the grocery store and restaurants just to see what he could find. Folks in this part of town tended to throw out some mighty fine victuals!

One day, a white man came out the back door of the grocery store and caught Shurley leaning over the edge of the bin, trying to snag a tidbit. Without a word, the man angrily grabbed Shurley by the nape of his neck, jerked him roughly out of the bin, and kicked him hard in the rear end. Then he threw him brutally to the asphalt, as he might have a cur dog.

"Get your nigger ass out of here and don't ever come back," the man yelled, with another hard kick for emphasis.

It was only a week or so later. Shurley was behind one of the restaurants, grabbing a bite from its garbage bin. This time it was a Negro employee who came out the back door, already in a rage and cursing. He jerked the boy out of the bin and began kicking and slapping him viciously.

"Nigger, you better keep your raggedy damn ass away from here, you hear me? I ever catch your black ass here again . . ."

And he kicked the boy again, hard, sending him bruised and crying back toward the Stringfellow place.

Those two incidents brought home a powerful point that would remain with Shurley. He knew how white folks treated the colored. He had experienced the worst that racism could bring. But he had also experienced equal meanness from those of his own color. Hell, even from his own blood kin.

White folk did not have a monopoly on cruelty or heartlessness.

There was good and bad in all people, regardless of their skin color. The Derryberrys clearly held the same racial attitudes as most other whites in that place and time, but they had treated Shurley decently and gave him a job and a place to live when he had nowhere else to go. They fed him and gave him access to schoolbooks and magazines. His own father and aunt had done none of those things. These white folks were already more of a family than any of his own kin had ever been.

Soon, though, Shurley Stewart would meet another man. A white man. This one would show him yet again that you could not define a man or his attitudes by his ethnicity. This man, one of the horse owners who regularly visited the Stringfellow barn, would help set Shurley even more confidently on a path toward the promise his teacher first saw in him.

"Shurley? Your name Shurley? Come over here. I want you to read something for me."

7

PaPa Clyde

Shurley had noticed the man before. He always dressed well, parted his sandy hair in the middle as was fashionable at the time, wore flashy diamond jewelry on his hands and wrists, and drove a big Packard convertible with a thundering engine he liked to rev up as he approached up Euclid Avenue toward the Stringfellows'. He kept several beautiful and expensive Tennessee Walking Horses in the barn and often took them to shows around the southeast. Some of the stable boys told Shurley that Clyde Smith had plenty of money. He had several businesses—two motels, a restaurant, real estate he developed—but he also was rumored to have some less-than-legal enterprises, including moonshining and "policy making" (small-time lottery or numbers games) in black neighborhoods all over Birmingham. Shurley noticed that Smith never engaged in the hateful racial comments of the other white men; still they all seemed to like and respect him.

By this time, Shurley had begun to do more than eavesdrop. He had gotten over his reluctance to speak and would sometimes pipe up with a comment on whatever the men were talking about: current events, the world war that was about to enter its second year, the stock market, and more. And he would use his deepest little-boy voice with as near-perfect diction as he could muster. The first few times Shurley joined the white folks in conversation, Bubba poked him, frowned, shook his head, and tried to get him to quiet down. He was supposed to blend into the background and stop putting on his show for these people.

But Shurley liked the attention. He considered it an opportunity to put on a different mask and show a side of himself that he knew would shock and impress the men. Besides, he never grew tired of being told how smart

67

he was—at least, smart for a colored boy. Indeed, the stable's visitors took great delight in hearing such grown-up discourse from this little "nigger boy" who spoke so surprisingly well on so many subjects. They enjoyed asking him questions, quizzing him, allowing him to perform a mental tap dance for them and demonstrate just how deep his knowledge went.

On the day when Mr. Smith asked him to read something, Shurley did not hesitate to show out for him. He had a magazine rolled up in his back pocket. He took it out and picked a paragraph from a story he had been looking at earlier. He cleared his throat and read the words in an unexpectedly loud, strong voice.

Clyde Smith laughed heartily.

"That's pretty good, Shurley. Old Percy—he's a man who works for me—he says folks talk about the boy over at the colored school that's so smart. That's you. You still going to school?"

"Yes sir, boss man."

"How long you been staying in this barn?"

"I don't know for sure, boss man."

Smith rubbed his chin and grinned. Shurley watched as the sun glinted off the gold rings Smith wore on each finger. The white man looked around to make certain Derryberry and the other men could not overhear him. He lowered his voice.

"Look, I'd like to make you a deal. I want you to be able to keep going to school. I suspect it is hard on you working like you do and walking all that way every day. And I've been watching how hard you work. You could be a big help to me out at my place. It's a far sight better place to live than this barn and it's closer to the schoolhouse. But, see, I can't just take you away from Zollie or the Stringfellows." He looked around again and then leaned in just a bit closer. "On the other hand, if you were to leave here of your own accord and just walk on out the highway, I don't guess I'd be taking you away from Zollie, now would I? I'd just be picking up a hitchhiker."

Shurley had mixed feelings. He had wondered how long, with winter approaching, he could continue the long walk to and from Irondale. It sure sounded as if Mr. Smith was offering better living conditions, too. But the Stringfellows and Derryberrys had been good to him, even though they expected him to work hard—very hard—in exchange for only meager room and board, no salary.

His biggest concern, though, was that he would once more be separated from Bubba. Shurley decided he would let his brother in on the offer and see what he thought about it.

"Mr. Clyde, he's a good man," Bubba assured him, nodding.

"But I'm thinking I'll stay here, Bubba," Shurley confessed. "I go over there to stay, I won't ever get to see you no more."

"'Course you will! Mr. Clyde, he'll bring you over here when he comes to ride his horses. You'll see me then."

Smith confirmed what Bubba had told Shurley. Of course he could ride back to the Stringfellows' every time he came to visit his animals. That settled the matter.

THE BOY YET AGAIN gathered up his clothes and a few of the magazines he had not yet read. Then he set out across the pasture, walking the same route he took to school each morning, until he reached the highway. Sure enough, a few minutes later he heard the rumbling engine of the Packard convertible approaching and then sliding to a stop alongside him. The door swung open.

"Climb in, Shurley," the man said with a broad smile. As soon as the boy was settled in the seat, Clyde Smith gunned the motor and they roared away off down Highway 78.

It was a new sensation for the boy. His only other previous travels were in his uncle's Model-T and a couple of trips to horse shows, riding in the back of Mr. Stringfellow's big truck with the horses. The wind in his face was invigorating and the acceleration and speed were even a bit frightening. Frightening but thrilling, a mixture he had never experienced.

Smith lived with his wife, Bessie, in a huge rock house not far off Highway 78. He ushered Shurley through the back door. Miss Bessie, a tall, red-headed woman, was waiting, a cigarette in her mouth, arms crossed, and a mock scowl on her face. Shurley had no idea her frown was not for real. His stomach turned over. Had he just stepped into another mess by going to Mr. Clyde's place?

"Now, Clyde, who is this young man and what are you doing bringing him home with you?" she asked.

"This is Shurley Stewart, the one I was telling you about. He's going to stay downstairs in the basement."

Her scowl turned into a big smile and Miss Bessie's eyes sparkled.

"All right, then. Come on in, Shurley, and meet Mary Sue and we'll take you downstairs so you can see your nest."

Mary Sue was the Smith's twenty-something-year-old daughter, an attractive woman but a victim of polio, with withered arms and legs. She walked awkwardly with the aid of a pair of rattling metal crutches.

"Papa Clyde told us you like to read," she said as she shook Shurley's hand. "Books are what make being crippled like this bearable. Books are my greatest pleasure and I suspect you and I are going to get along just fine." She smiled at him.

Shurley could not believe what he was hearing. This white family seemed to be accepting him into their home, not just as a servant or hired help, but almost as a guest. He was even happier when he saw his new quarters. There was a cot in the corner near the coal furnace, a wash basin with hot and cold water, and—wonder of wonders—an inside toilet. He could not help but stare at the commode. How long had it been since he had used anything but a bush or a plot of grass when he had to go? Even at Mamie's and Henry's the only choice was a one-hole privy across the backyard.

The room also held a pool table (where he would pass many hours by himself, refining his game of eight-ball or cutthroat), a coal bin, and old, odd pieces of furniture. Among the furnishings was a tall, elegant, full-length mirror. That, too, was a novelty. Appearance had never been much of an issue for the boy. His looks, how he dressed, were not a factor when his concentration was on survival. Personal hygiene was something his father and aunts had never mentioned, much less taught him. There had never been much reason for a mirror before.

He stood and looked at his reflection for a bit. He was much taller now, and his arms were longer and muscled from shoveling all that horse manure. His teeth were yellow and his hair was long and tangled with bits of hay straw sticking out of it. He would work on all that, he told himself.

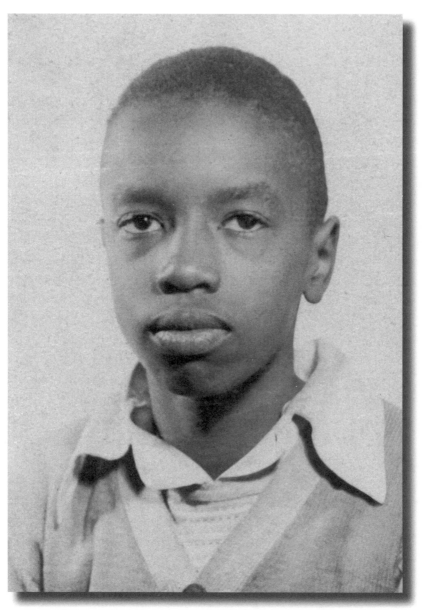

Shurley, 1944.

That first night in his new home, Shurley was as happy as he had been in a long time. There was coal dust on the floor, and he was on a cot, not a real bed. But it was a far better situation than anything he had experienced in his life since Mattie C. was taken from him.

He still quietly cried that night, though, as he drifted into sleep. Cried just as he had most nights since witnessing the death of his momma. Cried as he relived the turmoil that had befallen him and his brothers since.

He also thought about all that had happened to him that day since Mr. Clyde asked him to read him something from the rolled-up magazine. He wondered why Mr. Clyde had taken such an interest in him in the first place. Was he going to be like the others, his family members? Did Smith bring the boy home with him so he would have someone to beat and molest or work to death? Was he there in the basement of the big rock house because Smith figured this young, skinny nigger could not and would not fight back?

Shurley had a couple of homemade knives and an ice pick rolled up with his clothes. As he drifted into sleep, he swore he would not allow anyone to treat him the way Slim and the others had. He would fight back if he had to.

Lord, he prayed, *don't let me have to.*

Shurley would later realize that Clyde Smith was honestly impressed with the boy's eagerness to learn and with how quickly he picked up things. The boy seemed to have some ambition, too. Even at nine years old, he was aware of the importance of skills like reading and communicating when it came to surviving in a harsh world.

The next morning, Shurley learned that he would have chores to do, but nothing nearly as strenuous or smelly as what he had to do back at the barn, or as hard and dirty as his work when he lived with Aunt Emily in Rosedale. He was also to be company for Mary Sue and would help with housekeeping.

Before long, Mr. Clyde began to invite Shurley along with him as he toured the black neighborhoods, doubtless working on Smith's rumored illegal businesses. He also seemed to own several legitimate small stores and restaurants in those areas of town. Everywhere they went, though, blacks greeted Mr. Clyde warmly, as if they respected him, not just because they had to act that way to get along or avoid trouble.

As they rode through the hot city streets, the top down on the convertible, Clyde Smith shared his outlook on life with the boy. Though he was obviously quite wealthy, he preferred mingling with blacks and low- to middle-income whites instead of the blowhard big shots of the community. That was true even though he was certainly comfortable with all social levels.

He told Shurley over and over that he believed in "the good of the masses instead of the classes." He continually urged the boy to not lose his love and eagerness for learning, to absorb as much book knowledge as he could. But he also preached that he acquire practical knowledge at the same time. One of the traits that had made Shurley stand out to him was how the boy listened so intently to the conversations at the horse barn. And how the boy then boldly spoke up when he had something to contribute. He had never seen such a thing before, not just in a colored boy, but in anyone so young, Smith explained.

Smith made certain to take Shurley with him when he went to inspect work on the various housing developments he had under construction. He encouraged the boy to observe the carpenters, electricians, and plumbers, and to ask the workers questions about what they were doing and how they did it. The laborers never seemed to be irritated when the skinny colored kid got in their way or peppered them with questions, likely because he was with Mr. Clyde. And Shurley took advantage to learn all he could.

Even more enlightening to the boy was watching how Smith did business, how he treated others in the way he dealt with them. It was always the same, whether he was talking to a scruffy black man who was clearly helping with something illegal or with a store owner or banker. The boy would later realize that was the primary reason Smith took the boy with him in his rides through the neighborhoods, checking on his enterprises. Clyde Smith built his entire life—not just his businesses—on personal relationships. Relationships based on mutual respect, not skin color or station in life. Relationships based on doing the right thing, even if it was not always the easiest thing. Those lessons stuck with the boy as surely as the book learning and how the carpenters carefully measured the boards twice before cutting.

NOW THAT HE LIVED with the Smiths, Shurley's walk to the colored elementary school in Irondale was less than half an hour if he took the short way through the woods. However, he was afraid he might ruin the new clothes and shoes the Smiths had bought for him, catching beggar lice and briars in the shirt and pants and scuffing his shoes on rocks if he took that route. He usually took the longer way down the main highway, which was still far shorter than the journey had been from the Stringfellows'.

There was another reason he went that way, too. He wanted to make sure nobody at the school knew a colored boy was living with white folks. Such an arrangement carried a stigma that the boy already knew could cause trouble with both blacks and whites. Shurley knew his living there could raise questions and possibly ignite trouble for the Smiths as well as for him. Some days, when the weather was bad, Mama Bessie or Papa Clyde—they had insisted that Shurley call them by those names—would drive him to within a few blocks of the school. There they could drop him off behind a building so there was little danger of a colored boy being seen getting a ride to school from a white person. Shurley also knew he should never invite a school friend home to play after school. No use asking for trouble.

One of the few people who knew Shurley lived with the Smiths was Percy Kelley, a black handyman who worked for Papa Clyde. "Big Percy" was the one who had first told the Smiths about the smart boy down at the school, the one who always walked to and from Irondale from way over in Mountain Brook, no matter how hard it rained or how cold a day it was.

Shurley watched with amazement the interaction between Kelley and his boss. He had never witnessed such a thing. The two men acted more like friends than employee and employer. And certainly in a way the boy had never seen blacks and whites relate to each other before. The two men even passed around the same whiskey bottle, taking turns taking sips, and Clyde never wiped the spout before drinking after Big Percy. That astonished Shurley.

Two other black men came by the house several times a week. They apparently worked for Papa Clyde's policy business, likely collecting the bets and paying off the winners. One day Shurley overheard one of them advise

Smith that he should not allow a colored boy to live in the house of a white family. Such a thing would not play well in the black community if word got out, and it might be bad for business. It was one of the few times he saw Papa Clyde lose his temper. He told the man, in no uncertain terms, to keep his opinions to himself.

"Shurley's my boy. You do what you're supposed to be doing and let me mind my own business."

Still, from that day on, Shurley always tried to make himself invisible when those two men came to the house.

Shurley continued to go to school and do his chores as part of his agreement with the Smiths. He took out the garbage from the house, raked the leaves, and picked up trash in the parking lot at Papa Clyde's motel, which was just down the hill from the house. He also carried ice and clean towels to the rooms at the motel, which, he soon noticed, catered to some very short-term visitors. The boy noticed white men come in with their black maids or girlfriends, stay an hour or two, and then check out again. It occurred to him as well that he never saw black men check into the motel with white girlfriends.

Even if his living with the Smiths might have caused problems for some, Shurley continued his rides with Papa Clyde. The man ignored the stares and whispered comments of others—colored and white—who were curious about a black boy riding right there in the front seat of the big convertible, sitting next to a rich white man as if he actually belonged there. Some likely assumed Shurley was the child of a maid or handyman. Others speculated Clyde had fathered the child with some black woman and that was why this little nigger was treated so special. Regardless, Clyde Smith did not allow the curiosity, scrutiny, or speculation to bother him. If anyone said anything, he simply told them, as he had his numbers runners, that Shurley was "his boy" and they should mind their own damn business.

As they grew more comfortable with each other, Smith began to sense the melancholy and sadness that followed this smart little colored boy around like a cloud. Finally Shurley began sharing some of the hardships and abuse he and his brothers had lived with, from their momma's murder to the physical and sexual abuse from his aunt. He could not help crying sometimes when he talked about what life had been like for him. He noticed Papa Clyde was shedding a tear or two as well.

Later, Shurley learned that Smith had made some inquiries around Rosedale and confirmed the stories the boy told him. In their wanderings from then on, Smith made certain not to pass through Rosedale if Shurley was in the car with him. Slim Stewart sounded like the kind of man who might try to profit from his flesh and blood living and working for a rich white family.

Shurley had not mentioned his aunt and uncle in Collegeville, though. Several times in their ramblings they passed right in front of Mamie's house. Shurley just slipped down in the seat, though he doubted she or Henry would recognize him after the several years that had passed, especially if he was riding with a white man in a big convertible.

True to his promise, Clyde Smith always took Shurley with him when he went back to the Stringfellow barn to check on his horses. That meant he could see and spend time with Bubba. Then, in the winter of 1945, Papa Clyde got an offer for his horses that he could not turn down. There was no longer a reason for him to visit the stables. No matter. Shortly after, Shurley learned that Bubba had packed his few clothes and, after almost three years at the stables, left the barn in the middle of a dark night, looking for something else where he could make some money.

AGAIN, SHURLEY STEWART'S LIFE fell into an easy routine. He went to school, came back to the Smiths, did his chores, and finished his homework. Mama Bessie would tell him to bring in his workbooks and let her take a look at what he was doing. She pushed, corrected, and encouraged him but was often impressed with how bright he was. If he was assigned two chapters in a book to read, she insisted that he read four. Those were the terms of the agreement he had with the Smiths and he intended to keep up his end of the bargain. He could live with them but he had to learn, to do his best in school, and to pay attention to the more practical lessons the Smiths offered up for him.

The boy decided one day to take on a new project to keep his mind limber. He began reading a copy of the King James Bible from beginning to end. When he finished, he started over and read it all the way through again. And then, he started at Revelations and read the Bible backward, all the way to Genesis 1:1. It was good practice, reading the words and trying to comprehend the message they bore. But it also rekindled his interest in church.

Religion had been missing from his life since his mother's death silenced her gospel songs and he and Bubba had climbed into the trees outside the church in Rosedale. Shurley began walking down to a church in The Bends, the black area of Irondale, most Sunday mornings.

His first visit there he had walked right up to the door and started inside with the rest of the worshippers so he could get the full experience. However, an usher stopped him cold with a big hand on his shoulder and a withering gaze.

"Boy, you ain't dressed fit to come into the Lord's house. Get on out of here now. Go on back to your mammy."

Shurley took the rebuff in stride. It was nothing new. He simply walked around to the side of the church, climbed up into the limbs of a convenient tree, eased back into the crook, and listened to all the preaching and singing just as he and Bubba had done it in Rosedale. Now Bubba had disappeared. That fact and the songs—many of them about mothers who had gone on to be with Jesus—caused the boy to cry large tears. But he still got a blessing from the music and the strong-voiced words of the preachers. They made him sad and happy at the same time. They also got him to thinking.

One day, without even realizing what was happening, Shurley Stewart took a powerful new interest in that full-length mirror, the one he had noticed the first night in his little room, standing next to the furnace down in Clyde Smith's basement. Listening to the preachers, hearing how the people in the congregation responded to their potent message, the boy had already begun to form an idea about what his life's purpose might be, why God had put him here and given him the intelligence and desire to learn, and why He had led him through so many trials and tribulations.

Standing in front of that big mirror, Shurley Stewart would soon find his future revealed in surprising but puzzling detail. It was all there in the reflection that bounced back at him from the dusty glass.

8

the BREAKFAST GUEST

At night, after the Smiths had gone to bed, the boy grew ever so lonely. Except for his time with Aunt Emily, he always had Bubba to keep him company. Even in those miserable days at his aunt's house, she was there in the evenings so he was rarely alone.

Now, in his basement room by himself each evening, he had his regular good cry, missed his mother for a while and sometimes talked with her, and then tossed and turned on the cot. Maybe it was the bad dreams that would inevitably come that prevented him from resting. Maybe he simply had too much ache in his heart to doze off immediately.

Finally, he got up one night, pulled the string to turn on the bare overhead light bulb, and stood as tall as he could in front of the mirror. He studied his reflection and imagined himself grown up, standing straight, with an audience or church congregation looking up at him, waiting to hear what he was going to say.

Then he began to preach. Each night, he pulled messages out of the air, crafted them on the fly, and watched the faces in the mirror looking back at him, listening. He recited the Bible verses he had memorized or pulled out the Bible and read new ones in as deep a voice as he could find.

Shurley delivered the most spellbinding sermons imaginable to the looking glass. He started slowly, almost whispering, forcing his voice as low as he could, and slowly built momentum with inflection and nuance. Then, using his arms and hands for emphasis, shrugging his shoulders, doing a little dance on one foot, he amped up the energy to a frenetic pace. He laughed and cried, danced some more, used his modulation to emphasize the points he wanted to make, and used verses he had read from the Bible to bring them home. Sometimes his voice went full falsetto. Sometimes he found a surprisingly deep resonance somewhere in his skinny chest. Often he broke into song. But he practiced using just the right style and tone to get across the message he wanted to communicate to his imaginary and invisible audience.

The amazing thing was that he actually began to see that audience appear in the mirror. They watched wide-eyed as he performed, taking in his every word. Then they responded with shouts, applause, and standing ovations. That responsive audience he saw in the looking glass was as real as day, as genuine as all those faces at the church house looking up at the preacher, as tangible as the faces of the students in his classroom gazing up at their teacher.

"Shurley, I hear you talking to somebody last night?" Papa Clyde asked him one morning.

"No, boss."

"You sure. I got up and I could have sworn I heard voices."

"Just saying my prayers, probably."

Somewhere along the way, the boy realized that the mirror was giving him a clue about his future. At first, he thought it might be telling him he was going to be a preacher, delivering sermons and saving souls. Maybe a teacher, inspiring his students with his words so they would learn to read and go out and seek knowledge. Or a singer, moving an audience with his renditions of those old spiritual songs his mother loved so much to sing. He might even become a lawyer, persuading judge and jury of the innocence of his client with his oratorical skills and strong voice.

The more Shurley studied the crowds, though, the more he doubted any of those possibilities lay ahead of him. That was not a jury, a congregation, or a classroom full of students looking back at him. The only thing he could tell for certain was that he was destined to communicate with multitudes of people. Those people would heed his words and respond to what he was telling them, so long as he did his best and used his talents to move them. So long as he touched them as individuals, not just as a mass of people.

Shurley had no idea how to prepare for the future he was seeing in the mirror. Then he remembered what Mrs. Mamie Foster, his first-grade teacher at Union Baptist, had told him.

"You can be anything you want to be. You are going to be somebody."

Then there was someone else who reinforced the teacher's faith in the boy and his potential.

SOME NIGHTS CLYDE AND Bessie went out for the evening and left Mary Sue alone. Those nights, they asked Shurley to stay in the guest room that adjoined the handicapped young lady's bedroom, just in case she fell or needed something. Had she taken a spill she would have had a difficult time getting up. He often stretched out across the foot of her bed and he and the young woman read books and magazines together, or they talked about a broad range of subjects. One night, Mary Sue put down her book, looked at the boy, and frowned.

"You know, Shurley, I hate it that things are the way they are for Negroes," she told him. "I think I can imagine just how it is to want to do something special in life, to get any job you want or live anywhere you want to live, but you can't do it just because of your race." She glanced down at her crooked legs. "I think I know a little bit about how it must feel to want something you can't have just because of the way God made you when you were born."

Shurley did not know what to say in reply so he just kept quiet.

"You know what, though," Mary Sue went on. "I've been watching you, Shurley Stewart. If you have half a chance, you will reach your potential. You'll show people a colored boy can be just as smart as or smarter than a white boy. If you know you are right, don't let anybody else tell you that you are wrong. Maybe you'll change some minds about some things one of these days."

The boy still had no idea how to respond. Even though he liked Mary Sue, he also knew whites could get all cockeyed real quick if a colored person said the wrong thing or even looked at them the wrong way. Still, he felt something in his chest, a rising pride similar to what he felt when the crowd in the mirror cheered on his speeches.

After a year or so with the Smiths, Shurley still slept in the basement but otherwise pretty much had the run of the big residence. The only time he made himself scarce was when the Smiths had company, and especially if they were kinfolks visiting, or when the numbers-runners came by. He did not want to cause the family even a moment's uneasiness and he suspected even their kin might have a different idea about the propriety of a colored boy living in the house with white folks.

By then he also usually sat in the breakfast room with Clyde, Bessie, and Mary Sue as they ate their morning meal. Now that was a massive breach of commonly accepted decorum! Such behavior would have raised eyebrows among most whites and blacks of that time. A colored boy eating at the same table with whites!

One morning, a guest stopped by unexpectedly to visit with Papa Clyde while the family was eating breakfast. It was a man everyone called Doc. He was the blacksmith at Stringfellow stables. None of the Smiths thought anything of it and Papa Clyde invited Doc to come on, sit down, and have a cup of coffee while they got caught up on some business they needed to discuss.

As soon as Doc sat down, though, he stopped talking. He noticed Shurley for the first time, glared at the boy for a moment, and then poked a finger not at him but at the plate and coffee cup in front of the boy.

"Clyde, I expect you better throw away them damn dishes," the blacksmith proclaimed.

Smith looked over the rim of his coffee cup at the visitor, a questioning look on his face.

"Why's that, Doc?"

"That nigger boy's eatin' off of 'em. You usually let a nigger sit down with y'all and eat at your table?"

Papa Clyde calmly set his coffee cup down in its saucer. Then he drew back his hand and, like the sudden strike of a snake, unleashed a punch to the tall visitor's jaw hard enough to send him flying backward in his chair. The back of his head hit the floor hard.

The blacksmith rolled over and stood up, rubbing his chin and shaking his head, a dazed look in his eyes. "Jesus Christ, Clyde, what'd you do that for? All I said was you oughtn't let that little nigger sit . . ."

Before he could finish, Clyde stood and slugged him again. The man fell

Shurley, 1947.

backward, catching himself on the door to keep from going down again.

"Doc, you don't come into my house and use words like that again," Smith told him, his voice trembling with anger. "You understand what I'm telling you?"

"Hell, what words? Nigger? That's what we call 'em, case you ain't . . ."

Smith drew back his fist again. The blacksmith was much bigger and stronger than Papa Clyde but he did not try to fight back.

Shurley watched the sudden violence with eyes wide and mouth open. He would later decide that Doc had not retaliated because of his respect for Smith. And sure enough, in a few minutes the two men were outside in the back yard sharing slugs from a whiskey bottle as if nothing had ever happened between them.

Shurley never brought up the incident but Papa Clyde told the boy several times afterward to not ever allow anyone to use that slur around him. Clyde Smith was not a religious man, but he told Shurley that he lived his life by two standards: the Golden Rule from Matthew 7:12 and the Ten Commandments out of the book of Exodus. He strongly suggested that the boy do the same.

"You follow those rules and everything else will fall into place, Shurley," he told him. "I don't care who it is, you treat a man with the same respect you'd want to be treated until you determine that he is not worthy of it. Not worthy because of what's in his heart and head, not what color he is or how much money he makes or who his daddy was."

IN THE SUMMER OF 1947, a few months before Shurley turned thirteen, he and Papa Clyde were sitting in the yard beneath the shade of a big tree, trying to keep cool, talking about one subject or another that would have likely surprised an eavesdropper. The discussions between the grown man and the black twelve-year-old were typically far more advanced than anyone would have imagined.

Smith suddenly looked past Shurley, over the boy's shoulder and down the long driveway. He squinted hard into the brilliant sunlight. "There comes a big colored woman headed this way up the driveway," he announced. "Reckon what she wants?"

Shurley turned and looked in that direction. She was a big one all right, surely three hundred pounds of black woman. She wore a floppy bonnet and was huffing and puffing from the exertion of climbing the hill, fanning herself with a handkerchief. There was something familiar about the woman but the boy did not recognize her from that distance.

Then, suddenly, he did. His stomach turned over.

Aunt Mamie. It had been almost eight years since he had last seen his mother's sister. That was the day she and her husband Henry dumped Shurley, Bubba, Samuel, and David in the vacant lot next to Slim Stewart's house on Central Avenue and drove away. Two days before Christmas, 1939. A world war had been fought and won since then. The boy had lived through Marie and Slim and surviving on the open porch, his Aunt Emily and her strange, violent, and wicked ways, and being in the horse barn at the Stringfellows' with Bubba. There had been plenty of water over the dam since that day, but he recognized his Aunt Mamie for certain.

The boy's first impulse was to run and hide. But when he stood to do so, the woman called out to him in a voice as familiar as that staggering, stumbling walk of hers.

"Boy, you damn well better not run!"

"Hold on, Shurley," Papa Clyde told him. "You know this woman?"

"That's my auntie. Mamie. My momma's sister. I never told you about her. Her and her husband, they took us in for a little bit after Daddy killed Momma. Then took us and left us at Daddy's."

By then, Mamie Pickens was close enough to begin what was clearly a well-rehearsed speech, pausing between words to catch her breath.

"Mister, this here is my sister's boy. I come to get him. It ain't right that he be stayin' here with you white folks and I am truly sorry y'all have had to take him in and all." She wiped sweat from her broad brow with the handkerchief. "He's under-age, you know. And I mean to take him home where he belongs and take care of him and raise him right in the way of the Lord. We are family and we take care of our own."

Shurley still might have fled but Papa Clyde had a firm grip on his arm.

"I ain't going with her," the boy announced firmly.

The two adults discussed the situation for a bit while Shurley listened as his fate was bandied about. Papa Clyde ultimately lost the argument. Though he did not fully understand it at the time, Shurley later realized that Aunt Mamie could have caused a great deal of trouble for Smith. Not all his enterprises were strictly legal, and though the law usually looked the other way so long as he provided his services for colored folks and nobody got hurt, they could not ignore it if he was accused of kidnapping a colored boy from his rightful family.

It would be many years later before Shurley understood why Aunt Mamie was so determined to get him back with her and Henry. It seems that she got the news of the boy's situation through a complicated string of gossip. While talking with a teacher friend, a woman heard about an especially smart Negro boy out there at the Irondale Colored School. His last name was Stewart. That woman mentioned it to one of her friends, a lady who happened to know Mamie Pickens and lived in Collegeville. The lady also remembered her nephews from the brief time they stayed with Mamie. That lady was an acquaintance but no friend of Mamie's. She wanted to use the news to embarrass her. Especially after she learned the rest of the story: that the Stewart boy was, of all things, living with a white family.

"Mamie, whatever happened to them four nephews of yours?" the acquaintance asked one day, and then cocked an ear, ready to hear the answer.

"Aw, I put them little bastards out years ago," Mamie responded honestly.

The lady could not wait to tell Mamie the whole story. Especially the part about the white family taking the boy in.

Mamie was mortified. The situation reflected negatively on her in several ways. Her friends and neighbors would talk behind her back about how she and Henry were not taking care of her poor dead sister's child. Even white folks were doing more for her nephew than Mamie Pickens was doing. On the other hand, her generously taking in the boy—and raising him to be such a smart one, too—would actually give Mamie more social status in the neighborhood than she had before. Besides, there was just one of the Stewart boys left now, so far as she knew, and she could assume this one was housebroken by now.

Mamie would later tell Shurley that she "rescued" him from the white people, that they were raising him like a slave.

"Shurley, listen to me," Papa Clyde told him that day. "I love you. I'd love to keep you here with us and watch you grow up into a man and use that brain of yours to be successful. I really would. But this is your aunt. The law would be on her side, you can bet. Something tells me she would not hesitate going that route either."

Mamie only grunted in response. Then she tapped her foot impatiently as she waited for Clyde, Bessie, and Mary Sue to hug Shurley. All four cried as if at a funeral. She also waited while the boy packed up his clothes yet again, and while the Smiths and the boy hugged and cried some more. Then, as they walked off down the driveway, Shurley looked back, waved, and sobbed unashamedly as his aunt shoved him along down the hill in front of her.

The Smiths had been more of a family to Shurley than any of his kin had ever been. Years later, he would realize the most basic lesson he had learned there in that rock house on the hill: Love has no color. Prejudice, meanness, and discrimination are equally color blind.

It was ironic that it was a white family that first gave the black boy the kindness and love that he never received from his own family. It was a fact that was not lost on the boy, though. You cannot paint folks with such a broad brush. All white people are not the same. Neither are all blacks or other races. As Papa Clyde had taught him, people must be judged on their own merits, by the way they treat others, by what is in their hearts, not by their skin color.

The Smiths were still standing beneath the shade tree, Papa Clyde with his shoulders slumped, watching them go, Mama Bessie puffing on a cigarette and crying, Mary Sue leaning on her metal crutches, trying to wave to him as best she could manage.

Then they were out of sight and Shurley Stewart and his Aunt Mamie were standing by the side of the road in the hot sun, waiting for the Number 17 street car to haul them back to Collegeville.

9

the BIRTH CeRTIFICATE

Shurley Stewart did not have such a negative memory of living with Aunt Mamie and Uncle Henry. Not compared to some of the other places he had laid his head over the past eight years. It was the way the whole thing ended that left such a bad taste in the boy's mouth.

He had been so young when he rode away in the old Ford after his momma's funeral, he and his brothers stayed there for such a short time, and life in Collegeville, as he remembered it, had not been so bad. The house on 34th Avenue North was in a black, working-class neighborhood. It was warm, neat, and clean in Mamie's home.

However, on his return, Shurley quickly discovered that he was not to have his own bedroom even though it was a two-bedroom house. He would have to sleep on a cot set up in the living room and it had to be folded up and put away each morning. Though in the midst of a thriving city, the house still did not have indoor plumbing, which meant no bathtub and no toilet. There was an outhouse along the back fence of their yard. Henry and Mamie also kept a yard full of chickens and goats and a pig pen on their little city lot.

The surprising part to Shurley was how out-of-place he felt now that he was surrounded by black people. He had grown quite accustomed to Papa Clyde Smith's world.

On his first night back, Aunt Mamie sat him down and told him bluntly how things were going to be. Henry, still clearly henpecked, merely sat back, listened and nodded to whatever his wife said, nibbling all the while on the matchstick he perpetually had stuck between his lips.

Shurley was to be up at 3 A.M. each morning so he could bring in coal to heat the water for the washtub. Bringing it in the night before left too much dust and mess, Mamie explained. Each night, Shurley was to bank the coals in the stove and carry out the ashes to get it ready for the next day. In between, he was to sweep and mop the linoleum floors, dust the furniture, slop the hogs, and feed the chickens and goats.

"Henry works his fingers to the bone down to the wheel shop and you are going to help him out around here," she told the boy, her jaw thrust out for emphasis. "We gone see just how damn smart you are."

She also instructed the boy to never tell anyone he had lived with white folks. If he did, she would see that Clyde Smith got into a peck of trouble. Shurley was also not to let Jerome know where he was now. She did not want to take in any more of Slim Stewart's "little bastards" if she could help it.

Shurley was not to leave the yard except to go to and from school. While home, he was to do his chores to pay for the food he ate and the roof over his head. Once again, he was a prisoner in an aunt's house, though this one had not beaten him with an electric cord and poured salt in the welts. At least not yet.

Shurley listened, all the while wondering how his sweet mother could have emerged from the same family or shared the same blood with her sisters Emily and Mamie.

Mamie also made it clear to the boy that neither she nor her husband was the least bit interested in his pursuing an education. They were both illiterate and they were making it just fine, thank you. Colored folks only wasted their time getting educated. Whites would make sure no educated Negro got ahead in life. They best just get whatever job they could at the steel mill or L&N or one of the other industrial sites in this booming town. That was the best they could hope for in this life.

However, the law still required that children—white or black—attend school until they were 16. Shurley Stewart had two more years of compulsory education whether his aunt liked it or not. Then he could drop out and get a job.

So it was that his aunt bought him new shirts and pants—it would not do for her neighbors to see him going to school in clothes purchased for her nephew by white folks—and sent him off to eighth grade at Hudson

Elementary. After a few days, the principal sent word to his teacher that he needed to talk to the Stewart boy. There were problems with his school records. The most serious discrepancy, other than exactly where he had lived since entering the first grade over in Rosedale, was that he did not have a birth certificate on file. Nobody had thought to ask for one at his previous schools.

Shurley talked his way around the residence issue but he had no idea where a birth certificate might be.

The truth was, Shurley had already been roaming the neighborhood, all the way to downtown, regardless of his aunt's admonition never to leave the yard. As he had done since first grade in Rosedale, he knew how to take the long way home from school, and he also knew when his aunt would be away from home. If he brought up the birth certificate to Mamie, she might simply stonewall getting a copy and get him thrown out of school. If he could get one, he would do it himself.

Shurley found out from the school office where to go to request a copy and he would not have to even mention it to his aunt. The boy walked all the way to the Jefferson County Department of Health, marched up to the counter, and told the clerk who he was and what he needed.

"Shurley Stewart. S-H-U-R-L-E-Y," he said.

The clerk wrote his name down on a slip of paper and then disappeared for a long while. Eventually she came back with a frown on her face.

"Who is your momma and daddy again?"

"Mattie C. Johnson Stewart was my momma. Huell Stewart is my daddy." He spelled both names once more for her.

"And what's your birthday?"

"September 4, 1934."

The clerk looked sideways at the papers she held in her hand for a while, her lips pursed.

"I got Huell and Mattie C. Stewart all right. But it says your name is 'Shelley,' and your birthday is September 24th, not the fourth."

For his first thirteen years, the boy thought his name was "Shurley." And his birthdate—though it had never been acknowledged or celebrated—was off by three weeks, too. Apparently Slim had given the wrong spelling of his name and the wrong date of birth when he signed the boy up for first grade.

Jesus, the boy thought as he jogged back to 33rd Avenue with the official piece of paper in his pocket, *I don't even know who the hell I am!*

When he told Mamie and Henry what he had learned, they took no interest. He was still "Shurley" to them and forevermore would be.

Shelley's time at home was mostly taken by doing his chores. Lights went out every night by 8 p.m, both to save on the electricity bill and because there was no point wasting illumination on such things as homework or reading. Sundays were spent at Gaines Chapel A.M.E. Church, and the boy enjoyed not only the preaching and singing but also the opportunity to get outside the close walls of his aunt's house. School offered the same kind of precious escape and Shelley threw himself into his studies.

Then one day the boy found a new means of escape. This one turned out to be a lifeline he did not expect but certainly welcomed. Shelley got himself a job.

As USUAL, HE WENT with Mamie and Henry on their once-a-month trip to purchase groceries—staples like flour, meal, and sugar—at Yielding's, one of the city's first department stores. The establishment occupied most of a city block on 2nd Avenue North downtown. They needed the boy to help them lug the heavy bags back home or he would likely have been left behind to work. He also understood that his aunt and uncle bought those staples at Yielding's because it was one of the few stores that extended credit to blacks.

One of the store's owners, Milton Yielding, noticed Shelley doing something he had never seen a black child do before. He was telling Henry and Mamie the prices of items and reading for them what the signs along the aisles said.

"Young man, how are you doing in school?" Yielding asked the boy.

Aunt Mamie, though, pulled Shelley behind her and jumped in to proudly answer the question.

"He is doing fine, Mr. Yielding. Just fine. Me and Henry make sure of that. Yes sir, we do, sir."

Shelley would never know for sure what prompted him to do what he did then. Maybe it was a gentle nudge in the back from a ghostly hand.

But looking around from behind his rather ample aunt, he noticed that a long line was forming at one of the cash registers. The lady running the register was having to also sack the groceries because there was no bag boy available at the moment.

When Shelley felt the push in the small of his back, he stepped around his aunt and to the end of the counter. He began to fill sacks with food items just the way he had observed the other bag boys doing it.

"Bread and eggs on top now, boy," Mr. Yielding advised as he watched the skinny boy do the job for a moment. There was a smile on his face. "You know, you make a good sacker. How old are you? Thirteen?" He turned to where Uncle Henry watched wide-eyed. "I might want to put this boy to work, Henry."

If a white man said it, Henry and Mamie were obliged to grin, nod, bow and go along with it. And from that point and with or without his aunt's approval, Shelley had himself a job each day after school and on Saturdays. He was now a grocery sacker at Yielding's Department Store. His ten-dollar paycheck went straight to Mamie each week but he managed to stash away the penny and nickel tips. Shelley's paycheck eased the sting for Mamie of losing her live-in "employee" for several hours each day. She also made certain her church friends heard what the store manager had said about Shurley and that they knew that her nephew had been hired by and was now working for Mr. Yielding himself.

At first, it seemed to Shelley that this new job only intensified his labors and gave him none of the spending money he craved. It took more hours away from his studying and reading. Also, part-time job or not, there were no fewer chores waiting when he walked home each night.

Soon, though, he would come to the realization that he was doing much more than merely bagging groceries and earning tips. The job was teaching him valuable new lessons. At the same time, it gave him entry into a whole new world, one that included some very important people.

All Shelley had to do was pull on the appropriate mask, and once again he found a way to make the most of the situation in which he had landed.

10

MOViNg the BOARd

Shelley Stewart understood segregation about as well as any other black person in Birmingham, Alabama, did. He had seen it, felt it, and lived it. However, he did not worry about it or dwell on it. It simply was the way it was. It was as much a part of growing up in Birmingham as the pink-hued steel-mill smoke and the summertime heat lightning. It was just a part of being black.

There came a day, though, when it suddenly came home to him with full force. That was the day when he climbed aboard the Number 22/Boyles/Tarrant City street car to ride from Hudson Elementary to his job at Yielding's downtown. Some days, Shelley used his tip money to treat himself to a ride to work. This day it was hot and humid and he decided to ride.

The car was crowded that day. Or at least part of it was.

The back of the street car was crammed with blacks. The few seats back there were full and the rest of the colored passengers were so packed into the aisle they could hardly move, until the car came to a stop and they had no choice but to lurch forward as one mass. Shelley looked around as he got aboard.

The usual moveable board—the official demarcation between white seats and Negro seats—was in its arbitrary place. On this day, it designated only four rows at the very back where coloreds could sit. Or stand if all the seats were filled. And they were. Up front, amid row after row of empty seats, sat only two or three white passengers.

Only the driver could move that board. That was the law.

Shelley did not understand why one of the black men had not already asked the driver to open up more seats for his Negro passengers. They had almost certainly worked harder that day than the few whites had. Even so, he stood in the aisle with the others, with hardly room to breathe.

Then something spoke to him. An inner voice told the boy to be strong, to take charge and see what he could do about the situation. He walked down the aisle and stood behind the car's operator.

"Sir, would you please move the board up so those folks back there can take a seat?" he politely asked, smiling.

The driver ignored him, though Shelley was certain he had spoken loudly and plainly enough to have been heard and understood. Hours spent in front of that mirror back at Papa Clyde's had left him with a strong voice and good diction. He also had on his mask, the one that usually worked with white folks when he asked for something.

"Sir, please," he repeated respectfully. "Could you move the board and open some seats for those tired folks back there?"

There was again no indication the white driver had heard Shelley's request. The man stared straight ahead. Then, without hesitation, the boy turned, marched back down the aisle, boldly moved the board several rows toward the front, and sat down in one of the seats that was now behind it.

The street car whooshed to a sudden stop. Shelley could see the man's face in the rear-view mirror growing red with anger.

"Boy, you move that board back where I had it and you get your ass out of that damn seat!"

Shelley responded clearly and firmly. "No sir."

"Did you not hear what I told you? You move that board!"

The boy was suddenly aware of the tension filling the street car like thundercloud humidity. He could see the reactions to the sudden show-down, not just on the faces of the few white passengers but on the black faces, too. Several of the black passengers—and especially the women—had a look of fear or pain.

Shelley knew what they were thinking. Why was this tall, skinny boy causing problems on their ride? All they wanted to do was get home from their housekeeping or mill jobs, get off their feet and have some supper, maybe go to preaching down at the church. They wanted no hassle with the white driver.

Why didn't the kid just move the board back before the driver called the law? Then they could be on their way.

Shelley was having his own doubts by then. What if the driver did get the police involved? No doubt how that would turn out. Or what if the man simply grabbed Shelley up by the collar and threw him off the car? Did Shelley dare fight back if he did?

However, a couple of the colored men walked forward and settled down into seats near Shelley. They motioned for the others to do likewise and they did, women first.

The white passengers stared straight ahead the whole time, clearly hoping something would defuse the showdown before there was violence. The driver glared at all of them from his seat, his eyes squinting in the mirror. He recognized that he was now outnumbered. It was not just the brash kid defying the natural order any more. Those nigger men might be carrying knives, too. Didn't they all? He decided not to make a stand and simply drove on to the end of his day as well.

That successful but simple act of defiance filled Shelley Stewart's heart with pride. He kept a straight face the whole ride and said nothing when he exited the street car past the stony-faced driver. Later, the boy would think more about what happened that afternoon on the Number 22. Then again much later, when Rosa Parks refused to give up her seat on a city bus in Montgomery, Alabama, starting a fight that would eventually be settled in the U.S. Supreme Court. If one boy's simple action had caused a street car full of tired people to risk getting arrested simply to have a seat, what bigger things could black people accomplish if they worked together?

SHORTLY AFTER BEGINNING HIS job at Yielding's Department Store, Shelley had come to another realization. He was, as his mother might have said, "in high cotton." Many prominent people in Birmingham frequented the store and he was in a prime spot to eavesdrop and even to contribute to their conversations, much as he had done with the horse owners back at the Stringfellow stables. He also made certain these important men knew who Shelley Stewart was and that he could hold his own with them or anybody else.

One of Milton Yielding's brothers was on the Jefferson County Commission. Other commissioners and officials were regulars in the store, either stopping by to visit or to shop. The city hall and courthouses were just up the street. Jefferson County Sheriff Holt McDowell—who would have the longest tenure in that office in county history—was also a frequent visitor, as were other law enforcement personnel.

They all got to know Shelley Stewart, the bag boy who would also at times jump behind the counter and run the cash register, make quick and accurate change, and do far more, all while keeping up an amazing line of happy patter. The boy was something else!

Mr. Milton allowed Shelley to take breaks and go into a nearby stock room to do his homework or read. Sometimes the other bag boys—all of them white—asked him to help them with their studies. Shelley was happy to do so, even though the other boys were several grades ahead of him.

Often, the important visitors to the store stepped into the stock room to discuss business or politics, or they lurked just outside the door. They paid little attention to the boy with his nose buried in a book. They assumed the colored boy would never understand what they were discussing. That is, until he began to pipe up and join their chats.

That was another of Shelley's masks he so often slipped on. He had the knack to become someone totally different from what was expected, a person to fit the occasion. Now he was the "smart nigger," the "popular colored boy" who shocked average customers and important visitors alike with his grasp of current events and his ability to speak and articulate his opinions. Already Shelley had come to the conclusion that doing anything in life required developing relationships with white and black. Connections that could be put away, saved, and then used when needed. He had watched how Papa Clyde dealt with people, how he relied on relationships that were not just on the surface. They were sincere and they ran deep. It had worked out pretty well for Clyde Smith so it would do just as well for Shelley Stewart.

One day Sheriff McDowell looked at Shelley as the boy bagged his groceries and asked, "Young man, what do you hope to do when you grow up?"

Without hesitation, the boy looked the sheriff right in the eye—another trait that separated Shelley from most colored folks—and answered, "A lawyer. I want to go to law school and be a lawyer."

It was the first time he had ever said those words out loud and it felt good to finally do so. The boy had seen the lawyers who came into the store, how they dressed, how they held themselves. They invariably had a gift for gab. They seemed to have the respect of everyone around them. Surely being a lawyer was the ultimate white-collar job, a sign of intelligence and accomplishment. Shelley figured that would be the perfect occupation for him. He also reckoned that if he studied hard enough and made good enough grades, he could earn a scholarship that would make it possible for him to go to college and then continue on to law school so he could realize the dream. Granted there weren't a lot of black lawyers coming into the store, but he guessed there had to be some out there. Regardless, he would one day reduce that shortage by one.

The sheriff laughed and said, "Well, I don't doubt you will become one, then. Don't doubt it for a second."

However, when Shelley, bolstered by the sheriff's positive reaction, told Mamie and Henry of his desire to go to law school, they almost fell down laughing.

"Boy, you a mess!" his aunt cackled. "Forget school, Shurley. Ain't nothing good going to come from school. You make a lawyer?" She laughed even harder, as if he had just told her the funniest joke she had ever heard. Then she suddenly turned deadly serious, her mouth firmly set. "Boy, you ain't shit! You turn sixteen, you get yourself a job at the pipe shop or over at Stockham. Then maybe you'll be able to feed your wife and babies. Leastways you get your ass out my house. School ain't going to do no good for you. White man's going to make damn sure of that!"

One night Shelley woke up with a cramping in his gut. Normally, on a chilly night, he would just use the slop jar they kept in the corner. This night, though, he decided to go on out back to the privy. He was wide awake and the trip to the outhouse would give him the chance to think about the direction his life had taken. And the direction it was about to take when he moved on up to high school at Parker. As he usually did, he talked to himself as he sat there and did his business.

Nobody was out at that time of night so he left the door of the privy ajar. As he sat contemplating the future, he noticed the eerie yellow glow of the distant streetlight, the barking of dogs way off somewhere, a far-off police siren almost lost in the low, constant hum of the night-shift production at the mills. The streets were deserted at that hour and the mist and smoke concealed the moon and stars. There was only the yellow street light, haloed in the murkiness of the fog.

Shelley felt an odd sensation, as if he was not alone. His skin crawled and he felt a sudden chill run up his spine.

Just then, through the crack in the door, he thought he saw the slightest of movements in the shadows over close to the street light. Probably one of the chickens frightened off the roost by Shelley talking to himself, he thought. Or a stray dog. Wouldn't be anybody out here this time of night. Mostly working folks in this neighborhood and they didn't do too much cattin' around at night.

Still, he reached to pull up his skivvies, ready to make a run for the house if somebody meant to mess with him.

Then, clear as day, he heard someone say his name.

Shurley. The voice was so familiar. Achingly familiar. *Son.*

Through the narrow opening, he could just make out a dark form, out there beyond Aunt Mamie's property line, beneath the streetlight on the corner of 34th Street at 33rd Avenue. The dark shape seemed to be moving closer. Then he saw the familiar old coat, the small, furry hat, and the wire-rimmed glasses.

"Momma?"

Shelley did not know whether to run or not. His underwear was still down around his ankles.

Don't be afraid of me, Shelley, she told him in her gentle, soothing voice. *I'm not going to hurt you. I'd never hurt you.*

"But, Momma, I saw Daddy when he . . . you can't . . . I saw . . ." It had been ten years since he witnessed Slim hit her with that ax, knocking her out the window and into the clutches of that tree. But it was as if it had happened the day before. His momma was dead. He knew that. But there she was, standing in the fog beneath the street light talking to him.

Listen to me, Shelley. I've been with you all the time. You know you are my special angel, Shelley. I've been trying to guide you and you've mostly done what I told you to do. I'll still be coming to you from time to time and I'll tell you what to do. Obey me. I know things have been hard for you but remember I helped you find Jerome that time. That ought to show you that I'm always watching. Do you believe me, Shelley?

The boy could not move his mouth. For once, the "smart nigger" could not speak.

Listen, son, I want you to go find my boys. Jerome, Samuel, and David. I'll show you where they are if you will listen to me. I promised you I would never leave you. Know that I am in you and with you. I have not left you, Shelley.

With that, the shadowy figure melted into the fog of mill smoke.

Shelley pulled up his skivvies and ran as fast as he could to the house, yelling all the way.

"She was here! She was here, Aunt Mamie! Uncle Henry! I saw her! She talked to me! Momma!"

Henry came out the bedroom door, rubbing his eyes, carrying his shotgun. "What the hell's wrong with you, boy?" he asked gruffly. "Who you see?"

Mamie glared at him through half-opened eyes as he explained what he had just experienced out there in the backyard. There was no doubt in his mind that his mother had stood there and talked to him.

Of course, neither of them believed a word of the boy's ghostly tale. His aunt chalked it up to the craziness of the teenage boy with all that male juice coursing through his veins. Henry just mumbled something about "damn crazy Stewarts . . . every damn one of 'em."

Shelley was ordered back to his cot in the corner. It was only an hour or so until time to get up and fetch the coal and feed the animals. Working folks had to get up shortly after that, too.

However, the boy was unable to sleep the rest of that night. He had actually been thinking a lot about his three brothers lately. He missed them, wondered what had happened to them, where they were, and how they were doing. He wanted to find out if the younger two had survived much longer with Slim and Marie after he left. He still felt guilty for having it as good as he did when they might still be living like animals on that back stoop. Or worse.

He curled up in a ball on the cot and cried. The ghostly presence talking to him through the privy door that misty evening had confirmed one thing Shelley had already come to realize. It had been his mother who had been pushing and shoving him along the way. Now she was not only verifying it but she was also promising to continue to guide him. Shelley did not question for a moment that she would do just what she vowed to do.

After all, his momma had never lied to him before.

11

RaTKiLLeR'S and RADIO

In the 1940s, Birmingham's Parker Industrial High School was the largest black four-year high school in the nation. That was because it was at that time the only black four-year high school in the entire city of Birmingham. When Shelley Stewart enrolled there in the fall of 1948, he was equally excited and nervous, unable to sleep the several nights before his first day of classes. A school that big with hundreds and hundreds of students was a bit intimidating, but the boy also knew that it would offer the greatest opportunities for learning and continuing to work on his social skills.

A legal career and a scholarship to get there were heavy on his mind as he climbed from bed— as usual at 3 A.M. to do his chores—that first school morning. At 6, he began the long walk to Parker High. His hike took him through Collegeville to Evergreen Bottoms and through the Acipco community—all African American neighborhoods—and then along the Louisville & Nashville railroad bed all the way to Smithfield where the school was. He had saved enough money from tips to pay the seven-cent bus fare, but Aunt Mamie did not know of his stash and might have grown suspicious of such an extravagance as a bus ride to school. Shelley decided to walk the eight miles whenever the weather permitted.

The boy's first few days at Parker were not pleasant. Other students kidded him about the condition of his hair, his lack of oral hygiene, the odor of the animals he fed, and the threadbare clothes and frayed long johns he wore beneath them. Fashion and hairstyle seemed to matter much more to the high school kids than they had at the elementary school.

With the goal of a scholarship, Shelley knew B-and-C report cards would not do, but his classes were markedly more difficult now and study time—with Mamie's eight-o'clock lights-out dictum—was hard to come by. He began stopping off at a female classmate's house on the way home for some studying—and his first feeble attempts at romance—before work. He also took greater advantage of Mr. Yielding's kindly offered study breaks at the store.

Shelley was most surprised to see that his fellow students seemed far more interested in fashion, sports, and dating than they did in their studies. Most of his classmates considered it nerdish or even "acting white" if someone—especially a boy—showed interest in school work. That led to more taunting, but Shelley had his mind made up. Scholarship. Law school. Law career. Let them make all the fun they wanted. Shelley would one day have the last laugh.

Gradually the boy became more and more popular at Parker. One good friend was the principal's daughter, Alma Vivian Johnson, who was duly impressed by a young man so serious about his studies yet so funny and interesting to talk with. That friendship survived a call to the principal's office where Shelley was told in no uncertain terms to stay away from Alma. To her credit, the young lady brushed aside her father's admonition and remained a good friend. Alma Johnson would later meet and marry an upcoming military officer named Colin Powell, the eventual four-star general and Secretary of State of the United States.

THE BOY STILL OFTEN cried himself to sleep at night. He lay on the cot in Mamie's living room and thought of his mother, his brothers, and all they had been through together. Kids at Parker talked of hard times, discrimination, and the like, but Shelley knew they had no idea what trials he had been through. He certainly never brought it up.

He wondered when his mother would next nudge him, when she would direct him to his brothers and send him off to find them as she had promised to do.

As valuable as his book knowledge would be to him—Shelley had vowed to become educated instead of remaining ignorant like so many of his people, sober instead of drunk like his daddy, peaceful rather than violent like his Aunt Emily—he was also smart enough to realize he needed some practi-

cal education as well to survive in the world in which he lived. Down on
4th Avenue North between 15th and 18th Streets, was the black business
district in Birmingham. Many of the business owners were there because
they could not find well-paying jobs elsewhere and certainly could not open
their companies in white neighborhoods. However, even in what was called
"Little Harlem" they had to rent their buildings and storefronts from white
owners in New York or Chicago and a few from nearby Mountain Brook.
There was Magic City Barbershop, Nelson Brothers Café, tiny hotels, and
the offices of lawyers, doctors, and insurance men.

Not all the black establishments were so squeaky clean. One of them
was Ratkiller's Shoeshine Parlor, a place that offered its patrons far more
than a shoeshine. Big-time pool hustling took place in its backroom billiard
parlor along with other types of wagering. Shots of untaxed whiskey were
available. Romantic encounters were sold and purchased. Various illegal
pharmaceuticals were dispensed.

A young man with big ears and a mind like a sponge could spend some
spare time in that part of town and gain a world of practical street knowledge.

Shelley began to hang out in the area, on a corner or in front of or
inside Ratkiller's, before heading home each day after work. There the boy
learned about prostitutes and pimps and how that commercial enterprise
operated, how to load dice and rig card scams, how to tap a till without
getting caught, how the whiskey-by-the-shot enterprise worked, and what
kinds of street drugs were in demand, their colorful names, how much they
cost, and how they were marketed to a ready clientele. He also refined his
billiard skills beyond what he had learned on Papa Clyde's basement table,
where he had mostly played by himself.

The more he learned, the more Shelley knew he would soon have to make
a fateful decision. There was no doubt, with his sharp mind and likeable
personality, he could be bountifully successful in the underworld commerce
down on 17th Street. The pimps and dope dealers who answered his questions and offered their own unique tutoring even told him how good at it he
would be one day when he began hustling. Relationships certainly worked
down there and Shelley had already begun building some in his spare time
at Ratkiller's. He salted away the things he learned on the street, figuring

they might still come in handy someday, somewhere.

HOWEVER, THE BOY HAD always promised his God and his mother that he would go the other direction, through school and to a legitimate career that would make them proud. He saw how the old hustlers—the few who lived long enough to grow old—turned out. Instead of taking that dubious path, what he saw in Little Harlem convinced Shelley to throw himself even harder into his studies and to make the most of the extracurricular activities at Parker.

The teasing had eased some. He was a hit in his first appearance as a comedian in a variety show. It was his first time up on a stage in front of people but it felt as natural as performing for the horse owners in Mountain Brook or the businessmen and politicians at Yielding's. Even the most popular students praised him for his work on the school paper, *The Record*, and Shelley sucked up the acclaim and the attention.

Then Shelley heard about a new distraction, and its pull would prove to be far stronger than any of the "black beauties," "red pearls," or other drugs sold on the street corner. It was called WBCO.

A white businessman was opening up a new radio station in the western suburb of Bessemer. Word was the station would put on programming aimed at a black audience, something that did not currently exist in the area. Though Shelley's only experience with radio was occasionally listening to one, he knew he had to get on WBCO's air. He was certain he could be good at it.

One afternoon, he rode the bus out to Bessemer, marched right into the station, and asked to speak to the manager. He must have caught the man on a good day because he readily agreed to sit Shelley down in the new station's recording studio and allow him to do an audition tape, read some news copy and a commercial script, and say a few words as if he were introducing some upcoming recording.

"Young man, you sure you've never been on the radio before?" the manager asked him when he finished the audition.

"No, sir, but I've done some school plays and variety shows and that sort of thing."

"Well, I like your audition," the man said. "But to give you a slot on the air, you would have to sell a sponsor for the show. You come back with a sponsor and we'll put you on WBCO."

Shelley was ecstatic and plotted his new radio career all the way back to town on the bus. He thought he knew exactly who his first sponsor would be. A new shoe store had just opened up on 3rd Avenue in the black business district. The manager listened to Shelley's sales pitch: for $20 per show, he would hawk the new business once a week on WBCO, a station aimed directly at the manager's potential customers.

"If you don't think it's working, selling enough shoes, we can stop anytime you want," Shelley promised.

The manager was so impressed with the plan and with his new radio spokesperson that he not only signed up for his show's sponsorship on WBCO but he also hired Shelley to work as a stock boy.

Shelley felt right at home the instant he sat down behind that microphone at WBCO. His "radio personality" mask was an amalgam of his life experiences so far. The on-air persona was a recipe consisting of the comedian he had become on stage at the Parker talent show, the preacher talking to the mirror in Papa Clyde's basement, the "smart colored boy" sacking groceries at Yielding's, and the streetwise hustler-to-be hanging out at Ratkiller's. Just as he had imagined the crowds listening and cheering in the full-length mirror, Shelley could picture in his mind his listeners tuned in to WBCO on the high end of the AM radio band.

He talked *with* them, not *at* them. His up-beat patter between the records he spun and his energetically ad-libbed commercials for the shoe store were aimed at the common black person, the blue-collar laborer he saw standing up in the rear of the street car, the maids and housekeepers and nannies like his momma, waiting at the bus stop to go to work. In a not-so-subtle way, he poked fun at the black middle class, with their often snooty attitudes and disdain for the more common colored people. Shelley alluded to the fact that they lived in their big houses overlooking North Birmingham even as they struggled to pay their massive mortgages and dressed their children in the latest fashions. Somehow he sensed he could ingratiate himself with the listeners he sought by going that route, and doing it in a way they had never heard before on the radio.

Shelley, age 16.

He enjoyed the R&B records he played, too. Songs by Johnny Otis, Little Esther Phillips, Howling Wolf, and Muddy Waters. Whether it was the saddest blues or the happiest love songs, each one of them had the power to reach out and touch the listeners to Shelley's short program. But most of the fifteen minutes on WBCO was claimed by the boy's patter and his commercials for his sponsor.

It was a liberating and exhilarating coming-out for Shelley. Soon his classmates—and even teachers and staff members—at Parker Industrial High were singling him out, telling him how much they enjoyed his show. The folks he knew down on 17th Street laughed and recited back to him some of the things he said on the air that had especially tickled them.

THERE WERE TWO PEOPLE, however, who were certainly not fans of the young deejay. Mamie and Henry Pickens.

"You are going straight to hell, Shurley Stewart," Aunt Mamie told him, waggling her finger in his face. "You can't make no living on no damn radio. Henry done talked to the foreman at L&N. You got a job waiting for you in the wheel shop soon as you can drop out of that damn school."

Of course, Shelley had no intention of giving up radio or high school, nor did he tell anyone that he was doing the show for no pay.

Later, he stopped by another new station that came on the air and was aiming at the black audience. WEDR was much closer to home and the boy was willing to work for nothing there, too. White station management allowed him to go on the air occasionally to spin records and that web of gab. It seemed to come so naturally to the boy any time the microphone switch was turned on. He was also the station's official teen reporter, bringing the latest news from Parker Industrial High School. Then he used the same stories that he wrote about in *The Record*, delivered in his deepening baritone voice and well-practiced diction, which was so much different from his slang-filled, street-wise disk jockey style.

Shelley reveled in the realization that he could move audiences with his voice, what he said and how he said it, and how he mixed the records together. He could entertain them, make them laugh and cry, shout and think, and even do his bidding. If he told them to, they would buy shoes or any other products he recommended to them on the airwaves. He could bring a message of hope to so many who had so little. From the very beginning, the power of that was not lost on the boy.

He had also become a personality at Parker Industrial. Academic honors came his way. Those who had ridiculed him in the beginning cozied up to him to get him to help them pass their classes and stay eligible for sports. They wanted to be friends with the radio personality. Lunchroom workers gave him extra food because he made them smile. The school's printing instructor—who also oversaw the school newspaper—took him under his wing and gave him more and more responsibility for writing articles.

Still, Shelley felt insecure. He hid in the choir and dramatic club where he could be someone else besides the homeless boy from Rosedale. But he never seemed to get the best roles in the school plays. Then he found out why.

Lead roles went to lighter skinned Negroes. Cheerleaders and majorettes were light-skinned, too, and they had to have the accepted hair texture. Not the abundant tight curls of African Americans but something that looked more like the hair of white people. Even in classrooms, lighter-skinned students sat up front. Darker ones were relegated to the back rows.

Shelley was amazed that a race that had always been saddled with discrimination because of the color of its skin had its own internal prejudices based on the same criterion. He recalled one of the deep conversations he had with Papa Clyde's daughter, Mary Sue, in which she used a term he had not yet heard: human rights. "Civil rights" was not yet a common phrase in the late 1940s, but Shelley had already made up his mind that it was not descriptive of what he and his race should be striving for. It was human rights. The same rights denied to Mary Sue because of her handicap. To women because of their gender. And obviously to blacks because of their race. Even more so to darker blacks for no other reason than the color of their skin.

When he was denied the opportunity to audition for a lead role in a play, a role that went to a lighter-skinned student, Shelley got the same feeling he had that day on the crowded street car when the driver refused to move the board. This was not right. If he did not challenge the unfairness of the system, who would? If he was not the best actor for the role, so be it. But

Shelley, 1950.

he should not be denied the opportunity to at least audition simply because his skin was blacker.

The principal as well as the superintendent of all the city's black schools—whose office was located at Parker—suggested he drop his complaint and simply accept a lesser role in the play. Shelley ignored them and went to a higher authority. On his trip to work each day, he passed the Board of Education building. The superintendent of the Birmingham Public School System—all schools, not just the colored ones—was a regular at Yielding's Department Store.

Shelley stopped in and had a talk with him. The man knew Shelley, of course, and sympathized with his plight.

The next day, the school changed the play they were going to do and gave Shelley a key part. In truth, it was a part in which he was to play the stereotypical black role of a janitor.

Still, Shelley felt he had made his point.

By HIS JUNIOR YEAR at Parker, things had begun to pile up on the boy. He worked hard to maintain an "A" average with a scholarship to college always at the forefront of his mind. He was working alternate afternoons at Yielding's and at the shoe store. He had a regular half-hour show on WBCO, way down in Bessemer, and still was called in to be on the air at WEDR on occasion. On top of that, he still rose every morning between 3 and 4 A.M. to do chores for Aunt Mamie and Uncle Henry.

There was also a strong internal conflict going on inside the boy. The happy, joking personality on the radio and around the hallways of Parker was offset by the real Shelley Stewart. He was actually the boy who was so brooding, thoughtful, and sad that he still cried himself to sleep some nights, thinking of his life so far, his brothers, and his mother. He was tormented by the ever-present vision of his daddy striking his momma with that ax, and of her hanging, bleeding, in the branches of that pecan tree in Rosedale. He still relived the torture and abuse at the hands of his Aunt Emily, sometimes waking in the middle of the night, sitting up in a cold sweat, heart racing, thinking she was ripping back the covers and whipping him with the electrical cord.

Even through those nightly tears, Shelley fought to keep his eye on the prize, the scholarship and a career in law, and rejected the easier route, pimping, hustling down on 17th Street. That degree and law license would earn him the respect he felt he deserved. He could also work to correct the other wrongs he had witnessed in his young life so far.

He would prove to everyone that hard work and education could rescue someone from even the cruelest upbringing. He would show them that doing the right thing and building strong relationships could overcome hurt, pain, and discrimination, no matter how pervasive and harsh.

There were, though, a few more setbacks Shelley would have to face, and these would hurt far worse than a beating with an electrical cord and salt rubbed in the open wounds. The fact that those kicks in the teeth came from those he trusted—and from people of his own race—made them so much more difficult to bear.

the GILLEYS

It was early in the school year, 1951, Shelley's senior year at A. H. Parker Industrial High School. He had treated himself to a ride on the bus that morning and was in such a good mood he hardly noticed the three or four thugs obviously waiting for someone there at the bus stop near the school.

The Gilleys were an especially brutal gang of bad boys, ruffians who used bullying, harassment, and beatings to stake their claim on a territory and make life miserable for others. Extortion was their primary game, but even the slightest provocation—an innocent flirt with a particular female, an inadvertent bump in the hallway—was enough to set them off. And set them off violently. Kids stole money from their parents to meet the gang's shakedown demands. No one fought back. No one ratted them out. Anyone who stood up to the Gilleys could expect to be beaten senseless. Rumors were that they did not always stop there, either.

Now, they had finally turned their evil attention to that "smart nigger." It was time for Shelley Stewart to cough up some money.

"Nigger, it's past time for you to pay up. You owe us back dues and they be real high for you, seeing as how you are on the radio and all and making big money. We ought to just kick your ass right now for holding out on us so damn long, but if you come up with the money by Thursday, we'll let you go for now."

All day at school and afterward at work at Yielding's, Shelley could think of little else than the gang's threat. A teacher's notes on the blackboard blurred through blinked-back tears. More than one customer at the store that afternoon noticed that Shelley was not his usual jovial self and asked him if he felt okay.

The boy had suffered merciless beatings at the hand of his daddy and from his Aunt Emily. He had promised himself he would never allow anyone else to physically intimidate him in such an inhuman way. Besides, if he gave in to the Gilleys, it would only get worse. They thought he made lots of money being on the air and they would keep asking for a bigger "dues" payment. Little did they know that he made nothing for those jobs.

Shelley made his decision. He would fight back against the Gilleys, no matter the ultimate cost. He had to.

On that Thursday morning, before leaving for school, Shelley darted into his aunt's and uncle's bedroom while Aunt Mamie was outside. He knew they kept a .32 automatic pistol under the mattress. He put the gun into his book satchel as he headed out the door. On the way to the bus stop, he inserted a clip filled with bullets and then shoved the gun into the back of his pants, so it would be covered by his coat, yet it would be easy to get to in a hurry.

Shelley knew what the consequences would be if he was caught with a gun at school. He also knew the ramifications of shooting another human being, Gilley gang member or not. Still, he had a plan. If it worked, nobody would be hurt and the Gilleys would leave him alone from then on. And his popularity at Parker Industrial High would achieve a whole new plateau.

Sure enough, four members of the Gilleys were waiting for him at the 8th Avenue North bus stop near the school.

"Hey, radio boy. You got our money?" one asked him.

Shelley stalled, giving the other kids the chance to dash away, out of range. They scurried on inside the building, assuming Shelley was about to become the gang's next beating victim.

"How much you say I owed you?"

"Five dollars. You know how much. You got it, nigger?"

"Yes, I have your five dollars. I pay you, we're square, right?"

"Square 'til we want some more," the punk said with a sneer. "You smart enough to know that, ain't you, Shelley? Now give us the money before we take it away from you and whip your ass just for good measure."

Shelley motioned for them to follow him around the corner, behind a little store and out of sight of the school and traffic on 8th Avenue. He turned and grinned his biggest grin.

"I don't have any money and you are not going to whip my ass," he told them in his best broadcasting voice.

"You damn well better know we are! Get him . . ."

Shelley yanked the .32 from the waistband of his pants, pointed it at the feet of the Gilleys, and fired three quick shots. It was the first time he had fired a gun since he had shot one of Uncle Henry's pigs between the eyes on slaughtering day. He did not hit anyone, nor did he intend to. But the brutes scattered in all directions, jackets pulled up over their heads as if that would protect them from bullets.

"That damn nigger's crazy!" they screamed as they melted into the neighborhood.

Point made, Shelley walked back around the corner, glanced around to be sure nobody was watching, and tossed Aunt Mamie's pistol beneath a shotgun house there. Then he walked on into the schoolhouse as if nothing at all had happened that fine autumn morning.

There was a cursory inquiry by school officials. Someone had heard the three shots and reported it to the principal. Police never came, of course. There was no blood, no bodies. None of the students said anything to the principal either. At the same time, word spread throughout the school and Shelley Stewart was instantly a hero among his classmates. He had dared to stand up to the Gilleys. Even the prettiest girls and the biggest football stars looked at Shelley with a new respect.

The plan had worked precisely as he had hoped. The gang members would not dare mess with him again. His fellow students put him up on a pedestal. And his teachers and the school administration had no idea what had happened.

AFTER THE DISMISSAL BELL, Shelley retrieved his aunt's pistol from beneath the house and hurried home. He knew he had to put it back beneath the mattress before they missed it.

Uncle Henry and Aunt Mamie were standing at the door, waiting for him as he bounced up the front steps. They had, indeed, noticed the pistol was gone. There was no doubt who had taken it. They were not interested in any explanation of why.

"Give me that pistol," Mamie hissed. She took the gun and aimed it directly at Shelley's gut. Then she ordered Henry to take his shotgun and hold it on the boy as well. She directed Shelley out the back door onto the porch. While a frowning Henry reluctantly kept the shotgun barrel aimed at Shelley, Mamie grabbed the electrical cord that went to her iron and picked up her broom, breaking the handle off cleanly across her leg.

"You are just like your damn daddy," she told him, so angry she spat out the words. "You are no damn good. You won't live to see twenty-one. You are a liar and a cheat. That's how you get them good grades. You cheat. You cheat and then brag about how damn smart you are."

Mamie drew back the broom handle over her head.

"I'm not going to take a whipping," Shelley told her quietly, holding up a hand, shaking his head side to side, his mouth firmly set. The vow he had made to himself, the one that he would never be beaten again, applied equally to the Gilley gang and to his Aunt Mamie. He would do whatever it took to assure it.

"You strip off them clothes we bought you with our hard-earned money. Take 'em off. I'm going to whip your brains out."

"I am not going to take a whipping, Aunt Mamie," the boy calmly told her. "Not from you and not from anybody else."

The woman's eyes grew wide, her anger as substantial as summer thunder.

"So, you going to fight me?" she shrieked. "That what you going to do after all Henry and me has done for your sorry ass?"

"Whatever happens, whatever it takes, I am not going to take a whipping."

She dropped the broomstick and tossed the iron cord back through the door. She could hardly talk. Her voice was little more than a whisper.

"You get the hell out of my house," she told him. "You will never come back to my damn house again. Never!" She turned and stomped away, ignoring the boy's nod of confirmation.

"Shurley, take the whipping and she'll get over it in a little bit," Henry suggested, quiet enough so she would not hear him.

"I am not going to take a whipping."

Mamie threw a few of his clothing items and personal things out onto the front porch but she kept some of them, just for spite. Shelley gathered up what was left, wrapped them in some twine, and set off walking down 34th Street. This departure, at first glance so much like the one from his daddy's house when he was six years old, was not the same at all. This time, the boy was confident he could make it on his own. This time, too, he knew exactly where he was going.

Rosedale.

THE LITTLE COMMUNITY HAD not changed at all in the ten years Shelley had been gone. The minute he stepped off the street car, he felt almost at home. He was confident he could find a place to stay, a family there who would take him in for a few days while he decided exactly what he would do longer term. People there would remember him and his brothers, his momma, his daddy, his dysfunctional family history. They would be willing to help him.

From the street car stop, Shelley walked up to the familiar street where his mother died. Where he had lived that awful existence with his Aunt Emily. Everything looked the same. Even Aunt Emily's old shotgun house with its wilted flowers and yard full of cackling chickens pecking and scratching in the dirt.

As Shelley stood there in front of Emily's place, he saw someone emerge from the front door of the house next door. The man waved to him.

"Man, oh, man! Look what the cat done dragged in." Boot Wimbush was still living in the same house as he had when Shelley lived with his momma across the street. "Hey, ain't it something else that you and Bubba done turned up here in Rosedale at the same time."

"What?"

"Your brother. Jerome. He be in the army, out on leave. He been here about a week, staying over yonder with Junior Cunningham and them but he got to go back in the next day or two, I expect. Hey, speak of the devil, yonder he comes now."

Shelley looked the direction Boot pointed. Sure enough, a tall, skinny man wearing green army fatigues was walking their way. As he grew closer, there was no mistaking the sharp features of his brother, Jerome. Bubba.

Shelley dropped his small bundle of clothes in the street and ran to meet him halfway. Bubba was just as surprised and thrilled to see his brother. They embraced and almost forgot to let go of each other.

Later Shelley would reflect on the coincidence of his being sent away from Aunt Mamie's house on that one particular day. The odds of him deciding to come back to Rosedale, of all places, to seek a roof over his head. The chances of Bubba just happening to be there on leave from the army with only a day left before he was to ship out again.

Shelley did not question it, though. It was beyond coincidence. Momma could well be at work here again.

The brothers walked back down the hill to one of the joints along Highway 31, the place called Waterboy's, laughing and talking all the way. Shelley sipped his first beer and sampled his first cigarette as the two of them caught up on what each other had been doing, where they had been. Bubba was on his way to an ugly war in a new hot spot, a place called Korea, somewhere on the other side of the world. Shelley tried to explain to him where that distant country would be located on the globe.

"You know I heard you on the radio," Bubba told his brother. "I thought it was real good, but I didn't know it was you. That feller called himself 'Shelley.' Your name is 'Shurley.'"

Shelley explained. Meanwhile, Bubba reported that he had been in and out of school and somehow had gotten as far as the seventh grade in Rosedale School. He had done odd jobs and paid rent to various families to survive. He also had become something of a tough guy with a reputation around the area. One fellow who had done Bubba wrong actually ran to the Homewood City Jail one day and locked himself inside when he thought Bubba was after him with the intention of serving up some red-hot revenge.

After he and Bubba finally left Waterboy's that evening, Shelley spent the night at the home of the Bullard family. As he knew, people in the neighborhood were more than willing to help one of their own, and especially one of the Stewart boys, considering what their daddy had done.

The next morning, Bubba showed up early outside Shelley's window, his duffel bag over his shoulder. He was on his way to the bus station and wanted to say goodbye. He promised Shelley he would send him his military pay to help him get his feet back on the ground. Shelley agreed to save as much of it as he could to give Bubba a stake when he got out of the Army.

The brothers embraced again and promised to keep in touch. Then Bubba was gone, off to a far-away war.

After a few weeks at the Bullard's, Shelley decided on a plan, primarily at the suggestion of Mrs. Bullard. The more he thought about it, the better he liked it. After all, his situation would only last until he could complete high school, get his scholarship, and head on off to college.

ONE AFTERNOON, HE WALKED up to his Aunt Emily's house and settled down on the front porch, waiting for her to get home from her housekeeping job. When she rounded the corner and saw him sitting on her front steps, her face went cold. The boy she had beaten and abused was now over six feet tall and, though skinny as a flagpole, he likely could still fight back powerfully enough. She likely thought he was back to get some revenge from her for the way she treated him.

"What you want?" she asked him, with no other greeting.

Though a part of Shelley Stewart wanted to grab his aunt and show her what it felt like to be demeaned, beaten, and abused, he knew he never would do that. It would accomplish nothing, really, but could get in the way of his plans for law school if he accidentally killed the old lady.

"I need a place to stay, Aunt Emily," he told her. "I will pay you rent."

She listened, cocked her head sideways, and readily agreed to the arrangement. Twenty-four dollars a month. That was about what he was making at the shoe store since he had recently been promoted to salesman.

"You better not steal nothing," she told him. "I catch you stealing from me, I can have you killed. White folks I work for, they don't care nothing about killing no black man."

Shelley was happy to learn that Emily no longer kept chickens inside the house. And this time, Shelley slept in the middle room. The first night, sleep was difficult to find. He kept expecting Aunt Emily to burst into the room with her electrical cord, throw back the covers, hit him in the head with her big iron skillet, order him to strip down, and tie him up.

Once he had shelter, one of Shelley's first orders of business was to get back into school. Rosedale School had expanded by that time to be a high school but, there were more than five hundred in the senior class at Parker but a paltry two dozen at Rosedale. The facilities were rudimentary and the curriculum limited, even when compared to the other colored schools. Luckily, Shelley had taken most of the more difficult classes at Parker already so he settled in at Rosedale and was confident he could maintain the excellent grades that would soon lead to his scholarship.

The principal, B. M. Montgomery—called "Fess" by faculty and students alike—seemed to take a liking to the new student. So did the teachers, and especially Mrs. Carlotta Harris. Another teacher, Odessa Powell, even borrowed textbooks from a nearby black college for Shelley to use since he quickly grew bored with the used and tattered old books they used in their classes. It was not news to most teachers in the school of the conditions under which Shelley had been raised. They lived in Rosedale, too. The fact that he was such a good and eager student was even more amazing when that bit of family history was factored in.

One day, Shelley bumped into a familiar figure on the street. His daddy, Slim.

Shelley was surprised that the meeting did not cause him to feel anger. Instead, he felt sorry for the man, bewildered that anyone could stoop so low as to murder a woman like his mother. Or that any human could treat his own children the way this sorry man had done.

Slim did not even recognize his boy for a moment. Then, when he realized who the young man was, he only stared back at Shelley for a long, long time. The boy finally smiled broadly, turned, and walked away.

A few weeks later, when he ran into his daddy another time, Shelley decided to ask him directly what had happened to Sam and David, where they were, who was raising them.

"What the hell you asking me for?" was his snapped response.

"I want to know where they . . ."

"Get the hell away from me. Don't you come up here messing in my damn business."

Slim balled up his fists, as if he might throw a blow, but then slumped his shoulders and thought better of it. He was afraid of his boy now that he was big enough to fight back.

Shelley looked hard at his father for a long moment and then turned to go, sadly shaking his head. But his daddy was not finished.

"Boy. Hey, boy!"

Shelley stopped and looked back over his shoulder.

"What?"

"Listen. Reckon you got any money you can let me have?"

B irmingham, Alabama, was a simmering pot in 1962 and early 1963, ready to boil over. But suddenly, it was as if someone had turned down the heat. Demonstrations against the city's harsh segregation laws were flagging, disappearing from the national TV network news and falling off the front pages of the big newspapers.

The Reverend Martin Luther King had been lured to the city in the autumn of 1962 because it was considered—rightly so—as the most segregated city in America. And those who would defend its racist ways were the most blatant and heavy-handed there were. They would make great TV. That would attract the attention of the world. This was the place to make a stand.

King knew it would be a mighty and highly visible victory for the Movement if he could use his powerful voice to convince the city to come to a negotiating table, if those in charge began revoking the statutes that had so long enslaved his people. King spent time in Birmingham over the next few months, marching, preaching, leading rallies, meeting in various houses and motel rooms, always on the move so Police Commissioner Eugene "Bull" Connor's cops or the KKK and its branches—organized or not—would not know exactly where he was. King's failure—or even his demise—would be a highly visible victory for segregationists everywhere.

Local leader Reverend Fred Shuttlesworth was pushing to raise the intensity of the demonstrations to a new level. He was certain they would forever lose momentum if they relaxed now. Not everyone agreed with him.

King, for one, was not so sure. Bombs were exploding at the homes of ministers and other civil rights leaders so often the city had been dubbed by the press as "Bombingham." One neighborhood was hit so often it was called "Dynamite Hill." People were being hurt.

More moderate leaders in the white community were quietly telling King that things could not begin to change until blacks stopped forcing the issue so visibly in the streets. Not if they continued with more marches and protests over the upcoming spring and long, hot summer. Court cases were underway, they reminded him, in the wake of a public vote the previous November. Legal ac-

tions and a mayoral election would finally change the city's fundamental form of government. If the decisions and election went as expected, they would finally take power from Commissioner Connor and others determined to do whatever it took to maintain segregation. That would give the city more room to negotiate and bargain and ultimately reach compromise that would make life somewhat better for the city's colored citizens.

Not necessarily end segregation but make things better.

There was considerable discord among leaders and the various groups that made up the Movement. Some, like Shuttlesworth, were not interested in compromise or negotiation or simply "making things better." They wanted to push Connor's buttons hard while they still had some attention from the nation, the world. They knew Connor would, in his heavy-handed way, help keep the Movement in the national spotlight. They felt they could still rally the common folk and church congregations, those who suffered most from brutal segregation. They thought they could turn them out into the streets and fill the jails as King once promised, and as Gandhi before him had done.

Others, like King himself, wanted to go slow, not push into a corner the local businessmen—black and white alike—who were already feeling the ill effects of the fallout from the demonstrations and their coverage in the media. There were those in city government who honestly sought a way to fundamentally change their city once and for all, too, but they could not openly side with the protestors. They urged King to find a way besides marching in the streets, shouting slogans and provoking the ire of the police and the area's most racist citizens. King and others wanted to curry the favor of the press and President John Kennedy, not by being too confrontational but by continuing talking and preaching and protesting nonviolently. Meanwhile, the media's—and thus the nation's—attention had shifted westward, to Oxford, Mississippi, where violent and deadly reaction at the end of September 1962 to the desegregation of the University of Mississippi made for better television.

Regardless the reasons, the Movement was losing steam in Birmingham, Alabama, in the spring of 1963. Connor's tactics were working. Those common folk who marched out of the churches and into the streets had their pictures taken and those pictures were shown to their employers at TCI, Sloss, ACIPCO, and Stockham Valve.

"See where Willie was when he didn't show up for work last week? He tell you he was down there on 3rd Avenue causing a ruckus? That he spent the day making bail at the jailhouse?"

Lawyers, merchants, and others from over the mountain were reminded that their maids and nannies and landscapers were taking part in all that mess with King and them in the downtown streets. Those who were arrested often lost their jobs. Nobody else would hire them. It became more and more difficult to raise enough marchers to even resemble a civil protest. They still showed up in the church rallies, sang, clapped and shouted, but fewer and fewer had the stomach for the streets, jail, and the other consequences. It was getting more and more difficult to turn them out.

Dr. King still hoped for a victory much like Rosa Parks and the Montgomery Bus Boycott had been for him. A decision from the federal courts striking down segregation on the city's public buses was the win that first thrust the preacher into national prominence.

The truth was, though, that in early 1963, Birmingham was looking more and more like Albany, Georgia, where not even King's oratory and national prominence and brief jail stays were enough to keep the initially promising demonstrations going. It was no longer news when King went to jail, spent a night, and bailed out.

George Wallace had just been elected governor of Alabama. His inaugural speech set the tone for how things were going to continue to be—in the state of Alabama and in its largest city. Clearly Bull Connor and others in Birmingham were not going to allow all this desegregation nonsense and the lawless protest marches to continue. Racist groups were effectively frightening many—both black and white—into stepping back, remaining quiet, and letting whatever happened happen.

Unless something changed, the Movement in Birmingham—the most obvious and visible place in the nation to make a stand—might well shrivel and die. Maybe Reverend King could pick up the charge elsewhere. Maybe not. Maybe Reverend Shuttlesworth could rouse up congregations in some other Southern city and push buttons there. Maybe not. If they failed, where would the next leader come from? Whose voice would turn out the people?

Would the violent racist element, the ones that seemed to have the tacit approval of the city's police department, become even more vicious in trying to squelch any voice of protest? Were more people about to be hurt, about to die, because the Movement fizzled in the nation's most brutally segregated city?

Something had to change in Birmingham in 1963 to once again turn up the heat to a boil. If not, a powerful opportunity could well be lost forever.

the JACK-O-LANTERN & JEROME

Money had never been a problem for Shelley. He worked for his food and shelter, and when he had to he pulled sustenance from the dumpsters behind the restaurants and stores in whatever neighborhood he lived at the time. When he worked at the shoe store and Yielding's, he managed to put back just enough to be able to afford precious few extras, the things many of his classmates at Parker took for granted.

Now, though, living back in Rosedale, he felt the need to make more. Because of the distance to Yielding's and the drain on his time with school, he had given up that job. The rent he paid to Aunt Emily took what he made by bowing, grinning, and being polite to the black women who bought shoes from him. Radio paid Shelley nothing but satisfaction and with on-the-job training. The last thing he wanted was to have to rely on Emily's charity. He desperately wanted to keep that a strictly business relationship.

One weekend afternoon, Shelley was hanging out with some of the other younger neighborhood residents at Fess's Place, a café owned by the Rosedale School principal. Inevitably, the subject of jobs came up. Making extra money was always a concern. The prospects were slim. Yard work, bell boy, porter, ditch digger, common laborer. That was about it for young black men. The pay was so pitiful a man would have to devote far more hours to a job than Shelley could manage and still keep up his studies and the radio work. Shelley had even begun to consider approaching his old buddies at Ratkiller's to see if he could partake in some of their hustle. He had seen the kind of money a smart guy could make if he was willing to risk jail or getting his throat slit. But he also needed something to get him through the next few months, to graduation and college.

One of the older guys piped up.

"I know where y'all can make yourselves some serious money."

"Where's that?"

"The Jack-O-Lantern. I make plenty of money over there. Fifty, sixty dollars a week, parking them white folks' cars. And plenty of free whiskey, too. They leave the bottles under the seat or in their glove boxes and I make sure I get a nip for a tip, one way or the other."

The Jack-O-Lantern was an upscale restaurant that catered to the more wealthy white residents of Homewood, Mountain Brook, and Birmingham. Shelley's friend told him they were always looking for bus boys, and he might be able to work that into a waiter's job. And good waiters could earn big tips.

Shelley had no idea he was stepping into the most blatant display of racism he had ever encountered. It started with his introduction to the restaurant's owners.

"This here is Shelley Stewart," his friend told the owners. "Now this is one nigger that loves to work. He won't steal from you neither."

Certainly the boy had heard the word before. Blacks called each other "nigger" all the time, usually good-naturedly or as an expression that implied "we are all in this together." But never in front of whites. The few times Shelley had heard whites say the word were when they chased him out of their dumpsters. Or from the blacksmith visiting Papa Clyde that morning, and Smith had certainly shut that down.

"Hey, if our boy here says you are a good nigger, you are a good nigger," one of the owners told him, straight out and without hesitation. "That's the only kind we try to hire here at the Jack-O-Lantern. You act right and stay in your place, you can make some money."

Back outside, Shelley's friend explained what had just happened.

"You got to know how to work white people, Shelley. Learn how to play 'em. Grin and act ignorant. You better not let 'em know you smart or they come after you. They be scared of you. Mad at you and they going to get back at you. Play 'dumb nigger.' That's the way to do it."

Shelley gritted his teeth and frowned.

"I don't know, man."

"Look, I will call you 'nigger.' So will white folks. You can't let that bother you. Not if you want to take their money. Just because they call you one don't make you one. You know you smart. They don't have to know it, though. Best they don't, man."

The conflict inside the boy almost made him walk away. He had to make some money, however. He could not allow Aunt Emily the satisfaction of sheltering him for nothing. Of making him work as her own private slave as she had done before. That would put him right back where he was before he walked away from Rosedale.

Shelley quickly got the hang of balancing the big trays over his head as he cleaned up the mess the diners left on their tables. Then, maybe a bit overconfident, he suddenly dropped a tray, spilling remnants of food and drink all over the fancy carpet. He immediately began apologizing to patrons at nearby tables, but one man stood and glared at him.

"Nigger, look what you did to my lady's dress," he growled. "I ought to make you lick it off, boy, but I don't want you that close to her."

Play the game, Shelley thought. Swallow that pride. Bow. Scrape. Ignore the vile things the man was saying. Play the game like he knew all the middle class and educated blacks did. They somehow managed to stay quiet when a white person called them "boy" or "girl," even if they had gray hair and a college degree.

That was precisely what Shelley did. He also practiced with the loaded trays until he was perfect, avoiding any more spills. Soon he was making five or six dollars each night in tips. That, in addition to his three-dollar-per-night salary, was more money than the boy had ever seen before.

When he came in late from his job, Aunt Emily frowned at him, assuming he had been out drinking.

"You ain't no good, layin' out all night like your old sorry daddy," she told him. Shelley did not bother correcting her. He just made certain he gave her the rent money on time each month.

THINGS WERE LOOKING UP at school, too. Though some of the teachers continued to have a negative opinion of the scruffy kid, the one who had practically raised himself, others admired the hard work and good mind that had helped Shelley overcome all the tough times he had suffered. His grades slipped some because of all his jobs but he was still on track to graduate, to finish near the top of the class, and to earn his scholarship.

When it came time to elect the senior class president at Rosedale School, Shelley decided to run. He wanted the recognition and holding such an office would only cement the likelihood of receiving the grant that would make college a reality. To the chagrin of the principal and some of the faculty, Shelley won the election, beating out the school's football hero.

The owners at the Jack-O-Lantern somehow learned about Shelley's win. First, they were astonished that the boy was even in school. He was well past sixteen and could have dropped out long ago, like all their other black employees. The boy had worn his "dumb nigger" mask so effectively that his employers were further amazed that someone like him would be involved in student government, that he was approaching graduation from high school. For a while, Shelley was afraid this would cost him his job. But when the owners got over their surprise, they promptly hired him to be a server at a private party at the restaurant. He earned twenty-five dollars for the night, enough to pay an entire month's worth of rent to Aunt Emily. Then, because he did such a good job at the event, Shelley was asked to fill in the next night for an absent waiter, serving regular customers.

His first shift as a waiter provided the boy a new revelation on racial attitudes and further demonstrated for Shelley how sheltered he had been thus far from such ugliness. Most of the lack of human decency he had encountered had come from those of his own race, from the gang at Parker, and especially from his own family. Shelley was well aware Papa Clyde's attitudes were not the norm for white folks, but the boy had lived mostly in the black community or the shelter of the Smiths. He had not pushed back against discrimination from the establishment except for the incident on the street car, and had experienced little of the worst of Birmingham's brutal segregation laws yet.

His fight had been to merely survive, to find food and shelter. But that first night as a waiter at the Jack-O-Lantern showed him how blatant and foul some white folks could be, and how some of his own race retaliated the only way they felt they could.

The owner escorted a middle-aged, well-dressed couple to one of the tables for which Shelley was responsible. Shelley smiled, nodded, and placed menus before them with a flourish as soon as they were seated, just as he had been taught. He then promised to be right back and turned to go take an order at another table.

"Hey, you!" the man he had just seated called. "You, slim nigger. Nigger!"

Shelley noticed the other waiters—all black—were laughing, though they were also making certain the rude man and other white customers could not see them doing so. He wondered what the joke was, but he turned back to face the man.

"Yes sir?"

"Nigger, they told me you were waiting on my wife and me. So come on over here and take my order."

Shelley recalled the advice he had been given. He did not want to wreck the opportunity to earn a regular job—and the generous tips—waiting tables. The money could be very good. He swallowed hard, ignored the red-faced man's sneer and constant use of the word "nigger," turned, bowed slightly, and forced a smile to his face.

"Certainly, sir. May I take your order, sir?"

The man ordered two drinks. Tommy, the bartender, finally let Shelley in on the joke. This particular patron was a notoriously unpleasant man. He always addressed the staff by calling them "nigger" over and over, hammering home his disdain for blacks. He invariably found fault with everything he ordered. And he never, never left a tip.

Shelley was braced when he delivered the drinks to the man's table.

"Here you are, sir."

"Damn it, nigger!" the man exploded after one sip of his drink. "What the hell is this shit? You tell that boy Tommy to put some damn liquor in this drink. And to fix my lady's drink, too, nigger. You hear me? You able to understand what I'm telling you?"

Shelley again bowed, nodded, and smiled politely. When he dutifully took the cocktails back to Tommy and reported what the man had said, the bartender only winked broadly. He reached beneath the counter and pulled out a decanter he had hidden there. He then poured from it into each of the glasses and mixed it well with a stir stick. The boy later learned that the mysterious carafe held a distinctive concoction, reserved especially for this particular patron and a select few others who took delight in displaying so consistently and publicly their disdain for Negroes.

Members of the wait staff and the cooks had spit, peed and blown their noses into the decanter.

Had any of them openly objected to the racist attitudes or challenged the way they were treated, they would certainly have been fired on the spot. These were powerful men in the community, too. The backwash from such defiance—blacks openly challenging whites—could have meant even more serious retribution.

Still, the people who were the targets of these men's vile treatment had done just what blacks had done for centuries. They found a way to get even, to push back against the humiliation and degradation they experienced all their lives, but in a way that would not get them arrested, beaten, or lynched. It was small satisfaction but it was something.

"Sir, I told Tommy in no uncertain terms that he better take care of you from now on," Shelley told the man when he brought back the doctored cocktails. "I told him you my special man and he better take care of you or he will answer to me. See how that drink tastes now, sir."

"Now, that's better," the unpleasant patron said, smacking his lips after a big slug of his special-blend cocktail. "Now, nigger, see if you can bring me and my lady a couple of big steaks that's fit to eat. Cornelius knows how we like 'em."

Back in the kitchen, Chef Cornelius took two of his best T-bones from the refrigerator and, with a flourish, dropped them straight into the garbage can. He rolled them around in the mess in the can, pulled them out, and promptly dropped them onto the dirty floor, stepping on each, grinding his heel into the beef, and then flipped them over and did the same thing again. A cook spit on them and several waiters came by and blew their noses on them before sprinkling some seasoning on them and placing them on the grill. When Shelley served them up, he made sure to tell the man again how he made certain the chef had prepared them especially for him, seasoning them and grilling them just right. And he also complimented the customer's lady on her nice dress and the man for his choice in neckties.

The "nigger"-spouting diner gave Shelley a ten-dollar tip when he and his lady finished their meal and departed the Jack-O-Lantern that evening. The boy could only shake his head as he watched him go. The things Shelley and the black staff had done in retaliation might have been some satisfaction for them, but they would never change the man's attitude, or give them any hope for better treatment or basic respect.

There had to be a better way to counter such a hateful mindset, and not just to one racist restaurant customer at a time.

ONE COLD DECEMBER DAY, Shelley was trying to stay awake as he read a book as he sat on Aunt Emily's old, ratty couch. Going to school all day and working late nights at the restaurant were wearing him down, but he was determined to see it through to May and graduation. He tried to take advantage of any scarce spare moment to read and learn.

A knock on the front door shook him awake. Two white men were standing there, both in dress military uniforms.

"We would like to see Mrs. Emily Williams and any other relatives of Huell Jerome Stewart Jr.," one of the men told him.

Shelley's stomach flipped over.

"I'm his brother, Shelley Stewart. Aunt Emily!"

His aunt stepped out of the kitchen into the room, wiping her hands on a dish rag.

"Ma'am, Mr. Stewart, we are here to inform you that Huell Jerome Stewart Jr. has been declared missing in action in Korea on November 6."

Shelley closed his eyes. What did "missing" mean? Had Bubba simply not come back from a party one night? Was he wandering around the unfamiliar terrain, looking for the army base? Bubba could take care of himself. Gun, knife, or brickbat, his brother could use about anything to defend himself. He was savvy and plenty mean enough to fend for himself.

One of the soldiers, a chaplain, led the four of them in a brief prayer, and then they were gone, lost in the cold darkness. Aunt Emily clucked and headed back toward the kitchen.

"Damn fool probably got hisself cut, laid up in a juke joint somewhere," she mumbled to herself.

Christmas was coming and Shelley could not escape the memory of him, Bubba, and their younger brothers, dumped by Aunt Mamie in the vacant lot near their daddy's house. That was the same time of the year, a few days before Christmas.

He kept telling himself that Bubba would turn up, that he had found a way to survive. Still, Shelley cried himself to sleep. Some of the men down at Waterboy's were not so confident. They speculated that he was almost certainly dead. That's what "missing in action" usually meant. He was dead but his body would probably never be found. There would be no closure. It would be as if Bubba had simply stepped off the edge of the earth.

Shelley also found himself tormented by other thoughts. How much more tragic it was that his brother was way across the Pacific Ocean, fighting for a country that forbade him to go to Homewood High School, the white school, or to the University of Alabama down in Tuscaloosa. Locked him out of the all-white city swimming pools and tennis courts and golf courses. Would not allow him to sit in the lower section of the big, ornate Alabama Theater to watch a movie. Made him stand in the back of a street car or city bus, even if there were empty seats in the all-white section in front of the board.

Word came on January 5, 1952, that Bubba had been confirmed as killed in action. Shelley sat on his aunt's back porch and sobbed. Aunt Emily did not shed a tear. The boy later heard that his daddy showed up at Waterboy's and allowed the patrons there to buy him shots in memory of his oldest boy. He gratefully accepted them until he was drunk, and then he staggered home, though nobody ever saw him shed a tear. Slim certainly never came to Shelley to share his grief, though he surely knew where he was, just up the hill.

The casket arrived a few days later, draped in an American flag. Shelley borrowed a suit to wear to the funeral at Union Baptist Church. Slim was there, but he sat on one end of a pew and Shelley sat on the other. They did not acknowledge each other's presence. A few neighbors were there to see Shelley take possession of the folded American flag and his brother's Purple Heart, presented by the military honor guard.

As he sat there on the hard pew, wearing an ill-fitting borrowed suit,

Huell Jerome Stewart Jr., 1951. Killed in Korea, November 6, 1951.

a strange calm came over the boy. His heart was still breaking, still aching because he now knew that he would never see his brother again. However, he had already heard that sweet inner voice that still spoke to him at times.

Don't cry, Shelley. Jerome is here with me. Everything is going to be all right. Don't be afraid. Don't give up.

As they lowered the cheap, simple casket into the ground at Grace Hill Cemetery, Shelley looked off into the distance. He could see some of the taller buildings in downtown Birmingham, the ones where the white lawyers and bankers and businessmen worked. The structures cast such long, dark shadows across 17th Street and the rest of the Negro business district. He could also see the sun falling behind a shroud of red smoke, back toward the west where the mills cranked out steel and pipe and wire.

Job, from the Bible, must have felt the way I'm feeling, he thought. How many more trials will God put me through? But I still believe in God's mercy and blessing. I still believe right will win out. And I still believe there is a future for me, Shelley told himself.

After all, his mother had told him as much, many, many times.

Everything was going to be all right.

14

ScooBa

The late-winter sun felt good on his face as he lay back on his aunt's front step and looked up into the clear afternoon sky. Shelley was doing something he rarely did: playing hooky from Rosedale School. For some reason, on that particular day, he decided to leave the school at lunchtime and go on home. He had decided that he needed to rest a bit and maybe ponder Bubba's loss until he could figure out how to deal with it.

"How you doin', young man?"

Shelley opened his eyes, shielded them from the sun, and then he could see the postman standing there on the other side of Emily's hog wire fence.

"I am doing just fine, sir. How you?"

"Fine as frog hair split four ways," the postman replied with a laugh. The white mailman had always been pleasant enough, though he rarely had mail to put into Aunt Emily's rusty old box. Just the occasional postcard from Aunt Mamie, from all the way across Birmingham. This day was no exception. No mail for Aunt Emily, but the letter carrier seemed to be looking for conversation this day.

They chatted for a bit about the weather, the health of some of the neighbors.

"Say, I been meaning to ask somebody along my route about something," the mailman said. He came closer to where Shelley reclined on the steps. "I've heard you are a smart boy and you might be just the one that could help me, Shelley. We've had this postcard down at the office for about two years now that we keep pinned up on the wall. Some of the guys laugh about it. The writing is like a first-grader's hen scratching, they say." He nodded to the several pullets scratching in the dirt in the yard nearby. "See, the thing

134

they really think is funny is that it's just addressed to 'Rosedale.' No name, no street address. But it just occurred to me you might help me figure out who it could be that was supposed to get it."

"Well, I don't know." Quite a few folks lived in Rosedale. Shelley certainly didn't know all of them. He had not been back all that long anyway. Many others came and went, too.

"The only clue is it says something on the back like, 'To my bro Shurl.' You know anybody up here with that name, Shurl?"

Shelley's mouth dropped open. He felt dizzy. There were only a few folks left who knew him as "Shurl" or "Shurley." But who among them would be sending him a postcard?

The bigger mystery was the one that really left Shelley breathless. What was the likelihood of his leaving school early this particular day, being out there on the steps, having the mailman walk past when he did, and having him ask Shelley about a postcard addressed to him, but with a name practically nobody used for him anymore?

Momma, it's you, he thought. Mattie C. was still orchestrating events in her boy's life.

When Shelley got home from school the next day, the postman had left the card in the mailbox just as he had promised. It felt hot to the touch when Shelley pulled it out and looked at it. Supernaturally hot.

"To my bro Shurl. I need lot help. Sam."

The card was postmarked "Scooba, Mississippi."

It had been ten long years since Shelley had seen or heard from his two younger brothers, David and Sam. His daddy had pointedly refused to tell him anything about their whereabouts. Now, amazingly, the curious mailman had presented him a slim clue as to where they might be. Or at least where they were two years ago.

Shelley looked up his father's old neighbor, the drinking buddy who had reported Slim Stewart to the police for feeding his boys fried rat meat. The man thought for a moment, remembered something, and shared that Marie had, he believed, once mentioned she and Slim shipped "them little bastards" off to somewhere. Mississippi, it might have been.

That was all the confirmation Shelley needed. He found a map at the library that showed him where Scooba was located, north of Meridian, just across the state line from Alabama. It might just as well have been California or Massachusetts. The clerk at the window at the Greyhound bus station informed him that their buses did not go anywhere near the place. Still Shelley figured he could walk fifty miles if it took it to find his baby brothers.

Trailways was more helpful. The tiny town was on their route, but the roundtrip ticket would cost him about ten dollars.

When Shelley hit up his buddies out front of Fess's Place for money, they laughed at first. Then, when they saw how serious Shelley was, they reminded him that the odds of finding his brothers, even in a town as small as Scooba, Mississippi, probably was, would be dismally long. They might not even want to come back to Birmingham with Shelley by now. Besides, Mississippi was a hazardous place for a young black man. A Negro with no specific reason to be walking alongside a rural roadway in Mississippi could easily end up in jail or swinging from a tree limb.

Still, when they realized how determined Shelley was to make his quest, each agreed to loan him a dollar or two. Now that he had enough money in his pocket to purchase the bus ticket and then some, Shelley collected several knives to carry, just in case he had to defend himself over there.

When he stepped up to the ticket window at the Trailways station downtown, Shelley bought one round-trip ticket to Scooba. But he also purchased two one-way tickets from Scooba to Birmingham. He was that confident that Mattie C. would direct him to his brothers and would show him the way to extricate them from whatever their situation might be and get them back home. Otherwise she never would have set up the appearance of that mysterious and plaintive postcard.

Shelley was in the back of the bus with the other Negro passengers when it pulled away from the station at 6 a.m., headed westward for U.S. 11 and, eventually, the Mississippi state line. As he breathed in the diesel fumes, it occurred to him that this would be his longest foray away from Birmingham by far. He had been to a few horse shows when he worked with Bubba at Stringfellows', and had gone down to Chilton County with Papa Clyde to look in on some of his construction projects. Not only would this be the greatest distance he had traveled but it would surely be his most dangerous trip, too.

Just to be cautious, he had carefully wrapped the knives in one of his aunt's old towels and carefully taped it to his body, beneath his long johns and work shirt. Then he pulled a floppy old cap over his ears and tugged on his brogan shoes so he would look like a field hand, not a waiter, radio personality, or high school student from the big city.

The bus made lots of stops at grocery stores, filling stations, dusty country crossroads, and courthouse squares with their usual Confederate soldier statues, but it finally pulled in to Scooba at about 11 A.M. Shelley made certain he knew the time for the return trip to Birmingham. The driver said it would be 3:47 P.M. and he was on time every time, without fail. He always stopped, too, to see if there were passengers or packages to pick up, but he did not loiter or wait for anyone.

Shelley double-checked the time on the watch he had borrowed from one of the guys at Fess's. He had never owned a timepiece. His aim was to find Sam and David, get them back to the little store where the bus stopped, and catch the return ride back to Birmingham that very afternoon. Otherwise, he would have to find a barn or a stand of trees for shelter to sleep over. Instinct told him the longer he remained in this strange land, the more likely it would be that trouble would find him.

The only problem was that he had absolutely no idea where to start looking.

The town of Scooba was made up of only a few stores, some stop signs, a feed store, some frame houses, and a handful of other small, one-story buildings. Shelley looked for black faces and deliberately avoided the white ones. Trying to appear as if he knew where he was going and that he had a purpose in going there, he began to walk along the town's main street. Soon, he saw an elderly black man coming his way in a wagon pulled by two mules.

"Hey, there!" Shelley shouted to him, waving, as if he had known the old man for years. "How in the world you been doin'?"

The man told his mules to "whoa" and squinted to try to make out the face of this tall, skinny young man who seemed to know who he was.

"Do I know you?" he finally asked, scratching his stubbly chin whiskers.

"I ain't going to tell you. You supposed to know me."

"Well, let me study on it," the old man said, obviously bewildered. "I'll figure out how I know you here directly."

"Listen, while you studying, I'm looking for my two cousins, Sam and David. They come over here a while back. They be about 14 and 12 years old now. Reckon you could tell me if you know where I might find them?"

The old man nodded.

"Matter of fact, there's two colored boys come and took up here some time ago. Better than two years ago, I expect. Couple of skinny boys, kind of like you. They be staying up at Alan Johnson's plantation. Just up that road there, but I suspect you know where Alan Johnson's plantation be. Everybody knows it."

Shelley played along.

"'Course I do. Everybody knows Mr. Johnson's plantation."

The old man pointed a finger at Shelley.

"Hey, I think I figured it out. You one of them Cooper boys from over at Giles, ain't you?"

"Yes sir, one of them Coopers."

"Then you tell your granddaddy he damn well better pay me that money he owes me!"

Shelley assured the man he would relay the message to his granddaddy. Then he trotted away, in the direction the old coot had indicated led to where his brothers might be. Once away from the little cluster of buildings and houses that made up Scooba, he was surrounded only by cotton fields bordered by tall, loblolly pine trees. Black workers—men, women, and children, even though it was a school day—were preparing the fields for the coming growing season.

It might as well be 1852 instead of 1952, Shelley thought.

AS HE WALKED BRISKLY along, Shelley realized how much he stood out, now that he was away from town. The only ones out here were busily working in the field, not walking along the roadway. It occurred to him that some of the field workers might report seeing him to their foreman, making the assumption that he was a worker who was trying to run away. That he was taking off like a runaway slave. At the least, a suspicious overseer who saw a stranger out here would report him to the law and that would certainly mean jail, even though Shelley was not doing anything illegal.

As he passed an especially big field with clumps of Negroes working busily, Shelley decided he should make himself less obvious. He stooped and hid in a clump of bushes alongside the narrow trail of asphalt to think about his next move. He lay there on his belly and watched the workers for a moment. He noticed one young boy, riding a mule, going from one group of field hands to the next, giving them a dipper full of drinking water from buckets he had strapped to the animal's flanks.

Impossibly, Shelley noted that the young boy looked to be about the age Sam would be, and that his mannerisms were eerily familiar.

No, it couldn't be, Shelley told himself. The first field he approached? The first person he saw would turn out to be his long-lost brother, Sam?

The boy on the mule passed a couple of hundred feet from where Shelley was hunkered down in the bushes.

"Sam! David!" Shelley said, just loud enough, he hoped, for only the boy on the mule to hear.

The young man stopped and looked his way. But so did several of the field hands who had apparently heard him, too. Shelley reached into his shirt and pulled out one of the knives, just in case the young man turned out not to be his brother at all. In case he called for the others to come grab whoever was lurking in the bushes, hollering at him. The truth was, Shelley had not seen his brothers in more than ten years. They were little more than toddlers when he left Slim and Marie's place. He had no idea what they looked like now.

"Sam! David!" he shouted again. The boy looked around to make sure his bosses were not watching and guided his mule over to near where Shelley hid in the underbrush. Still wary but curious, the youngster kept his distance. "Your name Sam or David?"

"My name is Sam," the young boy replied warily, still looking back over his shoulder.

"Sam what?"

"Sam Stewart."

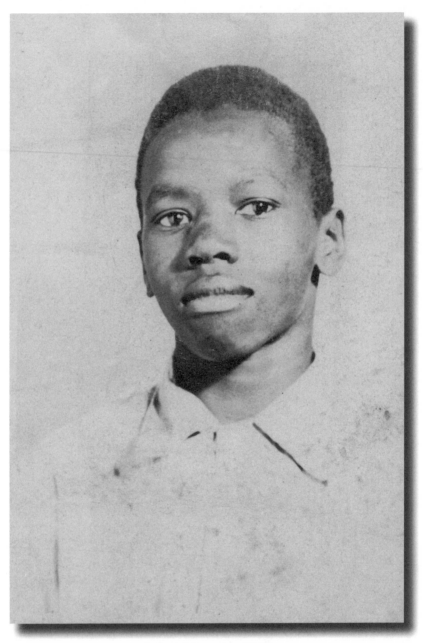

David Stewart, 1952.

"You got a brother?"

"Yeah."

"What's his name?" Shelley's heart was pounding.

"You done called it. David. His name is David."

Tears rolled down Shelley's cheeks. He pulled his old cap down farther so the boy on the mule might not notice.

"Where is David now? He out there in that field?"

"No, he up at the house. He fell off a mule and broke his leg and it ain't healed enough for him to work again in the fields yet."

Shelley got up onto his knees.

"Sam, do you know who I am?"

"No, but I reckon you could be one of my older brothers. Shurley or Bubba." Shelley stood and removed his cap. Sam looked hard at him. His jaw dropped. "Is that you, Shurl?"

Shelley knew he could not stand, run from the cover of the honeysuckle vines, pull his brother off the mule, and give him a proper hug, but he wanted to so badly that it hurt. Instead, he asked him how long it would take him to go retrieve David, and if his brother would be able to walk all the way back to Scooba.

Sam assured him it would not take long at all, and that David could hobble along pretty good by then. But Sam also told Shelley that it could go bad for them if they were caught. The overseers did not take well to their workers trying to run off. There might be beatings and even gunfire. At the least, there would be trumped-up charges and jail time just to discourage such desertion. Any one of the field hands might be a tattler, too, eager to alert the bosses in exchange for extra food or a reduced workload.

"I'm gone go get some more water," Sam shouted to the nearest group of field hands and trotted away on the mule, disappearing in the windblown dust from the bare ground.

Little more than fifteen minutes later, Shelley heard the clip-clop of the mule's hoofs and Sam's and David's voices, arguing with each other.

"I done told you, David, one of our brothers would come find us."

"You a damn liar! Shurley ain't here. I don't see him nowhere."

Shelley stood up then and stepped out of the honeysuckle, into the roadway. David slid down from the mule and stood there wide-eyed.

"Tie up that mule and we'll leave it here. I bet they hang mule thieves around these parts," Shelley told them. There was still no time for hugs yet. They had to get on down the road. The bus driver had assured Shelley that his bus always ran on time, and they had only about an hour and a half to get back to the stop. And no telling how many times they would have to dive into the underbrush and hide when vehicles came past. David's bum leg would keep them from making the best time, too. No doctor had been consulted about the injury. It would have to heal on its own. Shelley all but carried him at times.

As they walked, Shelley shared with them the news about Bubba's death in Korea. Neither seemed too sad about it. It had been too long since they had seen their older brother. Or their emotions had simply grown as calloused as their hands from the hard life they had endured so far in their own young lives.

Sam recounted that Marie and Slim had given them to a colored man who brought them to Mississippi. There, on the plantation, they were expected to do man's work—chopping and picking cotton, gathering corn, tending livestock, splitting logs, clearing new ground for crops—in exchange for food and shelter and practically nothing else. Even then, they had to kill rabbits and race the hogs to the slop bucket to have enough food to eat. Their shelter had been a shack in which they could see the ground through cracks in the floor and feel the knife-sharp wind in the winter. Of course, there was no inside plumbing and their only baths came when they swam in the nearby creek.

"We was slaves, Shurl, plain and simple," Sam told him.

Sam vaguely remembered mailing the postcard. He had long since given up on it summoning any help for them. He and David had resigned themselves to living out their years there on the Johnson plantation.

Watching behind them the whole way, fully expecting a posse to be coming to bring them all back to the plantation, they finally made it to the place where the Trailways bus would be stopping shortly. They hid between two buildings until the bus pulled in and the driver hopped down to go inside and check for packages and passengers.

"Go, now!" Shelley told his brothers when he saw the driver opening the store door, headed back to his bus. He presented all three tickets to the driver and they marched to the rear of the bus and sat down. They scrunched down behind the seatback, trying to hide, and then watched through the dust-covered rear window, looking for pursuers, as the bus pulled away from Scooba. There were none, and soon they were across the Alabama state line, then back on U.S. 11, a ribbon of concrete Shelley assured his brothers would lead them right through downtown Birmingham.

The younger boys watched with wide eyes everything around them and all they passed along the way. The cars and trucks might just as well have been flying saucers. Tractors plowing fields were a revelation. That work had been done by men and women and boys and mules where they had most recently been. It was as if they had been placed in a time machine and transported from before the Civil War into modern 1950s America. Still, the three Stewart brothers didn't allow themselves hugs and tears until they alighted from the bus at the terminal back in Birmingham and rode the street car over the mountain and into Rosedale.

Then, right there on the sidewalk in front of Fess's Place, they had a proper reunion with embraces, backslapping, and honest crying. Shelley finally ushered them inside the café. He pulled all the remaining money from his jeans pockets and bought hamburgers and French fries and Coca-Colas until there was not a penny left.

WORD QUICKLY SPREAD AROUND the neighborhood about the amazing re-uniting of the Stewart boys. Most knew the story of their horrid childhood, about the sudden disappearance of the two little ones, and now here they were, as if returned from the dead. A steady stream of neighbors filed into the restaurant to see the boys, to welcome them home, and to buy cakes and pies for them. Some offered to help, to take one or the other in for a few days, but Shelley knew most of the well-wishers barely had enough to feed their own families or beds enough to hold them. He had, of course, given the matter some thought already. From the moment he learned where they might be, Shelley had never doubted for a moment that he would bring his brothers back from Mississippi. He knew where they were going to stay

Sam Stewart, 1955.

now. Some place where he could see them and be with them every day.

"Thank you, but they'll be staying with me, up at Aunt Emily's house."

Never mind that he had not yet shared his plan with her. She would not like it, of course, but Shelley figured he could work a little harder, sell a few more shoes, grin and compliment the white folks at the Jack-O-Lantern to earn a few more tips, and his aunt would be happy to get some more dollars handed to her each month for her new tenants. It would be hard to get the additional money, but he would do it, at least until he went away to college. By then, he would have something else worked out for David and Sam.

Finally, gorged and growing sleepy after their adventurous day, Shelley urged his brothers to get started up the street toward their new home. They stepped out into the unusually warm March night, the stars already breaking through the night sky overhead. Shelley put his arms around each brother and they started walking up Highway 31.

Then, in the shadows ahead, there was movement. A tall, slim man stepped into the glow of the overhead streetlight. They stopped.

It was their daddy.

Neither Sam nor David recognized him. Slim stood there for a moment, glaring at them. Clearly, he too had received the word that his younger sons had somehow been rescued by Shelley from near-slavery way over there in Mississippi.

But, without saying a word, Slim turned and ran away as fast as he could until the blackness swallowed him whole.

15

FOUNd & LOST

As expected, Aunt Emily was not enthusiastic about having two more nephews underfoot in her little shotgun house. She made it clear to Shelley that
these two newcomers—her late sister's boys or not—were his responsibility,
to feed, clothe, and take care of. Anything extra she did for the boys, like
washing their clothes or changing the sheets on their bed, required payment,
promptly and in cash. Sardines and crackers, Vienna sausages and neck bones,
or whatever else Shelley could conjure up, were the staples of their diet. The
boys' clothes were falling apart. David and Sam had fled the plantation with
just the rags on their backs. One of the cooks at Fess's donated some items
her kids had outgrown, and that was all the boys had to wear.

Shelley considered it a first order of business to get both his brothers
into school. He knew only too well which way they would go without any
learning. Without even considering their lack of formal education thus
far, Principal Montgomery placed the boys in class based on their ages,
but down a grade or two just to make sure. Sam was in seventh grade,
David in sixth. That assured that they not only felt awkward because they
were older than their classmates but embarrassingly uncomfortable since
neither really knew how to read or write beyond, at best, a second-grade
level. It was not long before Shelley realized his tutoring would not be
enough, that his brothers were already playing hooky from school most
days and had gravitated toward others who shared their minimal interest in education. Others who sought to make their way with muscle and
guile, not brainpower.

Once again, the strain of it all was starting to take its toll on Shelley.
The pressure of paying Emily for rent and every little thing she did, keep-

ing his brothers fed, going to school and maintaining his grades, waiting tables at the Jack-O-Lantern, selling shoes downtown, and still trying to do his show on the radio stations was wearing him down. More than once, he prayed to God and called out to Mattie C., asking what they wanted him to do, wondering if they could help him get through. There was no immediate answer.

Then one April day he was headed to work at the Jack-O-Lantern, his stomach growling because he had not had time to get anything to eat. He caught sight of a brown paper bag lying amid some other garbage beside the highway. Maybe somebody had thrown out a half-eaten sweet roll or something edible, he thought. But when he picked up the bag, it was far too heavy to be nibbled-on pastry. When Shelley opened it and looked inside, his heart almost stopped and he was no longer hungry at all.

It was money. Lots of it.

He looked around but saw no one. Quickly, he shoved the bag inside his jacket and walked on, trying to look nonchalant even though his knees had gone wobbly.

The bills had not been bound with paper wrappers, as it likely would have had it been a merchant's bank deposit. No, it was almost certainly a bootlegger's take or the receipts from some neighborhood numbers game. Almost certainly ill-gotten gain and patently illicit, the boy decided. That would be a mixed blessing. Nobody would be talking too much about losing a sum of money that came from illegal activity. However, if anybody discovered Shelley had picked it up, the money's owner would likely slit the boy's throat to get it back.

After a mile or so, the paper bag seemed to be on fire against his ribs. He stepped behind a stand of trees, into a deep ditch, and counted the money. It took him a while. The sack held $2,700, mostly in ones, fives, and twenties. Shelley shook his head and tried to breathe. That was far and away the most money he had ever seen in one stash.

Shelley hid the money carefully and kept his ears open to hear if anyone mentioned losing it. A storekeeper or grocer would surely have put out the word. There was nothing said, further confirming it was likely whiskey, gambling, or drug money. Money from heaven, Shelley assumed. Money

from Momma. He promised her something good would be done with that
windfall she had provided.

EVENTUALLY SHELLEY PULLED $200 out of the bag and went on a shopping
spree to one of the dry goods stores on 3rd Avenue North downtown. He
bought new pants and shirts for his brothers and for himself, too. Then he
splurged on a new pair of Edmund Clapp shoes he had been eyeing. Diners
at the Jack-O-Lantern would certainly tip better if he was wearing something
besides his old scuffed brogans when he served them.

But somebody else noticed the new duds first.

"You ain't stealin', are you?" Aunt Emily accused, her chin jutted out for
emphasis. "You stealin' and go to jail these little bastards ain't staying here.
You stealin', you damn well better not get your ass caught!"

Shelley had a dream for how he might use more of the money. He heard
that one of their neighbors in Rosedale had purchased some land south
of town, near a little town called Sterrett in neighboring Shelby County.
Because it was most of an hour's ride from Birmingham down U.S. 280,
and because no bus or street car went that far out into the country, land
was cheap there. Word was, too, that the seller did not mind taking colored
folks' money. Shelley reasoned that one day the area would be more easily
accessible to the big city. The suburbs were already expanding southward
beyond Red Mountain, Shades Mountain, and Double Oak Mountain and
would only continue to do so, he figured. A simple but comfortable cabin
built there would assure he and his brothers would always have a roof over
their heads, if nothing else. And besides, the Lord was not making any more
land and it would be a better investment of his heaven-sent money than
just about anything else he might find.

With $1,200 pulled from the brown paper sack, Shelley bought a little
more than eighty heavily wooded acres near Sterrett. Since he was still only
17 years old, he had to have the deed issued in Aunt Emily's name. Shelley
knew the issues that could crop up with that entanglement so he drew up a
document in which his aunt acknowledged his ownership of the land. The
deed also carried a survival clause making certain it was Shelley's property
and his alone in the case of his aunt's death. She squawked and accused him

House on the 80 acres Shelley purchased in Shelby County, Alabama.

again of robbing somebody to buy the land, but she also reasoned the cabin down there would be a place for her to live now that she was getting too old to work as a housekeeper and had started to draw the Social Security. She went along with the way Shelley structured the land deal.

He waited a few more weeks before purchasing lumber, tools, and nails. When he had the time, and with the help of Sam and David, he hitchhiked back and forth and began building a small, simple three-bedroom house on the property. Even though Shelley's plan was to allow her to move there and live for free, Aunt Emily was quick to challenge even the rustic structure he was putting up.

"You making this place too damn fancy," she told him. "White folks down here won't like coloreds trying to live so fancy. Shurley, you always trying to live like white folks!"

At her insistence, Shelley stopped construction before painting the walls, inside or out, and she blatantly forbid him to put in an indoor toilet or electricity. Instead, she made sure there were a hog pen, a chicken yard, a cow shed, and a one-hole outhouse.

When it was habitable—to Emily's standards—Sam and Aunt Emily moved into the Shelby County house. Soon, mostly because of Emily's discouragement about anything to do with education, Sam stopped going to his new school in Columbiana and instead worked the land with a mule Shelley bought for $30. David remained in the house Aunt Emily had been renting in Rosedale and Shelley continued to pay the new tenant rent for his brother to live there. Without Shelley there, David soon rejected school as well and began spending more and more time with those who hung out on the street in front of the juke joints along the colored side of U.S. 31.

Shelley had moved in with another family nearby. He was too old to live with strangers in his aunt's old place but he did not want to stray from Rosedale just yet. He was centrally located for school and his various jobs and it was all temporary anyway. In a few months, he would be living in a college dormitory and enjoying good food in a cafeteria.

HIS GOAL WAS NOW firmly in sight. His senior year was winding down and at graduation he would learn which college he would be attending when his scholarship award was announced. Commencement was to be held at Friendship Baptist Church on Central Avenue, not far from where he and his brothers had once been dumped in a vacant lot and ended up living a meager existence on his daddy's and Marie's back stoop.

As he had for Bubba's funeral, Shelley borrowed a suit from the folks where he was renting the room. The lady of the house starched and ironed a white shirt so it looked just right. After getting help to put a neat and proper knot in his necktie and donning the suit coat and pants, he pulled on the long, dark commencement gown and carefully balanced the mortarboard cap on top of his head.

Then, grinning broadly, Shelley stood in front of a tall mirror and took a long look at himself.

Again, he imagined a crowd, cheering back at him from the edges of the looking glass. A throng congratulating him for defying about the longest odds anyone could have imagined and for not giving up. Before long, Shelley Stewart would finally realize the powerful dream that had seen him through so many horrible occurrences. He would be graduating from high school with honors. When Principal Montgomery called out the scholarship recipients, he would march up front and accept his. Finally his life would turn positive. All the hard work and sacrifice would have been worthwhile.

That new life lay ahead of him like a shining, colorful path. College. Law school. He had been so fixated on this night for so long, but now, finally, that bright future was within his grasp.

He almost cried when he thought about how proud Mattie C. would be if she could have been present. How she would have cheered and cried and laughed out loud when his name was called for the scholarship and when he walked forward to accept that hard-won diploma.

But of course, there would be no family members there to applaud what he had accomplished. No parent. No relative. The crowd in the mirror would have to do.

When it was almost time to go over to the church for the ceremony, Shelley had a sudden thought. At least one member of his family should be given the opportunity to see him in his garb. He walked down the street, still wearing his suit, his gown, and his mortarboard cap. But he made a slight detour from the route to the church. He turned toward the house on 27th Court where he knew Slim Stewart lived then.

Sure enough, his daddy sat in a chair on the porch, smoking a cigarette. He silently watched his son walk up and stop at the foot of the rickety porch steps. Marie was there, too, leaning back in the shadows in her cane-bottomed chair, spitting snuff into the dusty yard.

Slim did not say a word or even acknowledge his boy's presence. Marie simply glared at him, giving him the evil eye.

"I'm graduating tonight," Shelley announced. He noticed his daddy's hand trembling, the fiery end of his cigarette dancing slightly in the gathering dusk. "You told me I would never live to see 16 years old. Well, you were wrong. And I'm graduating high school tonight. They'll give me a scholarship tonight, too, and I'm going to college."

Slim continued to stare at his boy, his hand still trembling, a scowl on his face.

Then Shelley realized that his father likely was trembling because he was afraid of his own son. Afraid his boy had come by that day not to brag about his diploma and scholarship but to extract some revenge for the way Shelley had been treated by his own flesh and blood. The boy was certainly big enough to do it. Adept enough with a blade to do some damage, too. And he surely had the motivation. On the other hand, after years of drinking bad liquor, smoking, and coming out on the wrong end of so many fights, Slim was hardly in any shape to put up much of a fight. Slim knew it, too.

Shelley did not give his father the benefit of a smile. He stood there at the steps and stared stone-faced at both adults for a moment. Then, abruptly, he turned on his heels and marched on down to Friendship Baptist Church.

Everyone gathered in front of the church was excited, the air electric with anticipation. Family members, proudly dressed in their finest attire, gathered, cheered, and hugged their graduates, wiping away accidental smudges of face powder from graduation gowns and wetting palms to smooth down wayward strands of hair, just as they had done for their children since they were babies. Some of the family members had come from as far away as New York to celebrate this day. Others had bought new clothes just for the occasion. Graduating high school was a significant accomplishment in the black community, a milestone not achieved by many.

Shelley paid little attention to all the happy family members, though. He no longer felt bad about not having anyone there to cheer for him. It was nothing new, after all. For a moment, he had considered asking Papa Clyde to come. He decided that he did not want to put Smith on the spot if it might have made him feel uncomfortable.

When Shelley started into the church house to find his place among the pews up front, he noticed Mrs. Carlotta Harris, standing near the doorway talking with a group of parents and teachers. Mrs. Harris was one of the teachers who had taken a special interest in him when he first enrolled at Rosedale. Shelley walked her way. He wanted to thank her one more time for all her support, for being there to listen when he needed someone to talk with. She had been a valued confidante and had helped him through some rough times in the past nine months or so.

When she looked up and saw Shelley striding her way, Mrs. Harris's eyes immediately filled with tears.

"I'm sorry, Shelley," she told him, and turned away. "I am so very sorry."

The piano struck up then, signaling the graduates and their guests to their seats to begin the night's ceremony.

What did she mean? Shelley asked himself. There was no chance to ask her now. The ritual was about to begin.

There were songs and prayers and speeches and some more prayers. Finally, they came to the point in the program where scholarship recipients were to be announced, called forward one at a time, and recognized by the assembled crowd. Shelley sat there, struggling to remain still, as the excitement inside him rose. He only hoped his knees would not buckle when he finally heard his name called, and that he was able to go up there without dancing down the aisle or letting out a whoop of joy.

Several of his female classmates were called first. Scholarships to Miles College. Alabama A&M. Tuskegee. Of course, there were none for the University of Alabama, Auburn, or any of the white-only state schools.

Next to be called was one of the better male students, but one whose grades were not nearly as impressive as the marks Shelley had earned. Still, the classmate deserved the scholarship and Shelley was happy for him.

One of the school's star football players was called, the one Shelley had beaten out in the vote for class president. Shelley frowned. This student was receiving an academic scholarship even though he could hardly write his name and had, in fact, relied on Shelley's tutoring to even get his barely-passing grades.

There was even a classmate called who was known as the school drunk, a kid who skipped class more than he showed up and who usually slept through them when he did make it to school.

Then Principal Montgomery closed the book in front of him and turned to the pianist, signaling her to begin playing "Pomp and Circumstance." The announcement of scholarship recipients was complete. It was time for the seniors to march up front one at a time, near the altar, and receive their diplomas.

Shelley was struggling to find a breath of air. His head spun dizzily. What had just happened? What in hell had just happened?

He was still numb when his name was called to claim his diploma, but he managed to walk forward, take the rolled-up document with his left hand, and shake Fess Montgomery's hand with his right, just as they had practiced. The principal did not make eye contact with Shelley. He looked past him, focused on the next graduate whose name had already been called.

People in the audience shouted and squealed as each graduate trooped across the stage. There was only the sound of the piano as Shelley took his diploma.

But then Shelley heard a loud voice somewhere in the crowd.

"That's my boy! *That's* my boy!"

He looked up through the tears in his eyes. Standing in the back of the sanctuary, amid all the other friends and family members, was a familiar face. It was Mamie Foster, the elementary school teacher. The lady who had first believed in and gave special support to the rag-tag orphan boy when he started first grade. The one who had repeatedly told him he could be anything he wanted to be and do anything he wanted to do if he worked hard enough.

Shelley waved at her and forced a crooked smile. Mrs. Foster would never know how much her cheers meant to him at that moment. He marched back to his place in the pews. He could fight it no longer. A tear rolled down each cheek. He held onto the back of the pew in front of him to keep from collapsing.

As soon as the ceremony ended, Shelley headed straight for the principal. He had to wait until several parents had finished shaking the educator's hand and thanking him for shepherding their children through to this happy day.

"Mr. Montgomery, why didn't I get a scholarship?" Shelley asked him, point blank. He worked hard to stifle a sob.

Montgomery took a step back, as if he fully expected the boy to rear back and punch him in the face.

"Well, Shelley, you had some pretty good grades," he replied. "But the one thing you need for college is family support. You don't have family support. Look, Shelley, without that, you are just not college material."

MONTGOMERY EVENTUALLY PROMISED TO try to round up a scholarship for Shelley but nothing ever materialized. The boy would always wonder if he had erred by telling the principal so much about his dysfunctional childhood, but Montgomery had always seemed anxious to help, to listen, and to sympathize.

(Years later, Shelley talked with Principal Montgomery and told him that he had forgiven him for denying him the chance to go on to college. He also told his old principal that the disappointment, massive as it was, likely sent Shelley on a better path than college and a career in law ever would have.)

That night, when he got back to his little rented room, Shelley studied the fancy writing on his diploma. His faith in people had been severely shaken by what had happened that evening at Friendship Baptist Church. Still, he knew what his momma would tell him. He could not give up. He had a purpose. He would do great things.

But where and how? WEDR had already turned him down for a full-time, paying job for the summer. He was too young. Too inexperienced. He would never get ahead waiting tables at the Jack-O-Lantern. And swallowing his pride and kissing up to the white patrons just for tips had long since grown old and felt degrading.

Momma, show me something, he said into the dark night. *Tell me what I am supposed to do.*

The very next day, making his way down the hill and toward his job at the restaurant, he caught sight of a snazzy-looking car easing down one of the streets in Rosedale. Three cocky, well-dressed young black men were inside. Shelley had noticed the car and its occupants before, showing off for the neighborhood.

As they drove past him, the boy could see that the fancy automobile bore a colorful license plate, one much different from Alabama's with its "Heart of Dixie" slogan.

New York. The car had New York license plates.

16

HARLEM

New York City would be a different world for Shelley Stewart. With the stunning disappointment of his graduation night, plus the frustrations brought on by circumstance and racial discrimination, something dissimilar to Birmingham was exactly what the boy craved. Besides, the slicks in the car with the New York license plates painted the metropolis to be an exciting, vibrant place, one where black people did not have to put up with the white man's boot on their throats. There was money to be made up there for Negroes.

Had their sales pitch come at any time other than the morning after his graduation, he might not have gone. But it did.

With his old suitcase filled with a few changes of clothes and tied shut with a piece of rope, Shelley bought a ticket on the Silver Comet train a few days later. He was bound for Pennsylvania Station in Manhattan. As the train pulled away from Birmingham's grand old terminal building, he watched the familiar streets fading away into the smoky distance, climbing the hip of Red Mountain. He imagined Rosedale just over the other side of the ridge, beneath the Vulcan statue. He pictured Bubba and himself fishing in Edgewood Lake. And the cemetery where Bubba and his mother lay at rest.

Shelley did not feel bad about leaving. He had so much in Birmingham and yet so little.

Besides, Sam and David were getting along okay as far as he could tell. Try as he might, he could not think of anyone else he would really miss in this place, or anyone who would truly miss him once he was gone. Gone maybe for good.

It occurred to him that he might never return to Birmingham, whether or not he took to New York or New York took to him. He hoped to do well enough there to one day be able to send for his brothers and have them come up and enjoy all that the big city had to offer. But if it was not meant to be New York, there were places like Detroit, Chicago, St. Louis, and even California, any of which he figured would offer more opportunity for him than "the Magic City," Birmingham.

Twenty-four hours later, Shelley walked out into the chaotic streets of Manhattan. For the first time, the enormity of what lay ahead hit him squarely between the eyes. It was immediately obvious this place was different from the streets of Birmingham. He knew no one. He did not have a job. He had no idea which way to even head. He might as well have been six years old, walking away from Rosedale, from Mamie and Slim and Marie, looking for Bubba.

He smiled at a sudden thought. It was Papa Clyde who always said, "Boy, if you don't know where you're going, any road will take you there."

HARLEM. THE COOL GUYS in the car with New York plates had mentioned Harlem and suggested he would feel more at home there. He stepped back into the terminal and watched for a few minutes the doorways that led to the subway trains. Some had far more black faces than white passing through them. Shelley went in that direction. He bought a pass and followed the crowd onto one particular train that the sign indicated was the "7th Avenue IRT Uptown." The slicks in the snazzy car had mentioned "Uptown."

As the subway rushed away from the platform, Shelley was immersed in the most pungent mixture of accents and languages he had ever heard. Some of the dialects were almost musical. Though he was still timid and wary, he enjoyed the electric excitement of this place and its gumbo of ethnicities.

Most of the few white passengers on the train exited at the 81st Street or the 96th Street stations. Black riders started getting off at 110th Street and 118th Street. Shelley followed a big group and left the subway at 125th Street.

When he climbed the stairway and emerged into daylight at street level, he felt even more intensely the powerful energy, the rhythm of the city. Everyone looked like him, except, of course, for being much better dressed. The first thing that struck him, though, was a few black men with white women on their arms, something he would never have seen in Alabama. Police or the Klan would have put a stop to that with arrests, beatings, or worse.

Blacks up here drove convertibles and other fine cars, too. Blacks who were obviously not the chauffeur. Blacks worked right up front in the stores and they were desk clerks in the hotels, not just bellboys and maids.

There were no "White" and "Colored" restrooms. He needed to go and, for the first time, Shelley stood at a urinal next to a white man. Even that was a freeing experience!

Once his astonishment at the absence of blatant segregation wore off, Shelley realized there was still a back-door separation of the races going on, even there in the great city. Blacks lived uptown, in Harlem, and in other pockets around the various boroughs. Whites had their own neighborhoods. So did the Chinese, the Italians, and every other ethnic group one could imagine. Discrimination was much more subtle than back home, and often defined more by economics than skin color, but it was still there.

Shelley was so intently gawking at the bustling street scene and the names of the establishments—some of which he had heard of before, like the Apollo Theater and the Hotel Theresa—that he almost walked into the path of a car while he was crossing the street. It occurred to him he might as well have "rube" tattooed on his forehead. He tried to be more nonchalant and not so obviously a rank newcomer just off the train in a new world.

THE FIRST ORDER OF business was to find a bed for the night and hopefully beyond. The Cecil Hotel rented him a tiny room for $12 per week. Never mind that most of the hotel's patrons were men who were only there to meet up with the skimpily attired ladies who stood along the sidewalk in front of the hotel. Shelley watched for a bit as the men quickly closed the deal and ushered the ladies upstairs for a few hours.

Regardless, the place had a bed and a roof, and in one corner downstairs was a club named Minton's Playhouse, the place where jazz jam sessions in the 1940s gave birth to bebop. It suited Shelley fine so long as he could land a job and make enough money to pay the high cost of sleeping there.

The Cecil's desk clerk, a well-dressed black man with processed hair named Leroy, quickly saw that Shelley was not nearly as world-wise as he was trying to appear. He took a liking to the young refugee, though, and suggested he needed a back story that would keep some of the more experienced people in the neighborhood from taking advantage of him and his naiveté. The story Leroy suggested was that Shelley was on the lam for killing a black man down in Alabama. No, wait. Make that a white man, and he had beaten and stabbed the guy to death. That would give pause to anyone who might have otherwise taken Shelley for a chump.

Leroy also learned that Shelley could shoot a mean game of eight-ball, one of the courses he had taken during his schooling in the backroom at Ratkiller's back on 17th Street in Birmingham. That and all the practice he had at the pool table in Papa Clyde's basement. The desk clerk asked a coworker to watch the desk for him and ushered his new tenant around the corner to a sizeable and bustling pool hall. There Shelley not only got the chance to show his game but also to try out his newly created and lurid past.

"Yeah, we get lots of colored guys that have killed white folks and come up here to hide," Johnny, the billiard parlor's owner, noted. "I beat a white man almost to death back in California for spittin' in my momma's face. Are the rollers behind you?"

Rollers? Oh. Policemen.

"Far as I know, they ain't," Shelley told him.

"Well, Bama, you ever learn to shoot pool down there in the land of grits and greens?"

"Little bit."

"Tell you what. I ain't going to call you 'Bama' no more cause you running from the law down there. I'm going to call you 'Country.' Let's see what you can do with a stick and a good game of cut-throat, Country."

Johnny watched Shelley rack up the balls, break, and promptly sink a long run, calling each shot beforehand. Johnny winked at Leroy.

"What's this? Country is some kind of slick, a shark!"

With a bit of coaching, Shelley was soon adept at hustling other players who stopped into Johnny's place. Much as he had put on the necessary mask to converse with the important white men at Yielding's or Stringfellows', he played whatever role it took to convince his opponents that he was a mediocre pool player with no confidence at all. Or a big-talking windbag with an exaggerated opinion of his own abilities. Either way, the other players assumed he was a sucker and they were more than willing to take his money.

Then, when Shelley had set the hook, he could reel them in. Of course, he shared his winnings with Johnny, who had bankrolled him from the beginning. Soon Shelley was getting ten or twelve dollars per game. Of course, Johnny kept four or five times that amount, but he was providing the establishment, the tables, the stake, and the hustlers who ended up getting themselves hustled instead.

Shelley felt no remorse. Most of Johnny's customers were pimps and seemed to have plenty of money to lose. He knew they would have happily hustled him if they could have.

For the first time in his life, Shelley went to a barbershop and had his hair straightened with a powerful mixture of chemicals. Johnny, Leroy, and most of the men in Harlem wore their hair that way. So did black performers Shelley had seen, like Nat King Cole and Sammy Davis Jr.

IT WAS NOT LONG before Shelley lost even more of his innocence in the big city. He found a boardinghouse nearby that was less expensive than the hotel room at the Cecil. However, he soon found that his new landlord—an older, church-going lady—wanted to take her rent in something other than Shelley's hustle money. In exchange for money, clothes, and room and board, Shelley became her lover and, basically, her play toy.

He also held a couple of other jobs, first spray-painting metal cabinets and later working in a plastics factory. All the while, whether he was fully aware of it or not, Shelley was further developing his new, hip personality. He was expanding his amazing gift for gab, the style honed and developed at Yielding's, at Stringfellows', in front of the mirror at Papa Clyde's, in the Parker High School talent shows, and on the airwaves at WEDR and WBCO. Here it was one of the necessities to survive this fast-paced city.

The boy was not quite eighteen years old but he already knew his way around Harlem and most of Manhattan, knew the clubs and pool halls, was acquainted with everyone from street hustlers to backup musicians in the clubs to the blue-collar workers he met at his jobs. He also now smoked and drank liquor socially.

When he had time, he frequented the Minton Playhouse. All the top black entertainers in the country were making stops there whether they were booked or not. He saw Count Basie, Sammy Davis Jr., Pearl Bailey, and so many more.

The music and the sophisticates who frequented the venue fascinated Shelley. He missed being on the radio and playing the records by the black artists, many of whom he watched perform in person at the Minton. He also missed seeing the reactions of the crowd at the talent shows when he did his jokes and unleashed his distinctive and infectious patter. Sitting in the audience at the Minton, watching those great talents perform, brought back some of that same old feeling. Somewhere deep inside, he knew he was destined to do more in life than paint cabinets or make plastic drinking straws or hustle pimps in smoky billiard parlors.

One thing had not changed. Shelley still cried himself to sleep most nights. He still felt his mother's presence sometimes, but he missed her so much. He missed Bubba, too. And though he had hardly had a chance to get to know them, he missed his younger brothers and prayed they were behaving themselves, that they would not go bad without him there to guide them.

All he could do was stay busy. Keep his church-going landlady satisfied. Make sure she only saw his happy-go-lucky side. Work the hustle at pool halls all over Harlem. Ride the IRT out to the far side of Queens to the plastics factory. Save money so he could continue to live in this breathtakingly expensive place and maybe, one day, send for Sam and David.

He rarely thought about going back to Birmingham. Maybe he was still caught up in the excitement of New York City. Maybe he was actually beginning to believe that story about him killing a white man back in Alabama. Or maybe he was just waiting for Mattie C. to tell him what to do, where to go.

Then one night after work, as he walked from the subway station to the boardinghouse, he noticed something going on in the front window of the Club Baby Grand, on the corner of 125th Street, near the Apollo Theater. There were two microphones set up. Radio microphones. He recognized them right away. A pair of record turntables and an audio mixing board, too. And two men, one white and one black, playing records and talking into those microphones, seemingly having the time of their lives, broadcasting live on WHOM Radio.

Shelley stood and watched them for a while, unable to keep the broad smile off his face. It was only a little while before he built up the nerve to walk around the corner, through the door, and into the club. And only a short time after that before he struck up a conversation with the two radio personalities and introduced himself.

Standing there near the microphones and audio board, Shelley suddenly felt as if he was where he was supposed to be. He also knew it would only be a matter of time before he sent his own voice out over the airwaves by way of WHOM.

17

EASY GReASY

Willie Bryant told him, with a deep laugh, "You, my man, are a liar! I know for a fact they do not allow colored people to be on the radio down south!"

Bryant was known on the airwaves as "The Mayor of Harlem."

"No way, Shelley Stewart," Ray Carroll, his white partner, said in agreement. "It's against the law down there!" Carroll blew out a big cloud of tobacco smoke and winked at some of the crowd gathered outside the window on 125th Street, watching as he and Bryant broadcast their radio show on WHOM.

"But it's true," Shelley responded. He was still amazed that a black man and a white man could share the same broadcast booth, working together, right there in a very public place. "I had shows on WEDR and WBCO, and I had quite the following around Birmingham."

This time it was Bryant who winked at Carroll and, with a broad grin, said, "OK, Country, we are going to have ourselves some fun with Mr. Big Time Radio Announcer!"

The last notes of the recording on the left turntable were just dying out. Bryant flipped a switch on the audio console, moved closer to his microphone, and lowered his voice to a deep resonance.

"Ladies and gentlemen, we hope you enjoyed that number," he said. "But now, we have a treat for you. We got ourselves a country man, a farmer up from Alabama, who wants to go on the air and show you how they do it back home."

Meanwhile, Ray Carroll had slipped a big pair of earphones onto Shelley's head. It was the first time he had ever worn such a contraption, but they seemed to fit fine. He leaned into the other microphone, flipped on the switch as he had so many times, and went to work.

"Hell-o-o-o-o, New-w-w-w-w York City!" He was amazed at how comfortable, how natural, it felt. He was not nervous at all, though certainly the audience out there contained many times the number of listeners he had in Birmingham. "Now listen to me. I want to tell y'all something. Here's how we are going to do this thing, y'all! Understand? We are doing it e-e-e-z-z-z-y, g-r-e-e-e-z-z-z-y!"

Shelley went on with his rap, ignoring the open mouths and wide eyes of Carroll and Bryant. He fell naturally into the parlance of the street, the pool halls, the clubs.

"This is Bama from Alabama, coming to you from street side at the Club Baby Grand on 125th Street in Harlem, massaging the masses right here on WHOM." Without even looking, he had started the turntable to his right and, as the music started beneath his spiel, he turned the record's volume up and down as he preached. He matched his delivery perfectly to the tempo of the song. "A-w-w-w-w, let's go, Harlem!"

The vocalist on the recording started singing just as Shelley stopped talking.

The telephone in the booth lit up immediately with listeners telling the regular hosts how "bad" this newcomer was. "Bad," of course, was good!

The two began to allow Shelley to sit in with them on occasion and spin some records and carry on his energetic discourse. Not too often, though. Shelley assumed that was because they were afraid he might steal their jobs.

Shelley realized he still had a lot to learn about the business, though, so he enrolled in the Cambridge School of Radio Broadcasting in midtown Manhattan. He really did not know how to use the more elaborate mixing boards and newfangled tape machines or how to edit and deliver the news or write and record commercials. Cambridge would teach him those things, plus part of the enrollment agreement was that they guaranteed to find him a full-time job in broadcasting when he graduated.

Soon Shelley was asked to help teach some of the classes, especially those on how to sell products and services in commercial copy and how the message delivered over the air could be most effective.

MEANWHILE, SHELLEY STILL RODE the train out to the plastics factory each day. And on those nights when he was not at the broadcasting school, he haunted the best clubs in Harlem. The Savoy was a particular favorite.

There, Shelley quickly learned which masks to put on to make himself more mysterious and thus more attractive to the many women who were there. He worked on his character, as surely as he had in the drama club back at Parker High School. He also loved the music, the celebrities who stopped in, the emcees doing their spiels on stage, and the magnetic excitement the place offered.

But one night as he left the club, he was met in the street by his landlord, the church-going lady whose bed he shared. And after watching Shelley flirt with the women inside, she was livid with jealousy.

When she told Shelley that she had once cut the throat of a man for doing far less than he was doing—and produced from her purse a yellowed newspaper clipping to prove it—he knew his days at her boardinghouse would soon be over. One day, while she was away, he packed up his clothes and left.

Shelley found a room on 7th Avenue above a restaurant and bar owned by boxing champion Sugar Ray Robinson. The place was available and at a cheap rate because of all the noise and hustle and bustle just below its window. In the beginning, that was actually a plus for Shelley. He reveled in watching out his apartment window the many celebrities who pulled up in taxis and limousines, emerging with their entourages.

Robinson was then the middle-weight champion of the world, having beaten Jake LaMotta for the title, and was arguably one of the most famous athletes in the world. Anyone who was anyone stopped by his place to be seen while in town. Shelley was soon joining the crowd downstairs, rubbing shoulders with Robinson and other luminaries from boxing and other sports as well as musical stars such as Pearl Bailey, Louis Belson, Sarah Vaughn and others. Soon he was one of the regulars, and when they realized this tall, skinny, dark-skinned man had intelligent things to say, he was welcomed into their discussions.

People actually listened when Shelley talked.

"Hey, Bama, what do you think about that?" they would ask him, and that boosted his ego enormously.

That only contrasted with the loneliness, the uncertainty, the hole in his heart left by his lack of family. Those emotions almost overwhelmed him. How could anybody be lonesome with so many people around?

Shelley hoped to wash all that away with the sparkling exhilaration he found in the clubs. But when he was simply too tired to be there anymore, he found himself alone in his bed, the pain in his soul and the constant noise from the street below staving off any hope of hiding in sleep.

"Mama, what am I supposed to do?" he asked the ceiling of his room.

So far, though, there was no satisfactory answer to his question. Or at least any guidance from Mattie C. that he was willing to listen to and accept.

There was soon another woman in his life, Vera, the sister of one of the pool hall patrons. Shelley moved in with her in her apartment in the middle-income black community of Sugar Hill. She must have sensed his vulnerability. She quickly convinced Shelley to turn over his paycheck from the plastics factory each week. She promised that she would give him an allowance to live on while she put aside the rest of it for their future together, so they could one day travel and see the world.

Shelley fell for it completely, never realizing he was being hustled. He actually started to fall for Vera, to start thinking beyond tonight and the next day.

Then one evening he arrived at the apartment and realized that he was locked out. His key did not fit. Then he saw his clothes piled in a cardboard box in the hallway. Shelley knocked on the door and yelled her name.

"You don't live here no more!" Vera shouted back at him, refusing to unlock the door, to even talk with him.

"Then give me my money and I'll be gone," he told her.

"I don't give a damn about your money," she screamed. "Get away from my door, making all that noise."

Shelley pounded on the door some more and was on the verge of putting a shoulder into it when he heard heavy footsteps coming up the stairs behind him. It was a couple of big, solid policemen, and they were clearly in no mood to put up with any guff.

"That's him, officers," the woman shouted from inside. "That's the man that's trying to break into my apartment."

The cops had no interest in hearing Shelley's side of the story. Not even the part about Vera holding his wages from the last month or so. They made sure he and his box of clothes were outside on the street and told him jail was almost certainly in his future if the woman called them back.

Shelley, now calmer and thinking more clearly, knew that he did not dare fight back or risk arrest. Sometimes, based on some comments from some of the police officers he had run into in Harlem, he was afraid the totally made-up and oft-told story of his violent past might actually be drawing their attention. Some white man had certainly been killed by a black man back in Alabama, and the black man had surely been rumored to have headed north. Should he end up in jail, who knew what crimes they might try to pin on him?

Shelley leaned dejectedly against a streetlight post. A gentle snow had begun to fall. He checked his pockets. He had one dollar and some small change.

A wave of recollection washed over him. Cold. Hungry. Broke. Alone. No place to find shelter or sleep. Every stitch of clothes he owned in a cardboard box at his feet.

What had happened? He had recently shared a nice, comfortable apartment with a woman who seemed to care for him. He held a job that paid regularly if not all that well, frequented famous clubs, and mingled with celebrated people who called him by his nickname and invited his opinions and participation in their conversations. He and his lady had saved money from his job. The broadcasting school had made him an adjunct instructor and promised to find him employment in radio in the city when he finished the curriculum. Everything was finally falling into place.

Now here he was in a very familiar fix, asking himself a familiar question. What the hell had happened?

SHELLEY SPENT SOME OF that last dollar for a subway ticket, though he had no idea where he was going when he sat down on the next train that pulled into the station. He rode all night, allowing the hiss of the wheels against the rails and the rumble of the cars and the continual egress and ingress of faceless humanity to block out as much of his misery and loneliness as it could.

By the time dawn neared, he had come to the realization that the New York trip, and much that had happened there, was wrong. Not all of it. The radio seemed right. The naïve relationships with women did not. The clubs, the ego-boosting and forced relationships with the celebrities, the pool hustling, all seemed wrong to him now.

He realized that his mother had whispered as much, but, caught up in the exhilaration, he had stubbornly ignored her.

After a conductor ordered him off the train at daybreak, Shelley ended up in a homeless shelter on Broadway. At least he had a hot meal and a cot there. It was little more than what he had on Slim and Marie's back porch. Or at the Stringfellows' stables. But he was grateful for the warmth, the food, the chance to think and clear his head. Lying there among all those men, each down on his luck because of the choices he had made in life, Shelley began to wonder if he was doomed to spend the rest of his own existence in places like these because of his own choices.

Choices.

He could go back to Harlem, work the pool hustle, get some money. The church-going landlady would likely welcome him back if he put on the right mask, bowed, grinned, pleaded, and emasculated himself as surely as he had at the Jack-O-Lantern. He knew how to pimp, gamble, and, if it came to it, steal, if that was what it took to get by.

So what if that was not what his momma would want him to do? How many times did he have to get kicked in the teeth before he decided to take that darker path?

There had been no scholarship, no college, no career in law. Maybe the other side of the law was his destiny after all. He had even coincidentally run into the three slicks in the sporty car recently, the ones he had first seen back in Rosedale, the ones who suggested he go on up to Harlem in the first place to escape the suffocating blanket of the white man's segregation. He learned that those slicks were nothing more than mid-level hoodlums who made their living by stealing and hurting others, and mostly those of their own race.

No, he knew Mattie C. would never allow him to follow that path. She would haunt his every dream.

Instead, he decided, his six months in the Big Apple were nothing more than his freshman year in the College of Real Life. He was supposed to learn from his mistakes, gain power from disappointment, and choose a path in life that would coincide with all the other signs he had been given. The lessons had been harsh, but if he applied them positively, then they might help him do the right things later.

That mirror in Papa Clyde's basement. The crowds reflected back at him, responding to and cheering his words. His mother's admonition that he was meant to do great things. His first grade teacher's opinion that he could do anything he wanted to do if he only worked hard enough and properly used his gained knowledge and God-given talents.

Shelley took advantage of the cot in the homeless shelter for the next several nights, as much for a place for reflection as for sleep. Several times, he awoke during the night and jumped up, thinking he was back in Papa Clyde's basement, that he needed to get dressed and get down to Irondale School. During the day, he walked the cold, uncaring streets as the snow continued to fall, piling up against the curbs and storefronts, turning gray with grime like dirty cotton. As he walked he talked to himself, to his momma, to God, sometimes speaking out loud, ignoring the strange looks and wide berths given to him by those he passed on the icy sidewalks.

Then, on Monday morning, he happened to be standing, watching the cars, trucks and taxi cabs whirring around at a dizzying pace as they navigated Columbus Circle. Shelley wondered where they were all going in such a damn hurry. Then, for some reason, he looked up and caught sight of a billboard, one he would never have noticed had he been only a few feet either side of the patch of snow-covered sidewalk on which he stood.

The billboard's message urged young men to enlist in the U.S. Air Force. *Omen? Sign from God? Mattie C. talking to him?*

Whatever the billboard might be, Shelley knew then what he wanted to do. He walked directly to the address displayed on the bottom of the sign, to the nearby Air Force recruiting office. The Korean War still lurched on and men were needed to replace those leaving. Their tour completed, wounded, or like Bubba, in a flag-draped box, someone had to fill their slots. The mental aptitude test was so easy Shelley almost laughed out loud. The physical was no problem, either. He was skinny as a flagpole but in good shape.

Before he could even have second thoughts or question whether his enlistment was a desperate clutch at a straw, Shelley, a boy who had never even been on an airplane, was all signed up for the U.S. Air Force. He knew Korea and Bubba's death there was not a factor in his enlistment, even though he was almost certainly going to end up in that faraway land. It was just a chance to achieve some measure of security and structure until he could take whatever the next step was supposed to be. It was time for the next semester in the College of Real Life.

He was only 18 years old. Maybe the Air Force and Korea could teach him a few more things that would help him fulfill his promise in this world, whatever that might be.

Shelley opened the envelope the recruiter had given him. He was to take the train south and, in Cincinnati, get aboard the L&N Railroad's Hummingbird passenger train—maybe riding on wheels his own Uncle Henry Pickens had helped make at the L&N wheel shop back in Birmingham—and travel from New York City to his assigned induction station. Shelley grinned broadly when he saw where that was.

Maxwell Air Force Base in Montgomery, Alabama. And the Hummingbird would pass right through Birmingham on the way there.

There was something about the symmetry of it all, like the cars speeding and chasing each other around Columbus Circle, which convinced Shelley that he may have done the right thing after all.

The only way to find out was to climb aboard the Hummingbird and retrace his journey back down South.

18

EST

By the time the train stopped at Birmingham's Terminal Station, Shelley had decided he would not try to track down David and Sam during his one-night layover. He had not made the big time yet. He wanted the meeting with his brothers to be one of triumph, one where he could tell them to accompany him and return to wherever he was so he could take care of them, the way Momma had asked him to do. He had already decided to send them the bulk of his $72-a-month Air Force pay so they could get by easier.

Shelley's stop at Maxwell Air Force Base in Montgomery was brief, more for processing of paperwork than anything else. Soon, he was ensconced in barracks at Lackland Air Force Base in San Antonio, Texas. Despite all the snoring and late-night chatter of his fellow inductees, he slept soundly that first night, still tired from all the traveling.

But then, the early-morning screaming of the drill sergeant and the do-it-because-I-said-do-it nature of the basic training regimen was eerily too much like Aunt Emily's "I'm going to break you so the white man won't have to" tactics.

The new recruit bristled and got off on the wrong foot with Sergeant Smith. Later, though, Shelley shared some of his background with the drill instructor. They ended up on their knees, praying and crying together. Smith soon recognized this particular recruit's intelligence and leadership abilities and made Shelley a squad leader.

That promotion did not set well with some white members of the squad. One afternoon in the barracks, Shelley politely suggested to a white recruit that he do a better job of making his bunk and stowing his gear, all so the squad would get higher marks.

Shelley as an enlisted man in the U.S. Air Force.

"I ain't taking orders from you. Where I come from, Stewart, uppity niggers like you get their necks stretched," the recruit told Shelley. "You better stay in your place, and that place is with a mop in your hands, not out front of the squad giving orders to white folks."

Before he realized what he was doing, Shelley decked the guy. That set off a fistfight between black and white recruits. It caused such a ruckus that the Air Force police rushed in to break it up.

"That guy called me a nigger," Shelley told one of the policemen.

The man looked Shelley up and down and flashed him a crooked grin.

"Well, you are a nigger," he responded. "So go ahead and hit me, too."

Shelley considered the billy club and the pistol on the policeman's belt and swallowed his anger like bitter bile. It was not a war he could win in this one little skirmish. He backed down. There would be other ways he could fight back, and more effectively. But it still hurt to think that the military was still this way, too, even five years after President Truman had formally ended segregation in the armed forces.

The Air Force had been especially slow to change, Shelley learned. Blacks were relegated to traditional "Negro" roles: laborers in the motor pool instead of mechanics, broom pushers in the offices instead of clerks, kitchen and latrine duty instead of flight line jobs. Even black career men carried no stripes on their sleeves while whites with far fewer years in the service were promoted over them.

Shelley could not remain silent. He began to be vocal about what he saw as a basic lack of human rights for black members of the Air Force. Other blacks in his squad and a Negro sergeant all urged him to keep quiet. They explained that he had no hope of changing how things were and was, instead, only making it more difficult for himself and for the rest of them to get by.

Go along to get along, they suggested. Go along to get along and everything would work out.

White superiors took note of Shelley's complaints, too, but they only expressed their displeasure by making it harder on him during PT (physical training) and with stony expressions. They knew he would only be their problem for a little while. He would be in Korea shortly.

WHEN BASIC TRAINING WAS over, he was assigned to a school at Warren Air Force Base in Cheyenne, Wyoming. While he waited for a slot to open up in one of the positions that better suited him and offered him better skills training, Shelley worked as an assistant day clerk in the orderly room, keeping track of airmen's records. His new boss, who assured him such a job should be considered an honor for a colored recruit, told him he got the position for two reasons. First, he had received such exceptionally high evaluations, especially for a Negro. But mostly because the boss wanted to keep an eye on him. He had already been labeled by others as a trouble-maker.

However, Shelley still could not remain silent when he observed such blatant racism and discrimination. He felt the same familiar push in the back that had overtaken him on the Number 22 bus the day he defied the driver and moved the board to open more seats for colored passengers. He could not fathom putting up with the kind of ugliness that prevented blacks from getting jobs for which they were qualified. Where vile racial jokes could be told openly in the barracks, and where even blacks were expected to laugh at the gags without objection. Where the only entertainment was country-and-western music and where Air Force-sanctioned dances attracted plenty of women—practically all of them white—but black airmen were forbidden to talk with them, let alone dance with any of them.

It was the latter issue that got Shelley a summons to come visit with the base commander. Shelley and a group of other black airmen had attended an event and defied the ban. They openly danced with white women, even though the music being played was by Hank Williams and Lefty Frizzell with none from Count Basie or other black artists. Word quickly spread that Airman Shelley Stewart was the one who organized the colored men and led them to violate the inter-racial dance policy.

"Mr. Stewart, I would really appreciate it if you would tell me how you see things here at Warren," the colonel told him, his eyes serious as he studied Shelley's record. "I would really like to get your perspective."

The man seemed sincere enough, as if he really wanted to know, so Shelley proceeded to politely and calmly express his grievances. He also willingly shared his own background, his challenges growing up, and how things back home had only been made worse by the stifling discrimination so prevalent in Birmingham in particular and the Deep South in general.

Of course, he did not tell him that Mattie C., his late mother, still spoke to him and gave him guidance to push back against such things, or that Papa Clyde Smith had instructed him to never let a man get away with calling him a nigger. That he kept to himself.

The base commander nodded grimly as he listened to Shelley's story and made notes in the margins of the service record.

"It's remarkable that you have done so well, Stewart, considering your family background and history of abuse," he said. Then he looked Shelley in the eye and asked, "Have you ever had a psychiatric evaluation?"

Well, of course, Shelley had not. He told the base commander as much, and that he hardly felt that he needed such a thing. He saw mistreatment of colored airmen and wanted to help change things for the better. There was nothing crazy about that.

TWO DAYS LATER, THOUGH, he was ordered to report to the base hospital for a session with an Air Force psychiatrist. The doctor asked many, many questions and seemed to listen carefully to each of Shelley's sincere answers.

"Airman Stewart," he finally said, "I'll be up-front with you. You seem to possess excessive anger issues, and especially against white people. You are also deeply depressed. We will do EST. I believe that will make you feel considerably better and make you a much better airman, too."

EST? Shelley thought that meant Eastern Standard Time. He asked the doc what this "EST treatment" was.

"Electric shock therapy. None of the other colored airmen are acting the way you are. They seem to be fine with the way things are going here unless somebody like you, with your problems, gets them stirred up. We believe the EST will calm you down and make you far better able to serve your country in the Air Force."

"Do I have a choice?" Shelley asked bluntly. He suspected he knew the answer. He was just surprised at how barefaced it was.

"Well, obviously we would prefer you took the treatment willingly," the psychiatrist told him. "But the fact is, you are the property of the U. S. Air Force, Stewart. You don't really have a say in the matter, no."

The psychiatrist likely noticed the scowl on Shelley's face when he heard the word "property." Still, not fully understanding what this treatment was, Shelley did not protest the next morning when he was put in a wheelchair and rolled into a room. There were five or six other hospital personnel there waiting for him. Each wore a white coat. They were all males and burly enough to subdue anyone who objected to what was about to happen.

They instructed Shelley to lie down on a gurney. Straps were tightened around his arms and legs and a viscous salve was smeared on his temples and one ankle. Then something cold and metallic was attached to his head and leg.

Shelley began to squirm. This was not necessarily going to be a simple treatment. Plus he was already having flashbacks of being suspended by ropes at Aunt Emily's just before she ripped open his exposed back and buttocks with that electrical cord.

"Hold still!" one of the attendants barked. Two other big men lay heavily across his legs and abdomen, pinning him to the gurney. "You won't remember a thing when this is over, and you will feel much, much better."

With that, someone grabbed his chin and forced a rubber paddle into his mouth, between his teeth. Suddenly, without warning, a searing pain ripped through Shelley's skull. He mercifully blacked out, just when he was certain he had been sentenced to be executed in an electric chair.

He awoke hours later with a blinding headache. It lasted until well into the evening. He hardly felt like moving or even holding the plastic fork they gave him to eat with. He was dizzy, lethargic, and as tired as he had ever been in his life.

The next day, Shelley felt better and struck up conversations with several other men in the ward, all of whom were being subjected to the electric shock treatment. All were black. Each told Shelley that he had tried to speak up about the discriminatory treatment he had watched and received in the Air Force. Each had been told by the psychiatrist that the EST treatments were prescribed to help him become better "adjusted" to life in the service, to not buck chain-of-command, or try to change the Air Force way because of "anger issues."

After several more of the skull-splitting treatments, Shelley again had an audience with the psychiatrist.

"How are you feeling by now, Airman Stewart?"

"I have a headache."

"These treatments will help you feel calmer, and the headaches will eventually subside. You are bordering on schizophrenia, young man. You have to suppress the terrible things that happened to you in your childhood so you can work through your mental problems."

"I've tried to get past those things, Doc," Shelley responded. "It is hard to do."

"Yes. I'm sure it is," the doctor replied, his face showing sadness. Then he looked at Shelley over the tops of his half-glasses. "Now, have your views changed? Do you now see that you have just been imagining any discrimination and unfair treatment of blacks here at the base?"

Shelley thought of the agony of the electric charge pulsing through his head each time before he passed out. He desperately wanted to nod, grin, and give the psychiatrist the answer he wanted to hear. He thought about complimenting him on his tie, asking about his lovely wife and precious kids he saw in the picture frame on his desk, and telling him precisely what the psychiatrist wanted to hear. That would certainly end the agonizing EST and he would be released, "healed."

Shelley could not do it. He tried to form the words but they would not exit his mouth. Instead, Shelley heard clearly in his head the voice of Mary Sue Smith, Papa Clyde's daughter. "Shurley, if you know you are right, do not let anyone tell you that you are wrong." Shelley relaxed and smiled as he answered the doctor's question as politely and honestly as he could.

"Sir, I may be crazy, like you say, but I am not imagining what I see going on. I've seen it all my life. I know what it looks like and what it feels like. Now I see it here, and it is clear as day. I'm sorry. I can't pretend it doesn't exist, because it damn sure does!"

That answer sent Shelley back to the treatment room, to the straps and salve and cold metal attachments, and the searing, burning pain between his ears. Sent him back for twelve total sessions. Then, after a week's lull, to still more of them, for a total of thirty-six "electrocutions," as he had come to call them.

Instead of erasing the memories that haunted him, as the Air Force psychiatrist predicted, the EST only brought back more vividly the sadistic treatment he had received from Slim and Marie, from Aunt Emily. Brought it back as if it had only recently happened.

His so-called family had tried to break him back then. The Air Force was hell-bent on doing the same thing now.

Though he never dropped his claims that he had witnessed segregation and discriminatory conduct, Shelley's EST treatments were finally stopped. Shortly afterward, he was shipped off to Geiger Air Force Base, near Spokane, Washington. There he was placed in charge of handling maintenance records for the sophisticated F86-D Sabre Dog aircraft, a new jet that had recently broken all existing speed records.

This is a very important job for a lunatic, Shelley told himself.

He also took the opportunity to resurrect the base's silent radio station when he learned about it. No one had taken an interest so it had been shut down. He simply went into the studio, dusted off the turntables, mixing board, and other equipment and began spinning records and sending out his patented patter.

Shelley even led a group of black airmen to a dance on base, too, one where the women were mostly white, and the Negroes danced with them until someone pulled the plug on the music and sent everyone home early. Shelley thought nothing of it. Same old same old, he decided. Besides, he was having problems with pain in one of his legs and could not put on his usual dance moves.

A few days later, with the leg pain getting worse, he finally relented and went to the base hospital to have it checked out. The doctor took an inordinately long time studying his medical records. He quickly noticed the notations about his stay in the psych ward at his previous post and the electric shock therapy treatments he had undergone.

"I think what happened," the doc finally told him, "is that they strained some ligaments when that heavy guy laid down on you during the treatments.

Or you could have done it yourself, trying to get out of the restraints. We'll check you in and do some tests and see what we need to do to fix you up."

But when Shelley entered the base hospital, he realized right away that his bed was in his new base's psychiatric ward. There were other colored airmen there, too, with similar stories to the ones he had heard back at Warren. If anything, this place was even more restrictive than the previous one. Books and magazines were prohibited. Patients could only stare at the ceiling or play cards all day to pass the time.

There was not even a base radio station to listen to. With Shelley locked up, it was off the air.

A sympathetic nurse began to smuggle in books for him. She struck up a conversation with Shelley. "You know what?" she told him. "You are out of place here. You don't belong in this place."

"From your lips to God's ear!" Shelley responded. "Could you please tell the doc that so I can go on back to my job and the radio station?"

"You want to see me end up in this place?" she responded, but she did not laugh when she said it.

Before EST treatments could be resumed, though, Shelley was shipped out, farther west, to Madigan General Hospital at the U.S. Army's Fort Lewis in Tacoma. By now it came as no surprise to him that he went straight into that facility's psychiatric unit. Anyone who thought Negroes were not treated equally to whites in the military had to be crazy as a June bug!

ONE MORNING IN EARLY August of 1954, Shelley received word that Huell "Slim" Stewart had died at the age of forty-six. Shelley was not surprised at the news. Slim had been flirting with death all his life. Shelley was also not surprised that he felt no remorse, no sadness. In fact, he felt little emotion at all upon hearing about the death of his father.

The Air Force was amenable to allowing him to go back to Birmingham for the funeral. On the airplane ride to Chicago, though, Shelley half dozed and was overcome with a cascade of unpleasant memories. He saw again his daddy striking Shelley's mother with the ax, and her flying out the window. He dredged up memories of her funeral that hot, hot day, and of being hauled away to Collegeville, away from the only home little "Shurley" had ever known. Memories of fried rats and whistling wind and hissing sleet while living on the back stoop in the house on Central Avenue. Images of Slim's stone face when Shelley accidentally encountered him on the streets, when he stopped by his daddy's house all dressed up in his suit, tie and graduation gown, and when Slim saw Shelley with Sam and David, the very day they were rescued from virtual slavery in Mississippi.

During the stopover in Chicago, Shelley decided to deliberately miss his train bound for Birmingham. Instead, he walked to a nearby liquor store. He purchased a pint of cheap whiskey. Then he checked into a flophouse around the corner. There he ignored Mattie C.'s fussing and proceeded to drink until he had erased the dark images from his mind.

By the time Shelley sobered up and caught the train home, Slim Stewart had been in the ground for a full day. That did not bother the boy the least bit.

Instead, he tracked down his brothers, visited with them for a while, determined that they were getting by okay, and then rode the street car downtown to talk with the station manager at WEDR Radio. Shelley told the man that he would likely be out of the service soon, that he had been on the air up in New York City, the country's biggest broadcast market, and he inquired if the station may be able to use him. The manager readily agreed to hire him when he received his discharge and came back home.

Emily was still living in the half-built house out in Sterrett. His brothers assured him she was as hard to get along with as ever, still determined to live as if it was the 19th century. Shelley decided not to try to see her.

Sam and David did share with him the details of his father's passing, though. The death certificate put the cause as "alcohol poisoning." When he became so ill, someone took him to a voodoo doctor in Rosedale, and apparently the treatment consisted of more cheap, homebrew whiskey that was likely as poison as the rot-gut that had put him in such a fix to start with. That was what ultimately dispatched Slim Stewart to wherever his soul now resided.

Shelley never got by to visit his daddy's grave during that ten-day furlough.

From Birmingham, the next stop was Eglin Air Force Base in the Florida panhandle. Shelley's orders sent him directly to the psychiatric ward in the base hospital there. After a few days, the head psychiatrist came by to visit with him. The doctor had a frown on his face, his brow furrowed.

"Mr. Stewart, your records say you have been diagnosed as 'chronic schizophrenic—severe.' I have to tell you, though, that you just do not fit the criteria for that diagnosis."

The doctor went on to tell Shelley that, as far as he could determine, the Air Force had dealt him a bad hand, for whatever reason. The psychiatrist was willing to recommend Shelley be released with a medical discharge under honorable conditions. With that notation, the doc would make certain that Shelley's service record would never come back to haunt him in later life.

Shelley shook the man's hand and thanked him sincerely. The irony was not lost on him that he had to come back South to get fair treatment from the U.S. Air Force. The doctor was true to his word, and soon Shelley was on his way back to Birmingham, this time, he assumed, to stay.

He had the radio job waiting for him at WEDR. He had no dread any longer of meeting his father on the street. And something else—something important—was brewing in Shelley's mind.

He had been exposed to a lot of things while he was away from Birmingham. He had seen pure, ugly racism and found it was not relegated only to the South. He had also met white people who did not seem to notice the color of another man's skin but treated everyone the way he or she deserved to be treated. Shelley had felt just how wonderful that could be.

He could sense something electric in the air. Things were destined to change. Many things were changing much too slowly, such as what he had experienced in the "integrated" Air Force. But the wind was definitely starting to blow. Starting to blow hard. Stormy times lay ahead, but once they had passed, the air would be clear, finally.

That little voice in his head was telling Shelley Stewart that he should be preparing to help push things along. He was about to have a platform, and he could use that to build an even bigger stage. His voice could make a mighty difference if he used his talents properly.

The voice in his head made it clear. When the time came, he had damn well better be ready and willing to speak.

~~~~~~~~~~~~

J ames Bevel was a native Mississippian, born on the farm his daddy owned there. That farm was later taken away from his father because he was black and because he dared send two of his children to college. Bevel had worked his way up through the Movement and, in the spring of 1963, he found himself a key player in all that was happening—or not happening—in Birmingham, Alabama. Upon arriving there, he realized that the peaceful protests, the attempts to fill jails with peaceful protesters and force the city government's hand, were no longer working well enough to succeed.

Bevel saw the same thing others did. Dr. King's involvement in the demonstrations had taken focus off other leaders—especially those who were pushing the hardest against the city's harsh "Jim Crow" laws—and even from the nonviolent protests themselves. When King went to jail (the incarceration that resulted in the historic "Letter from the Birmingham Jail"), the impetus of all that the protesters had accomplished seemed to slow to a halt now that their charismatic leader was out of sight and mind.

At a mass meeting, Bevel unleashed some fire and brimstone in hopes of re-igniting the resolve of the big crowd gathered in the church that night.

"Some of you Negroes want segregation as much as Bull Connor!" he chided them. "You are afraid if segregation goes away, you'll have to compete with the white man."

Still, a call for "jailbirds"—people willing to be arrested and go to jail for the cause—from a congregation of more than 700 people netted just nine volunteers. By April, fewer than 300 people total had been jailed in Birmingham, and most were the same few over and over.

A visiting black minister noted, "More Negroes are going to jail for being drunk."

Police Commissioner—and also a mayoral candidate as well as overseer of the city's Fire Department—Bull Connor's brutal methods were working. He had predicted that Rev. King would eventually "run out of niggers," and it appeared he was correct. The hot summer was coming and Birmingham's white establishment was starting to believe that its colored citizens had lost their stomach *for protesting. Connor had succeeded in breaking the back of the most visible racial demonstrations in the country. At the same time, black businessmen and many of its clergy thought it was time to back off, to negotiate, to allow things to cool down just a bit.*

Even when Rev. King was released from jail, it was difficult to spark interest. He told a crowd in a mid-April meeting, "Don't think that we are going to lose Birmingham. Our destiny is tied up in the destiny of this nation."

But another minister, speaking to the same group, noted, "As soon as one of us gets to the top of the mountain, someone is there to pull us back down into the valley."

A call for volunteer "jailbirds" that night netted only ten people.

James Bevel thought he knew the answer. His experience with SNCC (the Student Non-Violent Coordinating Committee) and as one of the key participants in the Nashville, Tennessee, lunch counter sit-ins had taught him some valuable lessons. The fact that he was only 24 years old helped him in arriving at his conclusion, too.

However, once he decided what it would take, Bevel knew that he would have to go against the wishes of some of the established leaders in the Birmingham movement if he was to implement his plan.

He also knew it would be risky. Damn risky.

19

SHELLEY the PLOWBOY

Shelley Stewart settled back into the broadcast booth at WEDR and immediately felt as if he had pulled on an old pair of comfortable shoes. Ed Estes, the white manager of the station—no blacks could be in management or sales at that time—kept his word about providing a job for Shelley when he left the Air Force. Estes offered him $35 a week and carved out a mid-day slot on the air for him. Then he pretty much gave Shelley free rein to develop whatever kind of show and personality it took to attract an audience and sell products and services to Birmingham's Negro population.

Once again, Shelley called on his experiences. Without even thinking about it, he created an on-air persona unlike anything the city had ever heard. Once more, it was exactly the opposite of the real person Shelley Stewart was, the quiet, studious man who still suffered from grief, loneliness, and the pain of discrimination.

On the air, though, he was wild, bombastic, controversial, and colorful, as likely to toss out a Bible verse as to utter a thinly veiled ribald comment. He continued to gig those who deserved it—white and black, common man or upper-crust—but mostly he catered to the average man or woman, those who had suffered as he had the restraints of discrimination and class warfare. Only 21 years old himself, he knew the kind of personality that would appeal to young blacks—and especially to women. He pictured in his mind the girls who had befriended him at Parker High School and the older ones he flirted with in the Harlem night clubs. That was the basis for the character he became behind WEDR's microphone.

"Timber! Let it fall!" he screamed as he kicked off another "race" record, the name used for rhythm and blues music in the national music trade publications of the time. "Good googly woogly! There's a record for you if you are hurtin' because some *dawg* of a man has done you wrong, baby. Ole Shelley is hurtin' for you, too, sweetheart, playin' what you need to hear today to get yourself right! The mighty burner is here, just for you, baby, on WEDR."

Before long, adoring fan clubs began to blossom in various parts of the city. Shelley mentioned the names of their members on the air and played records by request just for them, further ingratiating himself to his most devoted listeners.

Shelley desperately wanted to parlay his new-found popularity and powerful platform into something more substantial than a one-hour-a-day radio show. But to make ends meet as he built his over-the-air following, he could only find menial jobs such as working as an elevator starter at one of the city's big department stores. Even there, the showman came out in him, and he entertained the tiny captive audience in that elevator with continual patter from floor to floor, up and down, several hours a day.

He hung out on the street corners much of the rest of the time. There he could hear what was on the minds of the people he talked to everyday on the airwaves. He also heard a lot about how things were changing rapidly in the realm of what many called "civil rights." The civil rights movement. While he was away in New York and the Air Force, the Movement had intensified its activities and was pushing hard.

In May of 1954, the U.S. Supreme Court issued its historic *Brown v. Board of Education* decision, effectively forbidding states to maintain separate schools for blacks and whites. School integration had become the law of the land, even if the Southern states vowed they would secede again before they would mix colored kids with white kids in the schools. As the Ku Klux Klan claimed, if you have them in classrooms together, next thing you know they'll be having babies together.

Closer to home, Rosa Parks defied the back-of-the-bus seating regulations in Montgomery, Alabama. The resulting bus boycott by blacks, as well as other acts of civil disobedience in Montgomery, led to a landmark Supreme Court ruling. They also attracted international attention, which brought to the forefront one of the Movement's most powerful and magnetic leaders, the minister of a black Montgomery church, the Rev. Dr. Martin Luther King.

Shelley Stewart already held strong views on the matter. He was all for pushing to the front of the bus in support of social justice for all. However, he strongly preferred the term "human rights" instead of "civil rights." Birmingham had "civil" laws already, but they separated and discriminated against one race. What Birmingham, the South, the United States, and the world needed was something more basic, the realization that every man or woman was born with basic *human* rights, just as the Declaration of Independence said: all men are created equal, endowed by their Creator with certain unalienable rights. Until everyone accepted that idea, and as long as the law demanded separation of the races, there could be no substantial change.

AMID ALL THE FUN and craziness of his on-air persona, Shelley began to mix in between the records some pronouncements about what he was witnessing right there in the streets of Birmingham. Again, radio listeners had never heard such declarations before. Between songs, Shelley talked about the need for blacks to register and vote, to begin resisting social inequities, and, maybe most prevalent, to denounce police brutality against Negroes. Blacks knew it was going on but nobody dared say anything about it.

Shelley became so adept at intertwining those messages into his over-the-top spiel that it took a while for even his most fervent listeners to notice how bold he was becoming. But the city's police commissioner, Eugene "Bull" Connor, certainly took note. Connor was a former broadcaster himself, having done play-by-play for the city's all-white minor league baseball team, the Barons, plus re-creations of other games using teletype reports and appropriate sound effects. Connor was a fervent segregationist. With his short, stocky stature, pugnacious expression, heavy Southern accent, and cigar firmly clamped between his teeth, he would become a powerful symbol of stubborn bigotry and oppression during the demonstrations in Birmingham in 1963. Unwittingly, he became the perfect stereotypical foil and focal point for King and the protest movement. However, in the mid-1950s, during his first term as police commissioner, the former Ku Klux Klan member and gubernatorial candidate oversaw a police department that was starkly and openly brutal in its dealings with the city's black citizens.

"Hey, y'all, let me tell you what I saw last night," Shelley would purr into the microphone. "Saw the Black Cat on the prowl on 17th Street, you know. Saw a couple of rednecks whoop up on a black neck, too, for the terrible, terrible crime of leaning on a lamppost. I know y'all appreciate them keeping our streets safe from lamppost leaners, don't y'all? That's what I saw, y'all, and y'all know what I mean."

The "Black Cat" was police car #13, a vehicle that notoriously patrolled only black neighborhoods, and especially the black business district near Kelly Ingram Park downtown. Its white occupants—all Birmingham police officers were white at the time—were "rednecks" or "KKK" when Shelley told his stories on the airwaves.

The officers assigned to the Black Cat gained their reputation of keeping the peace through brutality and intimidation. They would see a black man walking along or hanging out on a corner and ease up to the curb next to him.

"Hey, boy! Come 'ere. Lean in the window a sec, boy," one of the cops would order. "I need to ask you about something."

When the black pedestrian did as he was told—and his only choice was to do just that or run and risk a certain beating—the cop would suddenly roll up the window on his neck and, while he was pinned, give him vicious blows to the head with his blackjack. Then he would roll down the window and shove the victim out into the gutter. They needed no reason or cause, other than the victim's race. The purpose for such random, brutal attacks: to keep blacks in their place and let them know the police could and would do whatever it took to keep them meek and subservient.

There were many, many more examples, and the ruthlessness extended far beyond the Black Cat #13 and the downtown area. Much of it became between-records subject matter for Shelley.

Cops would roust men and women parked in lover's lanes in black neighborhoods, beat the man and rape the woman. There were no black hotels, and blacks were not permitted to stay in white hotels, so travelers or those who rented rooms for more short-lived excursions had to stay in boardinghouses or flop houses. The cops would observe black men taking their "dates" into such an establishment, wait a bit, and then, for no reason, break in on them. The man was sent on his way with the warning that he best not say anything about what had happened to anybody. Then, if the woman was attractive, the police had their way with her. Corruption was rampant and open. Shot houses and gambling establishments were allowed to remain open so long as the police received their generous bribes and were allowed to have their way with women patrons or prostitutes. Black men who even dared to look a white woman in the eye or committed other such dastardly "crimes" were beaten mercilessly by the police, or arrested on trumped-up charges.

Shelley had seen it all before but now he had the means to talk about it somewhere besides the street corner or inside Ratkiller's. Also, his popularity provided some insulation from any retribution.

"Shelley, you crazy," more than one listener told him when they met him on the street.

"I been told that many, many times before," Shelley would respond with a broad grin.

FOR MANY, JUST HEARING a black man on the radio was still something of a novelty. Most of the few black announcers stuck to the script, not wanting to offend anyone and lose their jobs. It was accepted that they could be happy-go-lucky, but they were reluctant to do anything that might be offensive to whites. Especially their white station managers or owners or the white-owned businesses that advertised on their air. Shelley had long since decided he would tell things the way he saw them, just as he had with the Air Force psychiatrist.

He would speak the truth and let the chips fall where they may.

The chips did fall.

One morning when Shelley arrived at the station, someone had smeared animal blood across the building's front window, spelling out the letters, "K K K." Shelley had to wash it away, but he also talked about it on the air that morning.

Another day Shelley was playing some tunes on WEDR, talking about the great bargains available at sponsor locations, flirting with his female listeners, and needling the police about some act of ugliness he had heard about. During the songs, he tried to always answer the studio telephone line because he wanted to stay in touch with his listeners, maybe play their requested songs. His intuition told him that communicating meant "talking with," not "talking to." It was a two-way street.

"Hello, Shelley speaking. What can I do for you, baby?"

"Shelley, what's wrong with y'all's station. We can't hardly hear you in Avondale."

"Shelley, you are all static out here in Bessemer. Is your radio station having some kind of trouble?"

After several such calls, Shelley phoned the station engineer at the transmitter site.

"Mr. Kirkpatrick, we are not at full power for some reason."

"I know," the engineer responded, short of breath. "There's a bunch of men out here in Ku Klux Klan robes. They've cut the feed line and guy wires to the tower and . . . there it goes."

"Can't you stop 'em? Call the police?"

"No, because I'm a member. I'm one of 'em."

The station was off the air for five days, until a temporary tower could be erected that would broadcast with reduced power. No one was ever arrested for cutting down the station's tower.

Shelley did not let up, though. If anything, this attempt to silence him and the radio station only made him more determined. And his targets were not just whites and the city's police and power structure. He also preached about discrimination within his own race, a residual he knew remained from the days of slavery. Light-skinned blacks worked in the big house. Dark-skinned blacks worked in the cotton fields. Light-skinned girls were the cheerleaders and majorettes and got the best parts in the school plays while darker-skinned blacks sat on the back row in the classrooms.

"If you are bright, you are right. If you are brown, stick around. If you are black, get back!" was a catchphrase he often used after a particularly biting diatribe on the subject, shouted over the opening strains of a record by B. B. King or Ruth Brown.

Before long, Shelley's show was so popular it expanded to three times a day, 6–8 A.M., noon–1 P.M., and 3–6 P.M. That was a good portion of the

Shelley, 1957.

station's broadcast day because WEDR was only licensed to be on the air from sunrise to sunset. Listeners could not get enough of that crazy-smart guy on the radio.

He was also starting to make extra money—and build even more of a fan base—by doing what were called "platter parties." He would set up with a microphone, a couple of turntables, a mixing board, and a PA system at a club or lounge and sell tickets for admission. Often his brothers, Sam and David, were his helpers and provided security. Shelley put just as much energy into these appearances as he did his on-air show, but in the personal performances he could readily see how his voice, his energy, and the music he played moved the crowd. He learned how to build momentum, bring it back down, and then build it up again, how to pack the dance floor and how to alter the mood with an inflection, a comment, or even by theatrics he could never do on the radio. When things got going, he threw off his jacket to reveal a shirt open to the navel and a remarkably tight pair of pants.

Soon, the boy from Rosedale who had been scorned by so many girls because of his family background, his quiet nature, his ragged clothes, and his personal hygiene was turning away women who literally threw themselves at him. Often, when he returned to his car after a platter party he found a naked female inside, waiting for him.

SHELLEY LOVED THE ATTENTION. However, he knew there would be trouble if he partook in what they so generously offered. They all had boyfriends, husbands, fathers. Still everyone made assumptions based on all the girls calling into his show, screaming at him from the dance floor, throwing themselves at him at the platter parties, and showing up outside WEDR in skimpy outfits, as well as the way he called them all "baby" and sugar" and "darlin'."

Shelley was certainly a lady's man.

That led to a new mask, one that would persist for years to come. Shelley Stewart evolved into the persona of "Shelley the Playboy." *Playboy* magazine had been on the newsstands for several years, becoming wildly popular by depicting a loose and free lifestyle and the relaxation of sexual mores. That fit the image Shelley had concocted on the radio and in his personal appearances at the platter parties.

He played the role to the hilt on the air, too. Students from area high schools called in each morning for a "roll call" segment. The black schools checked in—Ullman, Hayes, Parker, and Western-Olin—but so did many white schools like West End, Ensley, Woodlawn, and Mountain Brook. Even the University of Alabama, still all-white at the time, checked in from Tuscaloosa, even though the station's signal hardly reached that far. Shelley's unique brand of high-energy radio and the music he played—songs and artists that they could hear nowhere else because the white stations dared not play "race" records—were a magnet for young white listeners, too.

"Good morning, darlin'," Shelley would croon to female callers, whether they were black or white. "I love you madly, baby. You bet Shelley the Playboy is going to play that song for you and all the other sweethearts of mine at Parker High this mornin'."

It was all part of Shelley the Playboy's shtick, but some saw such carrying on as a violation of a longtime ban on interaction between black males and white females. In a town in which a black man merely looking at a white woman could get him beaten senseless or killed, uttering such endearments as Shelley the Playboy did was a serious offense.

Bull Connor—who derisively called him "Shelley the Plowboy"—certainly noticed what was going on there on the AM radio dial. In speeches and one-on-one, he warned white parents to crack down on their children—especially their daughters—and their questionable choice of entertainment. They should forbid their kids to listen to the "jungle music" the "Plowboy" played. That was the very kind of music and chatter that would soon lead to their precious darling daughters going to bed with "Nigras."

Shelley was walking along a sidewalk in downtown Birmingham one day when he was approached by a group of white students from Phillips High School, one of the schools that would one day be among the first in the city to integrate. They recognized him immediately and asked for autographs. One girl did not have any paper he could sign so she pulled up her skirt to the knee. Shelley signed "Best wishes, I love you madly" on her shin. Everyone laughed and went happily on their way.

Before Shelley had walked to the next block, two police cars pulled to the curb, lights flashing, and motioned for him to come over. He did as he was told.

"Hey, boss, what's up?" he asked with a smile.

"Boy, we heard about what you just did," one of the cops told him. "You best get your black ass on back to Niggertown and stay away from these white girls. You hear me, boy?"

Shelley retold the story a few minutes later to a group of young men hanging out in front of Ratkiller's. It only enhanced his star power. That crazy Shelley the Playboy, standing up to the police like that and not getting his ass busted!

But just then a half dozen police cars showed up there and the group dispersed immediately into nearby doorways and alleys. Shelley merely waved and smiled at the cops. Then he walked on down the street to the radio studio to do his noon show in which he would recount the morning's events and poke a little fun at "Bull's boys," bringing the full force of the law down on a poor, innocent disk jockey out on a morning stroll while burglars and murderers walked freely among them.

When Shelley turned 21 years old in September 1955, he decided it was time to back up all he had been preaching on about the power of the ballot box. Now he could finally go down to the Jefferson County Courthouse and do something none of his relatives had ever deemed important: register to vote.

There were two lines there at the courthouse, divided by heavy ropes. Signs designated the queues: "White" and "Colored." There were two tests given to all would-be voters, one written and one oral. Then, if the applicant passed both, he or she paid a poll tax and received a card designating the person as a registered voter.

The written test was laughably easy. Shelley could not wait to tell his listeners that afternoon how simple it was. As he stood in the "Colored" line to take the oral part of the process, he overheard the clerk ask a white applicant in the adjacent line the question that comprised the oral test, "Was the Declaration of Independence signed with an ink pen or a feather?"

The man thought for a moment and answered, "With a feather."

"That's correct."

When Shelley got to the front of his line, the clerk asked him the same question.

"A feather," Shelley answered confidently.

"No, that is not correct," the clerk told him and waved him on. He had failed the oral exam and would not be registered to vote. The same thing happened to the person in front of and behind him that day in the colored line at the courthouse. Such an outcome seemed to be the usual one, if you happened to be black.

Unfazed, Shelley came back a short time later, before the next opportunity to vote, and went through the process again. This time, with the same answer on the oral examination, he passed. Of course, the entire experience provided plenty of fodder for on-the-radio discussion.

THINGS WERE CHANGING FOR Shelley in his personal life. A friend introduced him to a beautiful young lady, a student at nearby black Daniel Payne College. Her name was Rebecca Ruth Jones. Despite all the platter parties and radio time that claimed most of his attention and energy, Shelley pursued Rebecca with the dogged determination with which he went after anything else he wanted. After a four-month courtship, they were married on the front porch of Rebecca's mother's house in Andalusia in south Alabama.

Now, with the two of them living there together, Shelley's tiny room in a north Birmingham boardinghouse became claustrophobic. Shelley had been a landowner and even a homeowner already, but the Shelby County property was still the home of his aunt and he would never feel at ease there so long as she occupied the place. With what he was bringing in for the personal appearances and his on-air work, and with the help of one of the few good things he got from his military service, the GI Bill, he and Rebecca purchased a home on Center Way Southwest, in the Titusville neighborhood. At least the Titusville place, though not fancy, had indoor plumbing and a den, and he was sharing it with someone he loved. Even better, there was a deed with his name on it and that meant he had accomplished something none of his relatives had.

Soon Shelley even arranged to broadcast many of his shows directly from his home. As far as he could tell, he was the first and only black radio personality in Birmingham to do such a thing.

Shelley was determined to make this marriage work. His only role model for such things had been Slim Stewart, but he figured if he only did the opposite of what his father had done, everything would work out fine.

There were soon problems, though. Rebecca had fallen in love with Shelley the Playboy, the gregarious, funny, devil-may-care personality that came out in public, whether on a date or on the radio. Though she knew snippets of her husband's upbringing, that his daddy had murdered his momma, that he had been homeless while still a small child, she did not understand why Shelley was so different sometimes in real life from his public personality. When he was home, he sometimes became the polar opposite person, melancholy, reflective, and quiet, happiest when he had his nose in a book. She also resented all the time he was away from her, doing the sock hops, platter parties, and the radio show three times a day. Maybe because she was so fond of her husband's public persona, Rebecca quickly became jealous of all the women who threw themselves at Shelley the Playboy. That was especially true when she heard the way he talked to them—on the air or at the dances—"Hey, baby," or "How you doin', sugar?" Even worse, some of the girls, their bold advances rejected by their favorite disk jockey, spread rumors about having had affairs with Shelley. Though he vigorously denied them, Rebecca tended not to believe him.

There were other issues, too. Only after they were married, Rebecca revealed that she was unable to bear children. Shelley wanted kids. He wanted to prove that he was not only a better husband than Slim but a better father, too.

Sam and David became an issue as well. They were rambunctious and often drinking, fighting, and running with low-level criminals and trouble-makers. Shelley tried to get them off the path they were heading by asking them to stay in his home for a few days at a time. Rebecca was cool to them, hardly speaking, making them come and go through the back entrance, and even mopping, spraying, and cleaning the whole house when they left, as if they were dirty animals. Meanwhile, Rebecca allowed her brother and sister to stay at the house. On one occasion, when his breakneck schedule caught up with him and Shelley was hospitalized with double pneumonia, she moved her mother in, too. When he was released from the hospital and came back home, it was only a matter of time until a terrible fight erupted. Enraged, Shelley chased his mother-in-law and brother-in-law from his house at gunpoint. With all the family friction, Shelley feared that things were deteriorating to a relationship that was eerily similar to the one in which he had spent his first few years.

At one point, Shelley considered that the Air Force psychiatrists may have been right in their diagnosis. Maybe he was schizophrenic. Maybe Shelley Stewart and Shelley the Playboy were two different personalities jockeying for control of the same body.

No, it was Mattie C. who told him about wearing masks, being whoever he had to be to survive. He vowed to work on being more what Rebecca expected him to be while he also tried to make her fall in love with who he really was. That is, if Shelley could ever figure out who he really was!

He could not allow his marriage to deteriorate to fights that might become physical and even violent. As badly as he wanted a family, that was not the life he desired.

There was another concern. Shelley's platter parties were getting to the point of being out of control. Often there would be 800 or 900 people packing a club or school auditorium designed to hold less than a third that many folks. In the clubs, alcohol—legal or not—always put the crowd on edge and it took only a small spark to ignite an inferno. Fights were common. Some were deadly.

At one gathering, a stabbing on the dance floor led to the death of a patron, a dancer knifed in the neck when he stepped on another dancer's blue suede shoes while Shelley played the Elvis Presley song. The man died in Shelley's arms as he tried to stop the blood spurting from the victim's jugular. Another time, a man was shot to death outside the doors of a high school sock hop. His brother, Sam, was almost caught in the crossfire, saved only when the gunman's weapon misfired the first time.

Shelley knew that with all the grief he was giving the police department on his radio shows, it was only a matter of time before such an incident bounced back and ensnared Shelley the Playboy. The cops were looking for an excuse to quiet their antagonist.

So it was that for the first time in a while, Shelley began thinking that a change of scenery might not only save his marriage but allow things to cool down just a bit for him in his hometown. That was when he received an offer from one of the pioneers in black broadcasting. It would not only send him to a new town for a while but would also lead to a chance encounter and a deep friendship that would eventually set Shelley Stewart off on a new and exciting path.

the TIe SaleSMAN

John McClendon had found himself a profitable niche in the broadcasting business. In his hometown of Jackson, Mississippi, he bought an AM station with a high dial position and decidedly weak signal. In a stroke of genius, he put programming on the airwaves that he knew would appeal to the town's black citizens, a mixture of preaching and gospel music, but also a generous mix of rhythm and blues and colorful deejays with even more colorful on-air monikers. McClendon was white and he took plenty of guff from his friends and the white-owned businesses for putting "nigger music" on the radio. However, he knew that he had found a gold mine, and many of those same business owners were soon buying commercials on his station. Soon, McClendon had purchased or signed on stations in a number of markets with large black populations, including KOKA in Shreveport, KOKY in Little Rock, WYOU in Tampa, and eventually WBCO in Bessemer, which he would promptly move to Birmingham. The call letters would be changed to WENN when he did.

McClendon had taken a liking to the star personality he heard about over in Birmingham, and when the company obtained a Federal Communications Commission license for the new station in Shreveport, Louisiana, he contacted Shelley Stewart and asked him if he was interested in moving there and managing the station until it got off the ground. With all that was going on, personally and professionally, and with the dollar figure McClendon tossed out, Shelley accepted. As much as he hated leaving the audience and happy advertisers he had acquired in Birmingham, he felt it important to do what he could to try to save his marriage. He also knew he could put a station on the air that would be an instant success while gaining some important and valuable experience.

He welcomed that opportunity to learn more of the business besides being a disk jockey. "Disk jockey" and "deejay" were terms he hated anyway. Anybody could start a turntable and let a record play on the radio. It took talent to be able to relate to an audience he could not even see, to carry on a conversation with listeners who had only limited capability to talk back, and even to select and mix music in such a way as to have an emotional impact on listeners. He considered himself a broadcast personality, a communicator. But Shelley felt he had that part of the broadcasting business down pat. His dream was to someday own a station or group of stations. Never mind that in the 1950s you could count on one hand all the black radio station owners in America. It had been less than ten years before that Jesse Blayton became the very first black man to own a station, WERD in Atlanta.

It was an exciting time, getting the brand new KOKA ready to go on the air. Rebecca seemed to enjoy the fresh environment, too, and things appeared to be getting better between them. After all, there were no platter parties or girls throwing themselves at her husband in Shreveport. At least not yet.

A FEW DAYS AFTER arriving in town, Shelley decided (at Rebecca's urging) that if he was to be a broadcasting executive, he needed to upgrade his wardrobe. He went into a clothing store on Texas Street to look around. No one seemed the least bit interested in assisting a tall, black man, even if he did have money to spend in their establishment. It was the same story in another couple of stores that day, too, and he was on the verge of walking out of the last one he tried when a man stepped through a door at the back of the store. He noticed Shelley heading for the exit and double-timed to catch up to him.

"Sir! Sir! Could I help you find something?"

Shelley stopped and looked around to see if maybe the clerk was asking someone else the question. No white man in that day, time and place called a black man "sir."

"Well, I was looking for a couple of ties, but . . ." Shelley answered.

Shelley, 1960.

"Well, mister, we have the best selection of neckties in northern Louisiana. Come on back and I'll show you."

Mister? Had this white store clerk just called him "mister?" Not "boy?"

Shelley was duly impressed with the clerk's personality and energy. It was not just that he had treated a black man with the respect he deserved. He simply liked the man's style. By the time Shelley had selected and paid for a couple of ties, he had talked the man into coming down to KOKA and talking to the sales manager about a job. He could make far more money selling radio spots than he ever could hawking ties and slacks. Although the salesman had no experience in radio, he was hired on the spot, based mostly on Shelley's recommendation to the station manager.

That was how Shelley met Cy Steiner and began a strong friendship and business relationship, one that would last for years and would one day open a lucrative new path for both of them. Shelley knew instinctively that Steiner was a rising star and had what it took to be successful.

Only a few months later, Shelley was recruited back to Birmingham and his old slot on WEDR for even more money. He also heard about a sales job that had come open at WBCO out in Bessemer and he convinced Steiner to come up and talk to the people there. He did and landed the job.

Shelley was delighted to have Cy in the same town. Not a week went by that they did not talk on the telephone several times or visit in each other's home, despite the fact they worked for competing stations. They sat for hours discussing what they saw going on, not just in broadcasting and advertising, but all that was happening in Birmingham. Their friendship would eventually result in a most unusual business relationship, necessarily kept secret due to the tenor of the times, but one that would be profitable for both men, in more ways than just monetarily.

Shelley was quickly back on top in Birmingham. It was as if he had never left town. The telephone in the announcer's booth at WEDR rang off the hook. People packed parking lots, auditoriums, and other venues, just to see Shelley the Playboy and dance to the music he spun out or the bands he hosted.

He had also begun to build quite a reputation in the music business and became fast friends with many of the artists and groups that were just emerging at the time. Such artists as Sam Cook, Bobby "Blue" Bland, and B. B. King even stayed at Shelley's home when they were in town, playing shows at black venues such as the Madison Nightspot or the Grand Terrace Ballroom. Berry Gordy, who eventually found fame as founder of Motown Records, was then a record promoter, pushing records by Mary Wells, and a friend of Shelley's. His brother, George Gordy, slept at Shelley's house when he was in Birmingham because he had little money and there were no decent hotels for blacks in Birmingham. The music industry folks were truly friends but they also knew that if Shelley played their records on his show, they would sell.

Late one night, after yet another platter party, Shelley came home exhausted, his flashy sequined outfit soaked with sweat. He called out for Rebecca when he stepped through the door, but something was wrong. The lights were out, the bed was empty, and the house was cold.

She was gone. His wife had left him.

Shelley sat on the edge of their bed, put his head in his hands, and cried. He saw this as an intolerable failure. He had never wanted anything so much as he had wanted his marriage to be the successful opposite of his parents' stormy union. Now, it was over. Shelley assumed she had returned to Shreveport because she liked it so much there, but he knew he would not go looking for her. He would not force her to do something she did not want to do.

Eventually, Shelley concluded that the marriage had come to an end for a number of very obvious reasons. It was likely doomed from the beginning. Theirs had been a whirlwind romance. They hardly knew each other when they said their vows on that front porch in Andalusia. He knew he had turned out to be someone very different in private from the person his fiancé had seen and fallen in love with in public. Rebecca had never been able to accept his dual personalities, not understanding the one she lived with at home and resenting the one the rest of the world heard and saw in the limelight. She, on the other hand, had known he wanted a family yet had concealed the fact that she could not bear children.

Still, it was another bitter disappointment for Shelley. It would take a long time and many talks with Mattie C. in the dark, lonely night before he could hope to recover from this latest blow.

SHELLEY LOST HIMSELF IN his work whenever he could. If he was carrying on about the buffoonery of the mayor or the city commission, if he was introducing the latest B. B. King song, he was not thinking about his marriage. Somehow, though, work was not as fulfilling as it once had been. He was basically telling the same stories over and over, and it appeared none of what he was saying into that microphone was changing the plight of his people one whit. He still got a thrill from seeing the audiences at his appearances react to his showmanship, but the crowd's response was not exactly the vision he had seen in Papa Clyde's full-length mirror. Here, he was sending them out onto the dance floor, but in the mirror they were responding to some other kind of call, clamoring for something bigger, deeper, and he could not quite figure out what that was.

Then Shelley got another call from John McClendon, who had hired him away from WEDR to go to Shreveport. He wanted Shelley to come to work for him again, this time to do an afternoon show on his flagship Jackson, Mississippi, station, WOKJ.

Shelley did not hesitate. He turned in his notice and again quickly found a tenant for his and Rebecca's Titusville home.

After his last show at WEDR, he packed up his belongings and piled them in the trunk of his new Holiday Oldsmobile, the one with his autograph, "Shelley Stewart," painted in big script letters beneath the driver's side door. He wrapped a do-rag around his big mane of processed hair and pulled away, not even looking in the rear-view mirror at the home he had hoped to share with Rebecca until they grew old together.

At 11 P.M. that night Shelley rolled into Jackson, the radio tuned to WDIA up in Memphis, one of the few black radio stations still on the air at night. He promptly made a wrong turn. He realized too late that he had wandered into an all-white neighborhood. He also knew the implications of that turn, honest mistake or not. Unless he was there to mow the grass, he was not supposed to be there. Nobody mowed grass after dark.

Shelley slowed to a crawl, peering at street signs, and tried to find the byways on the map folded in his lap. He hardly noticed the headlights in his mirrors when a car pulled up close behind him.

But he noticed damn quick when blue lights flashed and he heard the distinctive yelp of a police siren.

21

Daddy Long

The white policeman had his service revolver drawn and pointed directly at Shelley's face as he rolled down the car window. "Nigger, what you doin' prowlin' around over here? Where did you steal this car?"

"Hey, boss, what's the trouble?" Shelley asked, carefully keeping both hands on the steering wheel and in clear sight, feigning politeness even as his stomach turned at the vile attitude of the peace officer. The last thing he wanted to do was give the cop an easy excuse to blow his head off.

"What's your name, boy?" the policeman asked as he studied Shelley's Alabama driver license.

"Shelley Stewart." Shelley nodded downward, toward the door panel where his name was written in big letters. "You can tell easy that the car belongs to me, boss."

"We got us a smart nigger, here, Charlie. We ought to just pull your ass out and give you a good whipping right here." He motioned with the gun barrel for Shelley to get out of the car. "We gonna have to hold you."

"On what charge, boss?"

"We'll find something."

Sure enough, while Shelley sat in handcuffs on the curb, they located a mostly empty bottle of whiskey beneath the back seat. It had been there so long Shelley could not remember when or how it got there. Regardless, he was soon in the cage in the back seat of the patrol car. His vehicle was impounded, and Shelley was on his way to spending his first night in the town he intended to shortly own in the city jail. The outcome was actually something of a relief. Black men had died for lesser crimes than straying into a white neighborhood after dark.

Shelley was put into a holding cell with a collection of homeless men, drunks, and violent criminals, every last one of them black. There were cots scattered about and one of them would have to be his bed for the evening. He had to use his shoes for a pillow. A hole in the floor was the only toilet. It had to be flushed by a guard from outside the cell each time an inmate completed his business and yelled out, "Kick that mule!"

About 3 A.M., a trusty came by to count prisoners. Half-awake, Shelley heard him talking with one of the other inmates about the new dude that would be on the air over at WOKJ later that day. The station had been running commercials about it, and the trusty was excited about how this new guy was going to rock Jackson.

"That's me, brother!" Shelley told him.

"Naw! Go on back to sleep, slick, and quite making shit up."

"I got a rich white man's telephone number in my pocket so I ain't long for this hotel," Shelley responded and rolled over to try to get a little rest.

Shelley made his one phone call to John McClendon early that morning. Shortly, WOKJ's station manager showed up to bail him out. The manager launched into a speech about how Shelley was now in the Great State of Mississippi and he had better watch his p's and q's if he did not want to see lots of the inside of the jailhouse. He also ordered Shelley not to say a thing about his incarceration when he went on the air that afternoon.

"I won't say a thing," Shelley promised. He kept that promise, too, and did not mention the arrest on the air that afternoon. However, he certainly talked plenty about it the next day and many days afterward.

It was a given that black radio personalities had to have colorful names. Shelley had to have one before he started his show that afternoon and he had already decided that in an effort to start fresh, he would not use "Shelley the Playboy." McClendon wanted to call his new star "Daddy Long Legs," based on the image the station owner had of Shelley all folded up in the cage in the back of the squad car the previous night. Shelley settled on "Daddy Long" for his on-air nickname and McClendon, who knew a little about Shelley's family history, gave him the official on-air name of "Jerome Long" as homage to Bubba. That name would be used only when segueing into the newscast at the top of each hour. The rest of the time, as he played records and did his usual over-the-top thing, he was "Daddy Long."

Well, Jackson had never heard anything like Daddy Long.

"Good googly woogly! Timber-r-r-r-r! Let 'er fall! Hello, Jackson, Mississippi. I'm Daddy Long and I'm ready to burn, burn, burn!"

His subject matter between records was the same as back in Birmingham, using his bombastic style to take pokes at police brutality, racial injustice, voter registration, and well-to-do blacks who selfishly tried to quell any move toward equality.

John McClendon met him at the studio door after his first show. His face was red and carried a concerned look.

"Daddy Long, you are going to get everybody at the station killed by the Klan," he told his new personality. "We'll have night-riders throwing bombs in the front door in a minute!"

"Mr. Mac, this is what worked in Birmingham and it'll work here, too. Our people want that don't-give-a-damn attitude. The rednecks toss a bomb or two or chop down a tower, it just gets us more listeners and we sell more cars and groceries for our sponsors."

McClendon's eyes grew wide and he grimaced.

"Just tone it down a few decibels, okay? I don't necessarily want anybody chopping down my tower."

Shelley winked but made no promises.

The next day on the show, Shelley shared his welcome-to-Jackson experience with his listeners and wondered aloud if there was even a single black officer on the police force in his new favorite hometown. A short while later, two black officers showed up outside the booth window and gave him smiles and a thumbs-up.

"Well, I do declare! We got two Negroes in *po-lese* uniforms, all right. Y'all doin' better than Birmingham or Atlanta in that regard. But let me ask you something, brothers? Y'all allowed to arrest white folks if you see them breakin' the law? Huh?" The two cops looked at each other and nodded a no. "I rest my case, your honor! I rest my case! Hey, Fats! Fats Domino. Get walkin', yes ind-e-e-e-d, and walk old Daddy Long on out of here, baby!"

The hierarchy at WOKJ was identical to that at WEDR, WBCO, KOKA and every other white-owned, black-programmed radio station in the South at that time. All the on-air personalities were black. Managers and salespeople were white. The latter made most of the money. There were two restrooms in the station, one marked "Colored." In addition to their on-air duties, the blacks were expected to wash windows, sweep and dust, trim the hedges and cut the grass outside the station and at the transmitter/tower location.

From the beginning, Shelley refused to do those chores. He told the station manager that he had been hired to be an on-the-air personality, not a maid or landscaper. There was, though, another requirement of the job at WOKJ of which Shelley was not aware.

A FEW WEEKS INTO his tenure at the station, one of the other personalities stopped him in the hall and reminded him that Mr. McClendon was holding a big party that night at his home.

"In case nobody told you, we are all expected to be there," the man said.

A few minutes later, he saw McClendon passing by in the hallway outside the studio. The boss stuck his head in the broadcast booth door.

"Daddy Long, you will be at the house tonight, right?"

"I got the word, boss."

"Great! See you there."

Shelley was pleased. Maybe he had been wrong about McClendon and how he felt about the colored help. He wanted them to be present at a party for his rich and influential friends, even if it was only to show them off like trained circus animals. Still, the fact that he was invited to such a soiree so early in his employment meant that he had made it, that he had been accepted.

When he got home, Shelley picked out his most impressive shirt, tie and suit and made certain they were well pressed. He put extra pomade on his straight hair and combed it back so it lay perfectly. He checked himself in the mirror one more time and, satisfied, headed out to the party.

The driveway and streets around McClendon's big home were lined with fancy cars. Top businessmen and political leaders were there, including the city's mayor and most of the city council.

Once inside the impressive home, Shelley immediately began working the room like a politician on Election Day, introducing himself to everyone, shaking hands, complimenting men on their neckties and women on their nice dresses and hats. He might just as well have been at the Jack-O-Lantern angling for tips. Everyone he met seemed a bit reluctant to take his extended hand, to respond to his greetings, but that did not slow down Jerome "Daddy" Long.

Shelley noticed one of the station's other personalities standing behind the bar, preparing drinks, as if he was a bartender hired for the evening. Shelley assumed the fellow was moonlighting, picking up extra money tending bar at the boss's get-together. Shelley was hungry and thirsty from all the mingling and greeting he had been doing so he walked over intending to order a drink and a sandwich.

Just then someone tapped him on the shoulder. He turned to see John McClendon standing there, his face white and his eyes wide and worried.

"What are you doing? Didn't they tell you? You are here to be a waiter, serving my guests, not glad-handing them. Now get out there to the kitchen and get your jacket on and get to work."

"Boss, there must be some kind of misunderstanding," Shelley stammered, too stunned to speak. "I don't . . . I'm not . . ."

McClendon stepped closer to whisper so only Shelley could hear him.

"We will talk about this later. Get the hell out of here, right now. You are going to end up getting all of us killed."

So that was the deal. Black employees were not only personalities while on the radio and maids and gardeners when they weren't, but they were also the no-extra-charge help at the boss's parties. McClendon called Shelley on the phone later that night, long after the party was over and the important guests had gone home.

"Look, you embarrassed me tonight in front of my friends and some of the most important people in Mississippi, but it is not totally your fault," the station owner told him. "Either I or some of the others should have made it clear what was expected of you. Look, I know you are strong in your opinions when it comes to your people, and I think it's great that you want colored people to be accepted, but . . ."

"Mr. McClendon," Shelley interrupted, "I am not interested in being accepted. I want to be respected as a man. Getting invited to a party to put on some waiter's jacket and serve drinks is not my idea of respect. Not when I was hired to do a radio show and be a personality on the air."

Shelley was not asked to appear at any more parties at the boss's house.

The other black employees at WOKJ did grouse and complain about how they were treated at the station. That is, when they were absolutely certain none of the whites could overhear. They had never taken their grievances directly to Mr. McClendon though. Not even to the station manager. After the incident at the party, and after they heard about how Shelley had flatly refused to be a servant, they all nominated him to become their spokesman and talk with the boss about the way things were at WOKJ.

McClendon reluctantly agreed to a meeting in his office. The black air staff filed in. None was offered a seat. Shelley launched into his speech, enumerating the issues he and the other six black employees felt needed attention at the station. The others remained quiet and expressionless as they listened to their spokesman calmly and respectfully make their case, precisely as they had discussed it earlier in the day.

Shelley talked about the segregated restrooms, the menial jobs they were expected to perform after they had already completed what they had actually been hired to do, and, maybe most disturbing, how there were no blacks in management or on the sales force, nor were there likely to be any time soon. These were the positions where making more money and having a chance at career advancement were possible.

McClendon listened, his face red, but he did not indicate whether or not he agreed with what he was hearing. After a few minutes, Shelley summed it all up, looked his boss in the eye, and thanked him for agreeing to meet with them.

"Okay, Jerome." McClendon pointedly called Shelley by his formal before-the-newscast on-air name and not "Daddy Long," indicating it was now time for serious talk. "Is that all you want to tell me?"

"Yes, boss."

McClendon looked slowly around the office, lingering on the faces of the other half dozen black employees. None of them looked him in the eye.

"You know, Jerome, you have only been here for a short while. I would also like to hear from some of the staff members who have worked for me for a long time now. I want to hear what they think about all these . . . grievances."

He pointed to one of the announcers, a man who had been by far the most vocal grumbler about conditions at WOKJ. That is, he was most vocal when no white ears were around.

"Well, to tell you the truth, Mr. McClendon, I don't see as how things are so bad around here at all," the man said, studying intently the carpet pattern between his feet. "I don't really guess I have no problems, sir."

McClendon pointed, in turn, to each of the others. All of them responded similarly. All was well at McClendon Broadcasting so far as they were concerned. No grievances that they could see.

"Daddy Long, it appears to me that you are the only one that has a problem with working here," McClendon told him, a slight smile on his lips as he eased back in his big office chair and crossed his arms on his chest.

Shelley exploded. He cursed the others, drew back his fist as if he was about to punch the first man, the one who had been so eager to confront the boss man. Someone grabbed his arm. He cursed some more, called them all "field niggers," and told them how they were little more than slaves, refusing to tell the master that things would have to change, that they deserved respect.

Shelley's anger subsided as he realized what he was doing. He was trying to change hundreds of years of attitude and prejudice with one meeting. As he left the office, McClendon stopped him, allowing the others to quickly disappear down the hallway.

"At least you had the backbone to stand up and say what you thought," he said. "Next time you come forth like that, though, make sure you have it all together."

Shelley suspected then that he could not remain in Jackson. Another unexpected occurrence soon shoved him even harder toward the city limits.

One day as he walked along a street in downtown, mingling with his listeners as he loved to do, he looked up and stared directly into a face he had never expected to see again.

Rebecca.

She was just as startled to see him. She stopped, backed up a step, and watched him warily.

"You stalking me?" she finally asked, retreating another step. "What do you want with me?"

"No! I didn't . . . I never . . ." Shelley sputtered.

"What you doing here, then?"

Shelley explained what he was doing, that he was Daddy Long on WOKJ, that he had no idea she was anywhere near Jackson, Mississippi. Somehow she had not yet heard him on the air or she would have recognized his voice and style at once.

For a moment, Shelley actually thought about trying to talk her into a reconciliation, seeing if they might still make the marriage work, even after all that had been done and said between them. There might have been some deeper reason for this amazing coincidence.

He could tell, though, that she was not interested in such a thing. They went their separate ways, but Shelley felt an aching in his heart he had not expected. He also decided then and there he would have to move on.

He would later learn that she left Jackson shortly after their encounter on the street, and that she did go to Shreveport.

Still, Shelley saw their meeting as an omen.

About that time he got word that a new black-programmed radio station had just gone on the air in Columbus, Georgia. The owners were interested in hiring personalities that had a successful track record in other towns.

A new start sounded good to Shelley. A new start in a town far from Jackson.

There was something else, too, that drew him to the town on the east bank of the Chattahoochee River. Just across the river was Phenix City, Alabama, the place where his daddy was born. There was family and family history there in that old cotton mill town.

The happenstance of that particular radio job opening up when he was determined to leave the one he had in Jackson, and its being in a town where he had roots and family members was another powerful sign indeed.

It turned out to be a summons Shelley could not ignore.

22

MOMMa ROSa & THeM

Rosa Lee Stewart, Slim's mother, still chewed tobacco and the only time anyone saw her not wearing her apron was when she went to church. She kept a small bottle of some amber-colored liquid in a pocket of that apron but denied it was anything but sweet tea or her medicine. Even at her advanced age, she was well respected by black and white alike and was known to everyone as Momma Rosa. She had only recently retired from her job as housekeeper in the Patterson household.

Shelley had seen his grandmother once in his life. He and Rebecca—in happier times—took a trip to Florida and along the way down Highway 280—a highway called "the Florida Short Route" by locals—they stopped off in Phenix City to visit briefly with her.

As was her way, Momma Rosa was straight and to the point when Shelley showed up on her front porch and told her about his new job there.

"Where you going to live, boy?"

"I got a little money. I'll look around and . . ."

"Naw, looky here," she interrupted. "Your aunt owns this here house next door. You may as well live there 'til you find a place. It's sure better than where you growed up."

That was when Shelley learned that his grandmother had actually visited Slim and Marie at the Central Avenue house one day, but he and Bubba were gone, likely out scavenging for food or fishing in the lake, and they missed her. She also knew about how Mattie C. had died and how all of her grandsons by Huell had lived their lives so far.

"Granny, reckon why none of my family saw fit to come get us out of that," Shelley asked her.

She thought for a moment and spit tobacco juice into her cup.

"Well, here's the way it is, sonny boy. You got a heap of relatives. Some has trouble doing for their own. Some of 'em didn't want nothing to do with Huell or any of his'n. Some was flat out scared of him. Some of 'em just didn't like him or anybody he brought into the world. Some of your kin are just plain messy. Speaking of which, here comes your sister now."

Shelley's jaw dropped. His sister?

A young woman, maybe in her mid-twenties, staggered up the sidewalk and stumbled up the front steps. Her name was Lera and she was clearly drunk.

"You a tall one, ain't you?" the woman said when she noticed Shelley. "Hey, reckon you could give me some money? I need a drink."

She was Slim Stewart's offspring all right. However, this was the first that Shelley had known that he had a sister. There had been some talk about two boys visiting Slim and Marie in Rosedale one time, the product of Slim's youthful catting around before leaving Phenix City for Birmingham and his marriage to Mattie C. Shelley had been too young to notice or care at the time. Until that meeting with his sister on his grandmother's porch, he had no solid evidence that he had siblings left besides Samuel and David.

For the next couple of hours, various relatives showed up to take a look at Huell's boy. Shelley tried to remember names and connections but there were so many of them and it was all so confusing and complicated. He could not help but think that he had gone from being aware of practically no kin at all to being surrounded by a veritable flock of them, and it had happened in the space of only a few hours.

That was just one of the topics Shelley pursued that afternoon during his first show on WOKS. Station management had hung big banners all around the building with "Welcome Shelley the Playboy" printed all over them. A personalized song played every few minutes on the air, making sure listeners were aware a hot new personality was going to debut on the air at 3 P.M. that day.

As soon as he pulled the headphones over his ears and sat down behind the audio console, Shelley was back in his element. He morphed easily from introspective and quiet Shelley Stewart to electrifying Shelley the Playboy.

In addition to his new-found relatives and their penchant for hard liquor, he talked about whatever current events interested him and any blatant acts of discrimination or racist violence he had observed. Though he had just arrived in town, he was confident there were plenty of common denominators with previous stops like Birmingham, Shreveport and Jackson.

The telephones signaled that Shelley's chatter was exactly what the listeners wanted to hear. Many of the calls came from soldiers stationed at nearby Fort Benning. But by far the most were from women, young, old and in between.

"Lawdy, lawdy, lawdy," Shelley crowed. "Whooooeeee! I sure wish all you married women would stop calling me up on the telephone! That big old husband of yours ain't gonna appreciate y'all coming on to Shelley the Playboy, don't you know? I am not certain I can whip all of 'em! Besides, you ain't even seen me yet. I may be as ugly as a mud fence!"

MANY CALLS CAME FROM potential advertisers. Business was brisk. Sponsors wanted to jump aboard the Shelley the Playboy Show. The platter parties soon became as popular in Columbus and Phenix City as they had been in Birmingham. It was not unusual to have a thousand kids shimmying and shaking to records by the Platters, the Coasters, Jackie Wilson, or Brook Benton, or for Shelley to require a police escort into and out of the hall.

At one dance, one particular young lady caught Shelley's attention. He introduced himself to her during a break and they immediately hit it off. He quickly learned that Lucille Lemon was college-educated and taught school. He also soon found out that she had endured her own dysfunctional family situation growing up, though not nearly so dismal as Shelley's. Still it was common ground.

As love bloomed with Lucille, Shelley became more and more disenchanted with his newfound relatives. Their love for alcohol—especially Gilby's Gin and homebrew corn whiskey—was not nearly as funny to talk about on the radio anymore. In addition, the tendency to become mean-spirited when they were drinking did nothing to make him feel welcome in the family. Several of his relatives resented his popularity, too. They were not hesitant to goad him about thinking he was better than they just because he was on the radio. Others, assuming anyone in the broadcasting business had to be wealthy, constantly badgered him for money and became belligerent when he refused to loan or give them any.

Things were happening in radio back in Birmingham. Shelley learned that John McClendon had purchased his old radio station, WBCO, changed its call letters to WENN, and moved it to new offices and studios at 18th Street between 5th and 6th Avenues North in downtown Birmingham. They could literally look out on the black business district, Little Harlem, from there.

Despite the way Shelley had left his station in Jackson, McClendon was delighted to welcome a known star to his new venture in Birmingham. However, the move forced a decision for Lucille. She was hesitant to leave the only hometown she had ever known and move to a city she had heard treated black folks even worse than they did in Columbus. Shelley was persistent, though. He did not want to move back to Birmingham without her as his wife.

She accepted Shelley's proposal and they were married in November 1959. As man and wife, they drove up Highway 280 to the Magic City. The giant Vulcan statue on Red Mountain seemed to wave a welcome to them as they settled into a little apartment in the Fountain Heights neighborhood. As far as Shelley was concerned, he was back in Birmingham to stay. Also, though he was well aware of what had been happening with the so-called "civil rights demonstrations" in his hometown and across the South, he had no idea how hot it was about to get in Birmingham.

In addition, there was no way he could have known what a key role he was going to play in cranking up that heat.

The time was coming when Shelley Stewart would finally learn who those people were, those who responded to his voice as he preached each night to Papa Clyde's full-length mirror.

Shelley, 1960.

23

TEEN TOWN

Birmingham had a well-deserved reputation for being the most segregated and intolerant city in America. The truth was that other major Southern cities may have had equally repressive rules and regulations and blatantly maintained long-held discrimination against its black citizens, but Birmingham had by far the most visible resistance to equality. That visibility had taken a violent turn in the late 1950s and early 1960s.

Police Commissioner Eugene "Bull" Connor was easily the most prominent symbol of legalized segregation but he was only the very visible tip of a rather sizeable and dangerous iceberg. The Rev. Fred Shuttlesworth, the fiery leader of the protest movement in Birmingham, summed it up by saying, "If the Klan don't get you, the police will. If the police don't get you, the courts will."

Bombs had ripped apart black churches where meetings were being held, including Shuttlesworth's church and the parsonage in which he lived. A young black man, Judge Aaron, was picked up at random off the street by nightriders and castrated, just to send a message to Shuttlesworth and "outside agitators" they had damn well better cool their dissent.

Sadly, the threats were working. Even those dispatched to Birmingham on behalf of the various organizations that made up the Movement were urging Shuttlesworth and others to back off, to allow court cases and pending changes to the structure of the city's government to run their course. They were certain someone else was going to be killed, and it just might be Shuttlesworth, Martin Luther King, or someone equally prominent.

That was the atmosphere Shelley Stewart moved his bride into in late 1959. He went on the air at WENN-AM radio on January 3, 1960, earning

$135 a week, the most salary he had ever received. Of course, despite the tense atmosphere—or maybe because of it—he resumed his commentary over the airwaves about what was happening in his hometown and to his people. It seemed the *Birmingham News* and the *Birmingham Post Herald* daily newspapers as well as the other radio stations (including those programmed for blacks) and the two commercial television stations were unwilling to report much of the violence against black citizens. Instead, they made it appear that the protestors were merely goading the authorities, that outsiders were stirring the pot, and even that much of the so-called violence was being committed by the Negroes themselves to gain the sympathy—and money—of concerned Northern citizens and media. While somewhat sympathetic to the overall goal, the newspapers were more concerned about the negative image all the demonstrations and the violent reaction to them were giving to the city.

Shelley Stewart was still not afraid to talk about what was really going on. He was confident his popularity offered a protective cloak, at least when it came to the police. Bull Connor could (and did) rail on about "Shelley the Plowboy," but he and his officers knew better than to hassle him too strongly. Connor specifically ordered his force to not hurt the deejay.

Then, almost immediately upon settling back in Birmingham, there were distractions for Shelley and Lucille. Just after New Year's, they learned that Lucille was pregnant. At the same time, an old indiscretion came back to haunt Shelley.

After his first wife, Rebecca, left him, Shelley had a one-time encounter with a young lady after one of the platter parties. A few months later, an irate, middle-aged woman showed up in the lobby at WEDR demanding to speak with him. She accused Shelley of impregnating her daughter. He first denied it was possible because he honestly could not remember it. But when he saw the young woman, clearly with child, he recalled the incident. He offered to do whatever he could to support the child. Mother and daughter abruptly left the station and he did not hear from them again for over a year.

Not long after he began working at WOKS in Columbus, Shelley got word from the state of Alabama that the girl's mother had filed legal action against him. That was when he learned that he had a son, and that he was named Sheldon Collins. First order of business was to share this news with Lucille since they were engaged to be married by this time. Shelley had made it a point to be completely honest with her about everything, painful as some of it was to relate. She was understanding and supported Shelley's desire to do right by this child he had fathered in a one-night stand.

Shelley began sending money to the grandmother even before he attended a scheduled hearing in the tiny Bibb County town of West Blocton, where they lived. The baby's mother and grandmother were there, but not his son. He told the officials that he would certainly support the child, and even offered to take him in and raise him.

No decision was reached that day. On the long drive from Columbus up to Bibb County and back, Shelley could think of little else but his own father and how he had treated him and his brothers. He had to do the right thing when it came to this baby. This was not how he had wanted to bring his first child into the world. He wanted a baby with a wife he loved and who loved him, not as the result of a brief rendezvous with a girl he did not even know. He could fight the contention that this was his baby. He could demand some kind of paternity test. Certainly the grandmother did not have money for a legal fight.

But it was what it was. He was determined to do the right thing.

There was one more deciding factor. No matter how loud he cranked up the radio, he could still hear Mattie C.'s voice in his head, urging him to own up to his responsibilities.

Once he and Lucille had settled in Birmingham, they drove down to Bibb County one day to visit Sheldon. The place was a shanty, a ramshackle shack, filled to the brim with kids. They included the grandmother's half-dozen or so and an additional five or six grandchildren she was also raising.

The boy was so sweet and innocent, unaware of the nature of the circumstances that had brought him into the world or of the relative squalor in which he lived. Shelley immediately asked again if he could take him and keep him for a while. He was surprised when the grandmother agreed. The boy's mother apparently had little say in the matter.

Only a week or so later, though, the baby's grandma was calling Shel-

ley at the radio station and at home, raising hell, telling him she wanted
the boy brought back. And Shelley was to bring plenty of money when he
did. He again offered to take the boy in and raise him, to take him out of
the environment in which he lived, but the grandmother refused. Refused
loudly and finally.

From then on, when Shelley went back down to see his son, everyone was
hostile toward him, at times bordering on violence. Shelley considered legal
action, forcing visitation, but he doubted such an order could be enforced
with these people. Eventually there was little or no contact with Sheldon
and he did not hear from the mother or grandmother again.

AT ANY RATE, WITH Lucille growing bigger and bigger with their child,
Shelley decided he had to make more money. The platter parties were the
ticket. He could usually make in cash at one party over a few hours about
as much money as his weekly salary at WENN. In a good week, he could
book a couple of them, too. He hated the hours these events took away
from Lucille, and at a stage when she especially needed him there. There
was simply no other way to earn the money he felt he needed to give his
wife and baby all they deserved. Lucille would not have to clean white folks'
houses or take in ironing. No child of his would have to scrounge for food
or rely on hand-me-down clothes from neighbors.

The parties offered his best moneymaking opportunity. Becoming a
salesman at the radio station was not an option, of course. Any odd jobs
he might pick up on the side would have taken even more hours away from
his family and would have been for much less pay.

Besides, he enjoyed being in front of that audience and seeing how
they reacted to what he did. Something noticeable and new was going on
at the platter parties, too. Even from the beginning, there had been a few
white faces sprinkled in with all the black ones on the dance floor. Not
all younger white people shared their parents' disdain for "jungle music."
Rock and roll was now being played on the radio and many of its top artists were black. The white kids liked Hank Ballard, Little Anthony and the
Imperials, and the Drifters just as much as they did Elvis Presley and Dion
and the Belmonts. Shelley played it all while doing his high-energy act,

inciting kids—regardless their color—to get out on the dance floor and
have themselves a good time.

One night in the summer of 1960, Shelley was booked to do a party
at a place called Don's Teen Town near Bessemer. The crowd that night
was exclusively white, and so far as Shelley could tell, they were perfectly
happy to have a black man playing the music and doing exactly the same
kind of show he did for mostly black audiences. The party had been heavily
promoted and the club was packed. Everybody there seemed to know who
he was. Many likely listened to him on WENN.

Shelley launched into his usual frenzied show, much to the crowd's
delight. The young white patrons filled the dance floor and were having a
great time dancing to the music and reacting to Shelley's theatrics, just the
way his black audiences did. His brother David and a friend had set up the
big amplifiers and monolithic speakers and were performing their usual
security role. Things seemed to be totally under control, the dancers well
behaved and having a blast.

When Shelley took a break halfway through, David frantically motioned
for him to come over. He stood there with an obviously worried club owner.

"Shurl, they's a bunch of cars outside with the Klan in 'em," David told
him. "They wanting Mr. Mahoney here to send you outside. They's sheriff's
and state trooper's cars out there, too, but I don't know if they are there to
protect us from the Klan or help 'em lynch us."

Shelley nodded to David that they and David's friend should pack up
the equipment and quickly take their leave. The club owner gave Shelley
and David a chance to exit through a back door before he stepped to the
stage and turned on the microphone.

"Looks like the KKK has decided that our friend Shelley the Playboy is not
fit to entertain us here tonight," he announced. "So I guess the show's over."

"Like hell!" some of the people in the crowd shouted. Many of them
rushed outside angrily and confronted the men, some of whom were cloaked
in their white robes and masks. A serious melee—a near riot—broke out
in the Teen Town parking lot.

At one point, some of the Klan members spotted Shelley, David, and
the friend headed for the car with the sound gear. A group of white girls

rushed over and surrounded the three black men, protecting them. They informed the nightriders that they would have to hit them to get to their targets. The thugs lowered their chains and clubs and turned back to where the fight still raged on. Shelley and David made it to the vehicle, tossed the gear in the trunk and back seat, climbed inside, and cranked up.

By that time, the sheriff's deputies and troopers had moved in to try to break up the brawl. Shelley knew now was the time to flee, while the nightriders and the law were all distracted.

Even so, they were peppered with rocks and sticks as they sped away from the club's parking lot. Almost immediately they realized they were being pursued by someone. Someone with lights and a siren, not by the Klan. There was no reason to suspect that the lawmen would be any easier on them if they caught them than the KKK would have been.

Driving at breakneck speed on the narrow streets, Shelley made a tire-screeching turn or two and temporarily lost their pursuers. Then he saw something familiar as they raced through the town of Lipscomb. He veered into the driveway of a friend, switched off the headlights, and pulled around to the backyard, behind a stand of privet hedge bushes. The cops, lights flashing and sirens wailing, sped right on past as the three of them tried to catch their breath.

Word was already spreading, primarily on the police radio, that Shelley had incited a riot at the club and provoked some hoodlums in the crowd to attack innocent white bystanders outside the club. Bystanders who were there to help keep things peaceful should the "nigger music" and that damn colored deejay cause things to get out of control.

After a while, Shelley pulled some old clothes, head rags, and caps out of the trunk and the three of them did their best to look like laborers on the way to a third-shift job somewhere. Shelley put down the car's convertible top to confuse any vehicle description that may have been broadcast. He worked his way over to the Bessemer Superhighway, the main east-west route out of town. Within less than a mile they encountered a police roadblock.

"Hey, boss, what's goin' on?" Shelley piped up as he obediently pulled to a stop.

"Y'all know a nigger calls himself Shelley the Playboy?"

"He that one on the radio? I listen at him sometimes."

"You see him, tell him his ass is ours," the cop said. "He's been over there messin' with white girls and he got a riot going where some people got hurt tonight. We get him, he won't live to see daylight."

"Yes sir, boss. We'll tell him if we see him. We sure will."

They drove on to the Fountain Heights apartment. There they were surprised to see several armed black men outside, guarding the place. They seemed equally surprised to see Shelley alive.

Radio station WSGN had given a report that a white mob had killed Shelley the Playboy at the dance in Bessemer earlier that evening. Shortly, a reporter from the *Birmingham News* showed up at the apartment, seeking the "widow's" reaction. He, too, seemed surprised to see Shelley still living and breathing. The reporter asked Shelley if, considering the night's violent events, he still planned on being on the radio the next day.

"Yes! Absolutely! Why the hell wouldn't I?" was the response.

Still, when Shelley showed up at the station the next day, it was surrounded by armed men, too, making certain no one tried to keep Shelley the Playboy off the radio. Inside, someone showed him the early edition of the *Birmingham News*. There was a brief story about a scuffle at the dance and a quote from Shelley. It mistakenly said he had vowed to the reporter that he would never play a platter party for a white audience again.

Shelley tossed the newspaper in the trash can and proceeded to tell his listeners that he was fine, that the party had been peaceful until "some men with necks the color of the smoke that hovers over the Fairfield steel mills" had started a ruckus. He also reminded them that he saw no color in his audiences and he certainly would play for people who wanted to have a good time, whether they resembled "snow or coal."

He did, in fact, already have a booking for a party with a white audience for the next week at the luxurious Tutwiler Hotel downtown. He did play the party. There were no problems.

LITTLE SHERRI STEWART WAS born at Holy Family Hospital on August 28, 1960. That would have been Mattie C.'s birthday. His daughter's birth, on his mother's birthday and twenty-one years after her death, confirmed for Shelley that Momma still had a hand in what was happening, and that there was a circular order to how things occurred in life. The coincidence of the birth dates was a clear manifestation of the words Mattie C. spoke to Shelley that night so long ago as he sat in Aunt Mamie's outhouse in Collegeville: "Know that I am with you and in you."

The magnitude of it all was almost overwhelming. Yes, there had been Sheldon, his son. But he had not been allowed to be involved with his son's raising. Sherri was not only his flesh, blood, and bones but also his soul. She would depend on him for everything, from food and diaper changings to education, formal and informal. Now, he would finally have the opportunity to truly counter the kind of upbringing he had.

There was another benefit, too. The baby's arrival seemed to have firmed up his marriage to Lucille.

Now Shelley was going full bore on WENN. The Don's Teen Club incident had only increased his popularity, and not just with blacks. He and the other personalities had taken the station to the top and advertisers were lining up to buy commercials. Early in 1961, the station moved to bigger quarters in a storefront in the 1500 block of 5th Avenue North, directly across the street from Kelly Ingram Park. That was a peaceful one-city-block expanse of grass, shade trees, and park benches in the midst of the buildings of downtown and Little Harlem. On the other side of the park was the Sixteenth Street Baptist Church, a large, ornate structure with a distinctive neon sign that had become one of the prime meeting places for those involved with the civil rights movement.

From his studio window, Shelley could watch as people first gathered in the park and then entered the church for the spirited rallies. He could see Martin Luther King, surrounded by his "lieutenants," as they walked up the street and through the church house doors. Often he was accompanied by Fred Shuttlesworth, a firebrand even in comparison to King, and, coincidentally, a graduate of Rosedale High School, just like Shelley. There was also Edward Gardner, director of the Alabama Christian Movement for Human Rights, or other leaders affiliated with organizations most often identified by their initials: CORE, SNCC, SCLC and more. They all fell under the banner of the "Movement."

Sometimes the leaders would look in, see Shelley behind the microphone, and wave to him. Sometimes Shelley ran into them on the street and they always paused to speak with him, though, except for a brief encounter once in Montgomery, he had not yet had the opportunity to talk with Rev. King.

King, Shuttlesworth, and the others knew how valuable the black radio personalities were to what they were trying to do. Nobody had more of the ear of the community, and nobody could mobilize and inform better. The ministers and other leaders made sure Shelley and the others were aware of when and where the meetings were to be held. Then Shelley made certain his listeners were updated, though often cryptically.

He knew the police and the FBI were already well aware of which church hosted which meeting. The law enforcement agencies had salted in enough informants to know. They did not need a disk jockey to keep them informed. But he and the other personalities did not want to alert the Klan if they could help it. Let them get the specifics from their buddies in the police department. Or from the shadowy folks who straddled the fence, working for the FBI as informants even as they placed and set off bombs in churches and parsonages and attacked black folks on behalf of the nightriders.

Birmingham and Alabama were charged with kinetic energy by the summer of 1961. Freedom Riders, a mixed group of young and old and black and white people who openly challenged the segregated seating on interstate buses, had already thrown the switch. Even though the Supreme Court had struck down laws against separate seating for whites and blacks, the practice was still being observed south of the Mason-Dixon Line. Cities like Birmingham had hastily passed laws that stated the bus driver had the option to seat passengers anywhere he wanted on his vehicle, in the guise of maintaining the safety of customers.

Two buses carrying the Freedom Riders were attacked at Anniston, Alabama, east of Birmingham. One bus was firebombed by KKK members. Klansmen boarded the other bus and severely beat several riders before it continued on to Birmingham. There, Bull Connor had promised Klan leaders they could pick sixty men and they could have fifteen minutes without police interference when the bus pulled into the Trailways bus station a few blocks from City Hall. This would give the racists the opportunity to show the Freedom Riders that they should not be messing in the affairs of the people of Alabama.

Newsman Howard K. Smith, the only national journalist present that day, captured the eyewitness accounts of battered and bleeding victims for CBS. Other local reporters had their cameras seized and film ruined. Only one image survived and it appeared the next morning spread across the front page of the *Birmingham Post-Herald*, the city's morning daily paper. It clearly showed white men beating helpless Freedom Riders—black and white—in the bus terminal. When some of the victims staggered down to Sixteenth Street Baptist Church, they interrupted a service that was being conducted there by Rev. Shuttlesworth. He sent one of them—a white rider—to the emergency room at University Hospital. Later, Bull Connor phoned Shuttlesworth and threatened to arrest him because he had "harbored" white protestors.

Shelley certainly talked on the air about what had happened just up the street from the station. In his usual coded way, he let his listeners know that he knew that Connor and his cops had allowed the attack to happen on the Freedom Riders. Other media had politely asked where the police were before and during the brutal attack, but otherwise they mostly followed the line that the protestors had come to Alabama looking for trouble and they had found it.

The assault on the Freedom Riders was a turning point. It put Birmingham right back on the front pages of newspapers and magazines around the world. It was all taking place just outside the front window where Shelley Stewart did his daily radio show. He had a front-row view of the next few historic years.

Still, with all that was going on in this hot spot, it was some familiar bigotry inside WENN that soon occupied Shelley's attention, and it was a seemingly innocent venture that again altered his career path.

24

$\overset{\circ}{\text{S}}$HELLEY'S RᴇCOᴿᴅ MART

It was a familiar story. Whites had the better-paying jobs at WENN—management, sales, technical—and blacks had no hope of landing any of those positions. While it was the black on-air staff that brought listeners to the station and allowed commercials to be sold at higher rates, they received little respect. Managers were often hostile and impolite, refusing to speak with black employees or acknowledging them with, "What the hell do you want?" Blacks were required to use an unlocked toilet in the hallway while whites used the one at the back of the building, one that required a key.

The black restroom was occupied one day when Shelley had to go, with limited time while a record played. He proceeded to kick the door open to the unoccupied "whites only" restroom. He informed the station manager that he and other blacks were no longer going to tolerate such a condition, but nothing changed. Not with that manager or with any of the other bosses who came and went with regularity, each of whom seemed to believe that working with Negro employees was a necessary evil. The black deejays were to be tolerated, not treated with respect or professionalism.

Finally, confident this time that he had the backing of the entire black staff, Shelley asked for a meeting with Mr. McClendon the next time he was in town. He explained their situation and informed McClendon—with the solid approval of everyone present at the meeting—that they felt the best man for the currently open job of station manager was Joe Lackey, the office manager. Lackey was a mild-mannered man, liked by everyone. Though his opinions on integration were unknown, and though he never socialized with black people so far as the staff knew, they were certain he

228

would be more fair-minded and decent than anyone in the recent parade of previous but short-term station managers had been.

McClendon was flabbergasted.

"Joe? Joe Lackey! You have to be kidding me. He has no sales experience. Him?"

However, a few days later and to everyone's surprise, Lackey was promoted to station manager. Though he had been unaware that he had boosters among the staff, Lackey accepted the job and made sure everyone knew they could count on him. Things immediately became more tolerable around WENN.

During this time, Shelley continued to gain friends in the entertainment industry; he helped many establish and advance their careers. One such friend was the bus driver-singer for the group Johnny Jenkins and the Pine Toppers. The band stopped by WENN to visit with Shelley one afternoon while on the way to a recording session in Memphis. They mentioned how good a singer their bus driver was. The young man, a former roofer and construction worker, had recorded a couple of tracks that had not been hits. He sang for Shelley a verse or two of a song he planned to record if there was time at the Memphis session. Shelley heartily encouraged the fellow to record the song and put it out, and urged him not to give up. His voice was unique and powerful.

The young man did get the chance to record a couple of quick tracks on that trip. A plaintive love song called "These Arms of Mine" became the first hit for him, the first of many for legendary performer Otis Redding. That visit and Shelley's encouragement then and in the future led to a long-term friendship between the two men.

STILL SEEKING MORE INCOME to support his family and having recently obtained a mortgage on a newly built home, Shelley had a brainstorm one day. He decided to lease space on the ground floor of a building at 1607 5th Avenue North, just around the corner from WENN. There he opened Shelley's Record Mart.

As soon as the sign went up in the record store window, Shelley received a summons to the office of Joe Lackey.

"Shelley, what is this?" the manager asked.

Shelley with James Brown & friends.

"That's my record store, Mr. Lackey. Man's got to feed his family and since I can't sell radio time, I got to make it how I can."

The next day, the station manager informed him that Mr. McClendon had a big issue with an on-air employee also having a record store. He considered it a conflict of interest. Shelley told Lackey to inform Mr. McClendon that he saw no conflict at all and that he intended to keep his store open.

That evening, when Shelley completed his show, Lackey met him at the broadcast booth door. He had an envelope in his hand.

"Shelley, Mr. McClendon says you cannot own the record store and continue to work here. He is afraid you will become too independent. Is it still your intention to keep the store open?"

"Yes, boss, it most certainly is."

Lackey handed Shelley his final paycheck and wished him luck with his store.

"If you change your mind, you can come back to work."

Shelley had hardly informed Lucille of the situation that evening before the telephone rang. It was the manager of the top rival black-programmed radio station, WJLD. News traveled fast! The manager was calling with a job offer for fifty dollars more per week than Shelley had been making at WENN. And he would have the most listened-to shift on the station, morning drive time.

Shelley hesitated. Word around town was that the white manager at WJLD would not tolerate anyone with an activist spirit working there. He supposedly forbade his on-air personalities to even mention human rights issues or the things that were going on in Birmingham at the time.

Maybe he had mellowed, Shelley thought. He accepted the offer and went on the air the very next morning, surprising everyone by turning up on WENN's biggest rival.

Before long, Shelley convinced his new employer to set up broadcasting equipment at the record shop so he could do his show from there. They agreed.

As he had feared, all was not smooth sailing with the new station. The white engineer refused to come over to Shelley's store to maintain the broadcasting equipment. The manager made a big fuss over Shelley's refusal to address the younger white staff members as "Mr." or "Mrs." In the resulting shouting match, the manager told Shelley how much he disliked his "uppity" attitude and how his new deejay was precisely the kind that was causing so much discord in the South in those uneasy times.

Shelley did not back off one whit. If anything, the manager's attitude only made him more determined to get the respect every human being deserved, for himself and for everyone else. That was exactly what he told his new boss as they began a tense stalemate.

1962 would prove to be another very interesting year, and once again Shelley was in a prime spot to survey it all from the station and the doorway of the record shop at 1607 5th Avenue North, between 16th and 17th Streets. There, he could see passing by the faces that had so recently appeared on the covers of *Life* and *Look* and in the news stories each evening on NBC and CBS television.

ONE MORNING AFTER HIS show on WJLD, Shelley stepped outside the record shop for some fresh air. He saw a contingent of men walking his way up the street. He recognized the men at once: the Reverends King, Andrew Young, and James Bevel. Bevel was not yet as well known as the other two but Shelley certainly knew who he was; Rev. Shuttlesworth had introduced them.

He also knew that many in Birmingham's black leadership were not happy about having these men in their town, and especially King. Some of those black leaders were already successful businessmen and felt more protests and trouble could negatively affect their revenues. Others were simply scared, certain that any intensification of the demonstrations against the city's racist power structure would only lead to more black people being hurt and killed, more bombings and castrations.

It was Shelley's belief—and one he espoused constantly on the airwaves—that so long as the activists coming to town were there to change the ugly status quo they should be welcomed and supported. Just like convening the staff at a radio station to object to abuse, all black citizens and the whites who supported justice should present a united front, not give in to threats and bluster.

"Are you Shelley?" Young asked him, stopping in front of the record shop to shake his hand.

"Yes, I am," he replied and shook hands with each of the men.

"We were listening to your program this morning," King told him. "You are quite a personality. I want you to know that we really appreciate what you have been doing to help us."

"Thank you very much. I do what I can do, sir."

"Well, we need all the help we can get," King went on. "You know Commissioner Connor and his folks are putting a real scare into colored folks here in Birmingham. We have to walk and talk and pray all we can to try to gather up enough of a crowd to put pressure on them and impress the national media."

"Have you talked to the people down on the Square?" Shelley asked.

"The Square?"

Shelley explained that he was talking about the general area in the vicinity of where they stood, Little Harlem, the black business district. This was Shelley's neighborhood, the place where he loved to hang out and meet people, whether it was in their businesses, shot houses, offices, restaurants or just out on the street corners. Until the Black Cat or other patrol cars broke them up for no good reason, that is. Shelley told them that was how he kept up with what people were thinking, what the average person wanted to hear him talk about on the radio. He knew them. He knew they would be happy to participate if asked, but many would not necessarily darken the door of a church unless specifically invited for the purpose of demonstrating.

"Rev. King, I believe you could find you some demonstrators if you went into Ratkiller's over on 17th or Monroe Steakhouse, the pool halls and the whiskey parlors, or if you just stood there on the corner and let them see you and talk to you." Shelley smiled. It was the "masses and classes" thing he had learned from Papa Clyde. "Some of them may not be your most upstanding citizens, you know. But I know one thing. They would not be afraid of going to jail. Or afraid of much of anything else, for that matter. You can be sure they are not one bit worried about losing their jobs if they go to jail."

King and the other men thanked him once more and went on their way.

A few hours later, as Shelley stood in the door of the shop, he saw an odd assortment of characters coming around the corner, marching along

5th Avenue toward the Baptist church. The preachers, King, Young and Bevel, were out front leading a parade of hustlers, hookers, dope dealers, lawyers, businessmen, restaurant servers, and others, a group at least sixty people strong. Shelley knew most of them by first name. King slowed as he passed by the shop.

"You were right, Shelley," he said. "You have got to deal with the masses and then try to bring the classes. Birmingham is a hard city, but we will prevail." King walked a few steps and turned back toward Shelley. "I got a free shoeshine and the best breakfast I've ever eaten, too." Then he walked on.

Most of those people would be in Birmingham jail by nightfall, but before they were hauled away by Bull Connor's paddy wagons, they would have challenged the dreadful system under which they lived, and in the only way they knew how. Still, it was obvious to Shelley, Dr. King, Rev. Shuttlesworth, Bull Connor, Governor-elect George Wallace and everyone else that the nonviolent demonstrations in Birmingham were beginning to fizzle. It was becoming more and more difficult to gather enough of what Shuttlesworth called "jailbirds" to tax the arrest capacity of the police or to merit being up front on the nightly TV news or splashed across the front covers of the national magazines.

Shelley still did what he could.

"The heat is on, baby, down yonder at 17th and 4th, you know," he told his listeners. That alerted demonstrators that marchers had Bull Connor's cops occupied at that location so another group could take an alternate route to go downtown and conduct a sit-in at one of the lunch counters where Negroes were not welcome to eat alongside whites.

Then Shelley had another brainstorm. As he did his regular on-air roll-call with area high schools each morning on WJLD, he thought of a way that he might be able to help even more, maybe even kick-start the demonstrations and move things along. About the same time, he was approached by one of Rev. King's lieutenants with a similar plan and requesting his help in implementing it.

What happened over the next few weeks, in May of 1963, would be another of those history-changing events.

There is ample evidence that Martin Luther King expected to be killed in Birmingham, Alabama. It did not happen, of course. He remained the "face" of the demonstrations in that city. His jailing there in the spring of 1963, and the resulting letter he wrote to white ministers of the city while he was incarcerated, challenging their call for cessation of demonstrations, is a key event in those tumultuous times.

However, King's arrest was calculated by the authorities to take away the charismatic leader's visibility. It worked. King's jailing was hardly news anymore. And the historic letter, which so eloquently described the need for peaceful protest and detailed perfectly the purpose of the confrontations in Birmingham, would not be published for another two months.

Meanwhile, there was much disagreement among the leaders of the Movement on how to proceed. When King and his associate, Dr. Ralph David Abernathy, bailed out of Birmingham jail, they returned to Atlanta for a few days. Businessman A. G. Gaston evicted Movement members from an office building he owned, claiming they were carrying on there with whiskey and dope. Other leaders were facing trumped-up contempt-of-court charges and more serious jail time.

Meanwhile, Bull Connor was showing off his new "tank," a specialized armored urban assault vehicle specially designed to disrupt the kinds of street marches that were taking place. The Klan, bolstered by their attacks on the Freedom Riders and the fact that no one had been arrested, was bolder and more brazen with their threats. Confusion over court fights about the status of the city's legally elected mayor and council kept Connor firmly in charge of the police and fire departments and more moderate city officials off balance, working out of temporary offices in hallways at City Hall.

Rev. James Bevel was even more convinced that it had been a mistake to put so much of the spotlight on Rev. King, even if King could get the president of the United States on the telephone. Instead, Bevel felt, this should be a movement of the people, the locals. He knew the older blacks had tired of being arrested, jailed, and, in many cases fired from their jobs. They, too, were beginning to wonder what was being accomplished. College students had taken part in many of the *marches and prayer vigils, including some from all-white Birmingham-Southern College. But the* Birmingham News *had published the names and addresses of students who had been arrested at one event. Some promptly received visits from Klan members masquerading as police. Or police who actually were Klan members. One football star student at nearby all-black Miles College was badly beaten by men who did not even bother covering their faces. He recognized a couple of them as being policemen who had arrested him during the march. His mother, who tried to shield her son from the nightriders, was beaten even worse and almost died from her injuries.*

Bevel knew the cause was not lost, but he needed energetic marchers willing to fill the jails beyond capacity. He knew exactly where he could find plenty of them. He also knew he would have to defy many leaders of the Movement leaders if he went that way.

Bevel decided he had no choice. He also knew who he could get to help him turn those marchers out.

25

PACK youR TOOTHBRUSHes & WeAR YouR RaiNCOATS

In the few days since Rev. King had recruited marchers in Little Harlem, he and his lieutenants had stopped by Shelley's Record Mart several times. They were not there to buy the newest music. They had learned that an abandoned hallway led from the store's back door into the adjoining building which held J. Richmond Pearson's law office, one of the primary meeting spots for planning strategy. That meant King could shake the continual tail by local police and the FBI for a few minutes.

Shelley Stewart had also been working his music-industry contacts, raising money and influence to help support the Movement. He got immediate and generous response from Leonard Chess, the legendary founder of Chess Records in Chicago, as well as Don Robey at Peacock Records, and Jerry Wexler at Atlantic. There were many more.

Shelley already considered his program and the broadcasts of other black personalities to be like the ancient tribal drums in Africa. They kept their people up to date on what was really happening, not what the traditional media told them was going on.

Some called Shelley the community's "talking drum." He had already been using his influence to persuade blacks—regardless of their status in the community—to join in the marches, prayer vigils, and demonstrations, to keep pushing.

He used coded messages to alert people of the times of rallies. He might say, "All right, baby, it is 8:30 here on WJLD. No. Wait. That ain't right.

It may be 8:30 here at WJLD but it is 3 p.m. Wednesday at New Canaan."

Many in his audience listened and acted. Lately, many did not.

WJLD's station manager made it clear to Shelley that he was to shut up about the demonstrations.

"Boss," Shelley told him, "I am a man who sees his people suffering. I am not about to stop trying to help them win this fight for freedom. If you want to fire me, fire me!"

The manager continued to fume and sputter and fuss, but he knew he could not fire Shelley. Once word got out about why, the station would lose every listener it had.

Still, it was frustrating to Shelley that the marches were growing smaller and smaller. Weeks had gone by since anything had appeared on NBC and CBS about what was happening in the Magic City. He was not surprised when Rev. James Bevel showed up in his shop one morning just after Shelley finished up a truly rabble-rousing show on WJLD.

"Brother Shelley, what is going on?"

"You are, Rev. Bevel. What can I do for you this morning?"

"No, I think *you* are what is going on, Shelley. You and Rev. Faush and Tall Paul and the rest of them." Bevel explained his plan, then looked Shelley in the eye. "Look, I know this is risky for you. You work for the white man that owns the station. You live here and you have a wife and child. It could get rough. Some folks could get hurt. Will you do what we need to do?"

"Yes." Shelley did not hesitate. The preacher's plan was exactly what he had been thinking for a while now.

"I thought you would. Now, can you get some of the others to help?"

"Yes."

When Bevel left, Shelley locked up and walked around the corner to WENN, his old radio station. "Tall Paul" White was the town's other top black radio personality and he and Shelley had no warm relationship. Still, when Shelley explained what they needed to do, and asked White if he was in, the answer was immediate.

"Yes," he said in his deep rumble of a voice. White also recruited Erskine Faush, an ordained minister and popular personality on WENN, and others at his station.

The next day, Shelley and the others began recruiting—on air and off—some of the top leaders at the area's black schools. Shelley knew them from his platter parties, the morning roll calls, and the Shelley the Playboy fan clubs. And it included more than Birmingham city schools. Shelley had contacts throughout the area where WJLD's signal reached. Faush and a couple of others who primarily played black gospel music knew which young church leaders to talk to as well.

THE RADIO PERSONALITIES INVITED class officers, top athletes, majorettes, and valedictorians to attend a "hot lunch" at the Gaston Motel. At least thirty showed up for the meeting, conducted by Bevel. He incorporated his usual fiery message, explained why it was so important for them to participate, and told them how to start a "whisper campaign" in their schools and churches. He warned them it would be dangerous, that some could be hurt, and they would almost certainly go to jail. The young people also learned what signals to listen for on WENN and WJLD. Shelley the Playboy and Tall Paul White and the others would tell them where to go and when.

Finally, each student received a secret palm card, something that would make them feel as if they were doing something positively devilish and clandestine. One side of the card read, "Fight for freedom." The other side said, "Then go to school."

When the time was right, Shelley took to the airwaves and gave directions to his young listeners.

"Good googly-woogly! Checkin' in with Parker and Lincoln and Ullman and all you brilliant scholars listening to Shelley the Playboy. Old Eugene can even check in and make a request if he wants to!" Everyone knew "Eugene" was Shelley's pet name for Bull Connor. "Now I hope y'all know there is a field trip this afternoon at one o'clock down at Kelly Ingram and I expect y'all will learn a little bit about social studies down there. Now . . . timber-r-r-r, let 'er fall! James Brown is beggin' you, baby. Beggin'! *Please, Please, Please . . .*"

The whisper campaign confirmed what Shelley and the others were saying on the radio. Hundreds of high school students left class at lunchtime and showed up at Kelly Ingram Park. Bevel and a couple of other young lieutenants—college kids who were not much older than the high-school students—ushered them into Sixteenth Street Baptist Church. Then Bevel talked to them about as honestly as anyone ever had in their young lives. He echoed many of the same points that Shelley had been making on the air, that they were either part of the solution or part of the problem. He showed an NBC documentary on the Nashville lunch counter sit-ins, to emphasize what young people could do if their elders were not willing. Although a considerable number of knives and razors were confiscated at the door that afternoon, Bevel preached nonviolence and made sure the students understood their roles in what was about to happen.

As Bevel expected, the students soaked up the plain truth he was preaching and left the meetings aware that they could play a mighty role in achieving freedom for their people. Many, still fired up by Bevel's revival-like preaching, walked down the street to St. James Baptist Church and attended Rev. Fred Shuttlesworth's mass meeting that night. The church was packed and the fire marshal tried to shut them down. Later, when Shuttlesworth asked for "jailbird" volunteers, very few adults stood up. On the other hand, practically all the kids who came over from Bevel's meeting did.

Dr. Martin Luther King told the children he appreciated their enthusiasm but to sit back down. He was not in favor of them marching, getting arrested and jailed, and maybe even getting hurt. Few of the leaders favored the tactic. If children were injured, it could reflect on the Movement and its leaders who put them in harm's way. It also smacked of opportunism and he knew the media—local as well as national—would use that theme.

But Fred Shuttlesworth told King, "We got to use what we got."

On the last Monday in April 1963 leaflets were distributed to students at area black high schools urging them to leave class the next Thursday, May 2, and report to Sixteenth Street Baptist Church. Shelley and his associates spread the word in carefully coded messages. Of course, Bull Connor got word of what was planned and told the school superintendents that any student 16 years old or older would be permanently expelled from school if he or she left class to take part in the rally.

On the radio that morning, Shelley told his listeners, "Listen, baby, you better pack your toothbrush today. You know lunch will be served!" That meant they would need that toothbrush if they were going to practice good oral hygiene in jail.

More than a thousand students either did not show up for school that morning or left class during the day. One principal locked his school's front doors but students piled out classroom windows. Others scaled fences when gates were padlocked. Kids as young as six packed into Sixteenth Street Baptist Church. The atmosphere inside the church was like a pep rally, but once Bevel began preaching, the students were quickly focused on what they were being asked to do.

Around mid-day, Shelley played a pre-designated song on the air. That signaled a small group of young people to march, two-by-two, to a specific location. That immediately drew the attention of Connor's cops and the armored assault vehicle. Then, while the authorities were distracted, young people left the church a few dozen at a time, entered Kelly Ingram Park, and, as told to do, knelt and prayed. They pulled out signs that said, "Freedom," and, "We Shall Overcome."

The police finally realized that there would be hundreds of children kneeling, praying, and singing there in the park. No one had expected this response from the young people. No one but Bevel and the black disk jockeys.

Then Shelley and the others gave the next signal over the airwaves.

"It's c-o-l-l-l-d outside this afternoon!" It was actually approaching 90 degrees under a blazing sun but everyone understood this inaccurate weather report meant it was time to start marching.

The groups of school kids stood and broke into at least four different groups, each marching toward City Hall by different routes, singing the familiar spirituals and chanting the same slogans their elders had been doing for the past months.

Bull Connor and his officers had prior knowledge that there would be a "children's march" that afternoon. They had no idea there would be more than a thousand that would have to be arrested and hauled off to jail. As the apprehensions began, the paddy wagons and patrol cars were quickly filled up. Eager demonstrators practically ran gleefully to the nearest inmate bus. And then to school buses that were hastily brought in to help transport the "prisoners." Mortified cops could not believe they were arresting six- and seven-year-olds for the crime of walking up the sidewalk, singing gospel songs.

Shelley Stewart watched much of what happened from his record shop. He would later learn that more than 600 youngsters were packed into the city jail and into makeshift facilities at the town's baseball stadium, Rickwood Field, and the stock barns at the Alabama State Fairgrounds in the western part of the city. He also later heard that Martin Luther King had not been at the initial rally nor was he present at the march. He was in his hotel room still trying to decide whether or not to use children in support of the cause.

Shelley knew a few things without being told. The day's protests had been a success. He was proud of his role in it all.

"The whole world is watching Birmingham tonight!" Rev. Fred Shuttlesworth proudly told an excited church full of folks at a rally that evening. It was true. The film of young children being ushered into paddy wagons and hauled off to jail would be all over the evening news programs the next night.

But Shelley also knew that there was more work to do. He knew that once Bull Connor had been pushed into a corner, he would come out ferociously fighting. Shelley had noticed the fire trucks parked on several corners near 17th Street, the demarcation line between the black business district and "white" Birmingham. Their hoses were filled with high-pressure water, aimed at the marchers as they approached, but they had not been turned on and used on anyone that day. The urban assault vehicle had been parked most of the afternoon, more for show than anything else, and billy club-wielding shock troops had stayed mostly behind lines of squad cars. Shelley knew Connor's department had trained police dogs, too, but they had been held back that afternoon. The child marchers that day had been beautifully polite and peaceful, but there were others—gang members like the Gilleys and others—who might use the "nonviolent" confrontation with the cops as an excuse to inflict some of their own viciousness.

Shelley had seen firsthand and plenty of times just how malicious Birmingham police and Alabama State Troopers could be in their dealings with Negroes. How far would they go to try to win this battle, whether it involved children or not?

Shelley Stewart—and the world—would find out the very next day.

26

'Dogs & Hoses Repulse Negroes'

The official weather forecast for Friday was for hot and dry. However, from his broadcast position in the record store, Shelley Stewart could see the big fire trucks already arrayed along 17th Street. Riot police in hard helmets, squad cars, and yellow tape blocked the way of anyone who happened to be black. Shelley knew the plan for the day's demonstrations was for the children to march past that boundary, singing, chanting, praying, and waving their banners, and then on to City Hall and "white" downtown.

In his own way, and between the top records of the day, he made certain the kids understood what they would almost certainly be facing that afternoon—"OK, baby, you gonna want to wear your raincoats today if you don't want to get that pretty white senior dress wet!"

Rev. James Bevel had already termed that Friday's march as "D-Day." He was confident Bull Connor would play into the hands of the organizers and do something that would re-ignite the Movement. He prayed nobody would be seriously hurt, but he also knew it was a distinct possibility.

"I know some of y'all are listening out there at the Kiddieland this morning," Shelley announced. Kiddieland was the amusement park at the fairgrounds, a spot where blacks could only come play on designated "nigger days." Its rides were near the stock barns where some of the kids arrested the previous day were being held. "But I tell you, I suspect you are not going to be lonesome. No, baby! You got company coming!"

Again, using songs on the radio stations to signal them, some decoy marchers headed in a different direction from the church. And again, on cue, hundreds of school-age kids filed out the door and down the front steps, headed this time for City Hall. Connor used a bullhorn to warn the marchers, "Do not cross the police line. If you come any further, we will turn the fire hoses on you. You do not have a permit to parade and are in violation of the law."

The scenes of that day were powerfully documented in photos and on news film. The images of children and adults being blasted, knocked to the ground, and having their clothing ripped off by the high-pressure fire hoses would shock the nation watching on TV network news shows. Connor also quickly gave the okay to employ the K-9 corps against the young people. Pictures of a German shepherd ripping the clothes off a young black man horrified readers and viewers all over the world. Even the Russians picked up the story, ran images, and talked about how this typified life in the U.S.

The next morning, the *New York Times*—a publication that then rarely ran photos at all and especially on its front page—had the police dog image prominently displayed across three columns of page one. The headline screamed, "Dogs and Hoses Repulse Negroes at Birmingham."

Among those who were shocked by the pictures and stories was John Kennedy, the president of the United States. Kennedy immediately dispatched to Birmingham two attorneys from the civil rights division of his Justice Department. Their orders were to kick-start negotiations between black and white leaders and get this mess stopped.

By the weekend, journalists had raced to Birmingham to cover what was going on. So had celebrities like singer Joan Baez and comedian Dick Gregory. The police continued their winning ways by forbidding white reporters and entertainers to go anywhere near the black churches or even to enter the area of Sixteenth Street Baptist Church.

The next day, Saturday, more than 3,000 young people turned up at the church and once more staged a peaceful march toward City Hall. Again they were guided by Shelley, Tall Paul, and the others via radio. Connor obliged the demonstration organizers again by using the fire hoses and German shepherds against the children, elementary-aged up to college students. The mood was a bit darker that day, and some in the crowd of older black observers began throwing bottles and rocks. A sizeable group of whites gathered as well, and Connor, fearing a race riot and a park full of bleeding colored kids, told his cops it was time to disperse the whites.

Meanwhile, as school buses, paddy wagons, and squad cars hauled off hundreds of kids, Bevel decided they had made their point for the day. He, too, was afraid things might get out of control and someone would be badly injured. After all, the jails—real and makeshift—were already full. The media had done its job and captured compelling evidence of the brutality in Birmingham. Thanks to Connor's stubbornness, the "Children's March" had successfully created the images that would help accomplish the goal. So far, nobody had been seriously injured and the last thing they needed now was for Connor and his cops to create a confrontation that led to kids being hurt. Then the whites could blame it on the marchers.

Borrowing the police commissioner's bullhorn, Bevel instructed the demonstrators that the day's activities had successfully concluded and that they were to march peacefully back to the church. There would be no demonstrations on Sunday by the school children, but a large contingent of adults marched to the city's main jail and peacefully stopped to pray and preach. Fire trucks and police cars stood by but there was no confrontation.

Monday morning, Shelley announced, "Y'all gonna need your tooth-brushes again today. Maybe you want to put on that swimming suit under your clothes, too. Hot and wet, baby. It's gonna be hot and wet today!"

AGAIN, MORE THAN 3,000 students turned out. The fire hoses and dogs were not employed but a few compelling pictures resulted when a female demonstrator was roughly arrested by five officers. Some of the kids seemed disappointed that they would not get wet that day. Others felt bad because they were not arrested, even when they ran and lined up to climb aboard one of the jail buses. The police could not haul them in, though. There simply was no place to put them.

However, talks between black leaders and the city's white merchants and officials had privately begun on Sunday and, though there would be many fits and starts, those contentious meetings would soon result in an abrupt end to most of Birmingham's harsh segregation laws. At the same time, the marches continued and rallies kept the demonstrators fired up. Soon,

donated money from entertainers, celebrities, a few local black businessmen, labor unions, and others poured in and the arrested students were
eventually bailed out of jail.

Martin Luther King proudly told the press, "The activities that have
taken place in Birmingham over the last few days, to my mind, mark the
nonviolent movement coming of age. In a very real sense, this is the fulfill-
ment of a dream."

Shelley Stewart had watched it all play out. Though he was proud of his
role, happy that he and the other black radio personalities had been able to
so successfully turn out the children, he also had a feeling of dread.

Three or four days of children marching in the streets of Birmingham
had finally resulted in an unprecedented change in his hometown. It was a
victory for the civil rights of black people everywhere and for the movement
that helped bring it about.

However, Shelley was of the belief that it had done little to help in the
fight for the granting of human rights. Merchants had agreed to integrate
fitting rooms in the big department stores and to promote a very few black
employees to positions of more responsibility. There was a promise to integrate the schools, too. However, Shelley knew few hearts had been changed.
This was a major step for sure, but only the first one in a long, long stairway.

If all was well in Birmingham, why could he still not sell commercials for
the radio station to which he attracted so many listeners? Or be promoted
to become its manager?

And if segregation was over in Birmingham, why did he have to keep
secret a budding business relationship with an old friend?

He also knew there were dangerous people out there who would be
moved to fight back even harder now after this symbolic loss. A trapped
snake strikes. There were people in Birmingham who would never peacefully
accept a negotiated settlement between the "niggers" and the well-to-do
Jews and other rich white folks.

If the battle had been won, why was Shelley so certain more people
were going to be hurt?

~~~~~~~~~~~~~~~~

Summer 1963 in Birmingham's streets was not nearly as hot as it might have been had it not been for the Children's March and the resulting rush to the negotiation table. Still, the more radical among the segregationists were more determined than ever not to be beaten by Martin Luther King and his outside agitators. Nor were they going to be bound by the surrender of a bunch of rich Jews and panty-waist white politicians.

Shortly after the serious negotiations to end segregation began, a bomb ripped off the corner of the A. G. Gaston Motel. It was carefully placed to destroy Room 30 and kill the man who was supposed to be sleeping there that night. It was a blatant assassination attempt by members of the Ku Klux Klan against Martin Luther King. Had King not made last minute plans to be elsewhere that evening, it would have succeeded.

In June, Governor George Wallace kept his promise to "stand in the schoolhouse door" to block the enrollment of black students at the University of Alabama in Tuscaloosa. He did ultimately step aside—under protest—when President Kennedy nationalized the Alabama National Guard, but not before vowing to continue the fight against desegregation.

In July, Birmingham's new city council repealed a long list of segregation laws. King and Ralph Abernathy came back to lead groups who marched downtown to become the first to legally sit down and be served a meal in restaurants inside the big department stores. They marched past whites wearing Klan robes and shirts bearing the swastika emblem but the confrontation remained verbal.

In August, a black church not even associated with the Movement was burned to the ground by a Klan group. A few days later, a known KKK member set off a tear gas canister near the newly integrated lunch counter inside Loveman's department store. There were more bombings of black civil rights leaders' homes but no one was seriously hurt.

In early September, the Birmingham city schools were officially integrated, peaceably but not necessarily smoothly. George Wallace had prohibited the move, "for the sole and express purpose of preserving the peace." He was overruled by the courts, losing his second major battle of the summer.

On the night of September 1, the day before Labor Day, a black Civil Defense captain named James Lay saw something suspicious outside the Sixteenth Street Baptist Church. He noticed a car with two white men inside, parked near a stairwell of the church. A third white man carrying a black bag was standing on the sidewalk near the stairs. When the man with the bag realized Lay was watching him, he turned, rushed back to the car, and they sped away.

On September 15, a massive, timed dynamite bomb exploded near that same church stairwell. It was 10:22 a.m., between Sunday school and the morning service, a time when the most people would be inside the building. It was clear the terrorists who placed the bomb there wanted to hurt and kill.

Four young girls died. Twenty-two other people were seriously injured.

All the church's beautiful stained glass windows were shattered save one. It depicted Jesus leading a group of children.

27

a Good Beating

Busy as he was, Shelley still talked with his old friend Cy Steiner several times a week. Sometimes it was over the telephone, sometimes Cy dropped by the record shop, and sometimes they met over a meal at Monroe's or Apex. Shelley still believed that Steiner was a man on the move, a go-getter, and he was proving it by being a good salesperson at the radio station where he worked. Shelley also knew that Steiner, as did he, had greater aspirations. They talked about the future, about their dreams.

Shelley wanted to own a radio station or some other kind of related business. Steiner had thoughts of opening an advertising agency. They both knew the times would not permit a black man and a white man to be partners in such a venture. Still, the seed had been planted and they talked about finding a way to make it a reality.

Unfortunately, the turbulence of the times was mirrored in Shelley's personal life. The old rumors and innuendo of infidelity were finding Lucille. She was also jealous of her husband's time, too. Things were briefly better when she again became pregnant. Shelley Lamar Stewart (Lucille pointedly did not want their son to be a "junior" and insisted he be called by the nickname "Kip") was born in June 1963.

Still the Shelley the Playboy image kept gossip about a flamboyant lifestyle circulating throughout the community. No matter how many times Shelley assured Lucille he was the man she knew at home, not the rambunctious, flirtatious entertainer on the radio and stage, she was bombarded by stories and chinwag. By the end of the year, the marriage was on shaky ground.

There was another problem, a familiar one as well. Money.

As he prepared to file taxes in early 1964, Shelley realized what a mess the record store bookkeeping was in. His accountant had greatly overstated the store's receipts, maybe to make Shelley happy, but the result was a staggering bill from the Internal Revenue Service and the state tax collectors.

Then, to make matters worse, someone—Shelley suspected it was Lucille—informed the IRS that he had under-reported his income from the platter parties. They were a cash business, of course, and Shelley was aware that he had relied on a very informal pay system with no deductions. Soon, tax collectors were visiting each of the promoters who hired him for the platter parties, instructing them to garnishee his appearance fees until the tax debt could be settled.

Shelley saw only one way out. He had received a job offer from KATZ radio in St. Louis. The big-market salary was far more than he made at WJLD and the many platter parties.

Though not proud of his decision, Shelley left Lucille, dissolving the marriage, and moved to St. Louis, fleeing from the financial straitjacket and marital strife. His plan was to send her all the money he could after living expenses to take care of the children and try to keep up the mortgage on the house. Even so, the bank foreclosed on their home and Lucille moved back to Columbus, Georgia, with Kip and Sherri.

As usual, Shelley lost himself in work. He did the morning show on KATZ and immediately found a large, enthusiastic audience. Then, two nights a week, he performed at a bar, drawing several hundred people to a venue designed for seventy. Soon he had added a night gig at another club and was making, altogether, more than $600 a week.

Then one day he looked at his KATZ check and it was less than half what it had been. The IRS had caught up with him. Now, after paying rent on a tiny basement apartment and buying food, he had no money to send to his kids or to make his car payment. The Buick was repossessed and only through the kindness of a fan was he able to get a loan for a new car.

Shelley was losing himself in a different form of anesthesia, too. Liquor. Without realizing how far he had fallen, he would start his show each morning after having downed a couple of drinks. He drank before lunch, had a few while he ate, and had many more each night as he did his act at the clubs. Without realizing it, his bar tab at the clubs equaled the talent fee he earned. He was working for nothing.

With no other choice, he stopped making payments on the new car. Knowing repossession was imminent, he parked his vehicle blocks away from the station and walked in to work, and he left it at different locations distant from his apartment each day and hiked home.

The station tried to help, giving him part of his salary out of petty cash so he would not be flat broke each payday and arranging for him to eat at restaurants that owed the station money for advertising. Shelley's pleas to the IRS for a payment plan were ignored. Instead, they threatened to send him to prison. With nowhere else to turn, Shelley turned to more drinking.

ONE DAY, AS THE world closed in around him, Shelley asked a friend to drop him off on the Mississippi River bridge into Illinois to "do some sightseeing." For a while, he stood there at the railing watching the dark, swirling water far below. He had not been aware that he was considering ending his life, but as he stood there, trembling in the harsh wind, it did occur to him.

Something inside him quickly wiped away that thought. He turned and walked back into Missouri, straight to a liquor store. He bought the biggest bottle of cheap whiskey he could find and then checked into a fleabag hotel not far from the bridge. There he proceeded to drink himself into a stupor.

Almost immediately the visits began. Mattie C. She began to preach to him, to remind him that he had not followed her advice. She showed him reminders of his childhood, his daddy striking her with an ax and her flying through the window into the clutches of the tree, him and his brothers on Slim's and Marie's back porch, shivering in the cold wind and eating the fried gopher rats, the beatings and humiliation from Slim and Aunt Emily, the graduation ceremony in which his name was not called for the scholarship, the electric shock treatments in the military hospitals.

Look, Shurley! Look! You are not seeing these things so you'll feel sorry for yourself. Lord knows you've done enough of that already.

Then he also saw the times he stood up and promised himself he would make something of himself, saw himself speaking to the crowd in the mirror, heard the voice of his first-grade teacher reminding him how

smart he was and that he would be something someday, and her standing up and shouting "That's my boy!" at graduation, saw himself as he
worked a platter party crowd into a frenzy and brought them back down
again and worked the high school roll call on the radio station, saw himself before a big microphone telling the children marchers to wear their
raincoats and pack their toothbrushes as they went out to do something
important and lasting.

Those last images were even harder to watch than were the ones that
depicted misery, the beatings, the crushing disappointments.

Self-pity ain't going to get you there, Mattie C. told him, her voice becoming
angrier as she went. *You promised me that you was going to do so much better
than your daddy did, son. And look at you. Look where you are.*

Shelley thrashed in the sweat-soaked sheets. He pulled the pillow over
his head to try to shut out her voice and the images flashing before him.
Then, when that did not work, he turned up the big bottle and swigged the
bitter whiskey down until it was all gone. Then he passed out.

That did not stop it all, though. At one point, he felt blows being in-
flicted on him, fists pounding into his gut and chest, as if some frustrated
angry somebody was giving him a good beating. He struggled for breath
and writhed with pain until it all stopped.

Then, finally, he slept, dreamless.

Sometime late on the second day, Shelley awoke. He felt awful. Not the
least of it was his bruised and battered ribs and stomach. He finally pulled
himself up to sit on the edge of the bed, fighting nausea and struggling to
breathe. His chest hurt bad when he tried to suck in air.

He saw a slight movement out of the corner of his eye. Momma? Was
she back for more?

No, he had seen himself reflected in the cracked mirror on the tiny dresser.
The image was horrible. He looked terrible, unshaven, eyes bloodshot, and
his chest black and green with bruises. He blinked hard and tried to stand,
to remove that unlikely likeness of himself from view.

Then there was a knock on the motel room door. It was the maid. She
looked hard at him, her eyes wide, and Shelley thought for a moment she
might run from the sight of him.

"Sorry, sir. You ready for me to change . . . hey! You the one they looking for."

"Ma'am?"

"You that Shelley the Playboy, that deejay. They looking for you."

Sure enough, when he did not show up for work at KATZ that first morning, they notified the police. Then his friend came forward to tell them about leaving Shelley on foot on the river bridge. Everyone made the assumption that he had jumped into the Mississippi. The police had been dragging the river, searching for his body.

Shelley quickly got on the phone and informed the police and the station manager that he was still alive, though he still felt that he might perish any minute. A hot shower helped. So did a shave.

When he got to the station, he talked with the manager and explained that he needed to talk with his wife, to try to make things right. He had no telephone but the manager told him to use the station phone.

The chat with Lucille did not go well. She told him he was washed up, his career over, and she did not want anything else to do with him.

Even so, when he hung up, Shelley felt better. He had tried. And he would keep trying. He desperately wanted to be a part of his children's lives. At that moment, he decided that this quick sojourn to St. Louis was over, that he needed to move back closer to where his children—all three of them—lived.

At his last show at the bar, he put on what he felt was his best performance ever. The bartender as well as people in the audience kept pouring him shots of whiskey as reward for the job he was doing. Shelley did not touch a drink.

At the end of the night, at least a dozen glasses of whiskey were lined up along the bar. They were still sitting there when Shelley walked out the door, headed for the next chapter in his life.

28

OTIS

First stop on his roundabout trip back home took Shelley to Georgia. He accepted a job at WAOK, Atlanta's top-rated black radio station. The town billed itself as "the city too busy to hate," a direct slap at Birmingham to the west, where bombs still exploded in homes of black leaders, at the A. G. Gaston Motel, and even at the epicenter, Sixteenth Street Baptist Church, where four girls died.

Meanwhile, Atlanta was booming. Its airport, a major hub for Delta Airlines, was already one of the country's busiest by the late 1950s and major corporations were either opening branches there or moving their corporate headquarters there.

Again Shelley the Playboy was one of the most popular personalities on his station. He was soon getting reacquainted with some of the top artists of the day who made Atlanta a stop on their tour circuits. That included Aretha Franklin, Wilson Pickett, the O'Jays, the Temptations, Jackie Wilson, and others. He also developed relationships and had deep discussions with political figures like Andy Young and Julian Bond. Martin Luther King and his wife, Coretta, often hosted him for dinner at the Birdcage Restaurant, one of their favorite spots. There King made it a point to tell Shelley how much he appreciated his help in Birmingham. King admitted to him that he had never truly understood how to use local media in his movement and Shelley had taught him some things.

King always picked up the tab for dinner. That was a good thing. The IRS had quickly located Shelley in Atlanta and continued to take a large chunk of his weekly paycheck from WAOK. He could not have afforded an appetizer at the Birdcage.

Despite these relationships, it was a lonely time for Shelley. He fell into his usual work routine, determined to do a good job for the station and for the promoters who booked him for platter parties. Then he went home and thought of Momma, Bubba, his brothers, and his kids. It took an especially good friend from his past to help Shelley overcome the oppressive lonesomeness.

Otis Redding was quickly becoming a major star and he lived just down the highway in Macon. Anytime he was in Atlanta to perform or conduct business, he made certain to spend some time with Shelley. At one point, Redding gave Shelley a beautiful diamond ring to show his gratitude for his help and friendship. Though there were times Shelley contemplated pawning it to buy food and pay rent at the little boardinghouse where he lived on Fair Street, he never did.

Then Redding offered Shelley something far more valuable than a piece of jewelry. He offered him a job.

REDWAL MUSIC HAD BEEN started by Phil Walden. It was primarily a talent agency in Macon, mostly booking bands for fraternity parties around the southeast. The first major artist to sign with Walden for management was Otis Redding. Eventually RedWal Music was incorporated with Redding, Walden, and Walden's brother, Alan, as its principals. The company was revolutionary for its time because its ownership and management was racially integrated. That and the fact that few artists then had ownership in the company that managed them.

Soon, in addition to Redding, the company represented such artists as Sam & Dave, Percy Sledge, Johnnie Taylor, Clarence Carter, Arthur Conley, Al Green, Joe Tex, Albert King, William Bell, Eddie Floyd, and Etta James. Even more lucratively, they would hold publishing rights over the years to many of their artists' hit songs such as "Respect," "I Can't Turn You Loose," "Sweet Soul Music," "When a Man Loves a Woman," "I've Been Loving You Too Long," and "Dock of the Bay." By 1965 the company was second only to Motown—the company started by Shelley's old friend, Berry Gordy—when it came to management of black artists.

The Waldens and Redding hired Shelley as director of public relations—a significant step for a black man in the music industry at that time—and his primary job was promoting Redding. That entailed traveling with him at times to help out at shows and to make sure radio personalities who played his records had access to the superstar. Shelley understood how important that relationship could be.

One night on a long flight from somewhere to somewhere else, Otis asked Shelley a loaded question.

"Brother, you sure do seem down in the dumps sometimes. Anything I can do?"

Shelley never wanted to burden others with his own problems but Otis was enough of a friend that he felt moved to answer directly. He talked about being away from his kids and rarely seeing them. Redding understood. He also hated leaving his family behind for all the travel he was doing those days. Then Shelley shared with Otis the debilitating burden of the tax problems and how the constant pressure had bled him of much of his spirit.

Shelley was not asking for help, but Redding immediately offered it.

He set some of the company's high-pressure accountants to negotiating with the Internal Revenue Service on Shelley's behalf. They were not intimidated by the IRS's bluster. The same tax collectors who had threatened Shelley with immediate payment-in-full quickly accepted a fraction of the original lien as a settlement. The only requirement was that it be paid in its entirety. Then Redding gave Shelley a check for $6,000, the entire amount. It was a no-strings-attached gift.

Shelley was stunned by the star's generosity. It was true that the money was relatively not that great, considering Redding's success. However, his willingness to help an old friend was certainly not typical of all artists. Otis's unselfish kindness was even more important to Shelley than actually getting out from under the debilitating stress of the debt. There had been times lately when Shelley had renewed doubts about the basic goodness of mankind. This gentle singer of mostly sad songs had just restored his confidence.

Of course, Shelley worked even harder for the company once the burden of the IRS lien was lifted. He booked Redding into some of the bigger clubs in New York and was key in planning and hosting a major event for disk jockeys at the star's home in Macon.

THEN, WHEN HE LEAST expected it, radio called again.

Shelley confessed to the Waldens and Redding that he missed being on the air, reacting to his listeners, and told them that WJLD back in Birmingham had offered him a job as program director. Just the fact that his old station was offering him a management position was incentive enough to go back home. RedWal understood and worked out a deal in which Shelley could take the radio job and still work as a consultant for Redding and the company.

Shelley suddenly had the best of both worlds. He could use his creativity and innate ability to discern what listeners wanted on the radio so he could craft a successful station with WJLD. He could continue his affiliation with his friends at RedWal and assist Otis as his career continued to build toward the stratosphere.

Not long after settling back in Birmingham, Shelley had a conversation with Redding that would prove tragically prophetic. The artist had begun flying to most concerts, sometimes taking risks with weather and out-of-the-way airports. Otis believed flying kept him fresher for his high-energy performances than long, tiring bus rides would have. Plus, it let him get home more often to see his wife, Zelma, and his kids. Shelley had forcefully recommended against so many flights, using unknown pilots and rented aircraft with shaky maintenance records. Shelley offered to help redesign a tour schedule that would keep him from taking all those perilous trips and still give him time home with his family, and to write and record.

"No problem, Shelley," Otis assured him one day when Shelley was giving him a tough time. "I got it solved, man. I got me a twin-engine Beechcraft airplane. It's way yonder faster getting where I want to go and bringing me back home."

For some reason Shelley felt a twinge of dread.

TWO WEEKS BEFORE CHRISTMAS, 1967, Otis called Shelley at home. It was Sunday and Shelley was sleeping in, but his friend seemed excited.

"Shelley, I'm in Cleveland and I got a big show in Madison, Wisconsin, tonight. Why don't you let me swing down to Birmingham and pick you up and you can come up here with me and see what we are doing with the show? I'm gonna do 'Dock of the Bay' tonight. We can catch up and I'll have you home in time for your show in the morning."

Shelley would have loved to spend some time with his friend. However, something besides being up all night, flying back and forth, made him decline the offer.

Later that Sunday, word came that Redding's new airplane had gone down a mile short of the runway in Madison, crashing into a cold lake. Redding and six others died. Only one person aboard, the trumpeter for the BarKays, Redding's backup band, survived the crash. A song Redding had recorded only three days before in Memphis, "Dock of the Bay," was released shortly afterward and became his biggest-selling single.

Of course, Shelley cried, just as he had when he lost Bubba. He had lost a good friend, someone almost as close to him as a brother.

But he thought long and hard about something else. There had been that voice in his head yet again, advising him.

Was it Mattie C.? Was she the one who had given him the warning not to take the trip with Otis?

Regardless where it came from, the advice had certainly saved Shelley's life. Once again, he had been spared. But for what?

He vowed to use this new opportunity he had been given to do something special with his life.

29

BeACON of BIRMINGHAM

Birmingham was a lighthouse beacon for Shelley Stewart. No matter where he was, no matter the hardships he had suffered in that place, the city seemed to always beckon for him to come back. Each time he did, he realized anew that shoals and whirlpools awaited and they could do some serious damage.

Upper management had changed at WJLD, and Shelley was able to recruit top talent to the station to complement him and his show. Shelley quickly used that newfound clout to try to change things, insisting that a well-qualified black secretary be hired when there was an opening. One would need an understanding of the times to realize what a victory that simple hire was.

In April 1968, Dr. Martin Luther King was assassinated in Memphis. Shelley talked on the air about his experiences with King and openly cried in mourning. He had not agreed with King on everything, but he knew what the man had done for blacks everywhere with his nonviolent methods. Across the nation, flags were lowered to half-staff to honor the man who helped change history.

At least flags were lowered everywhere but over Birmingham City Hall. That flag simply was not put up at all the day after the assassination.

Shelley was furious. Why, of all cities, would Birmingham ignore this tragic death, especially after all that King had done right there? He blasted the city's new mayor during the morning broadcast on WENN. George Seibels was a moderate Republican but had built a strong reputation for fairness while positively leading the city away from its racist past. To Shelley, that made the city's lack of respect even harder to fathom.

The mayor was on the telephone by the time Shelley started up his next record.

"Shelley, George Seibels. I heard about what you were saying on your radio show this morning."

"Mr. Mayor, thank you for calling in. Now, you tell me why flags are at half-staff all over America for Dr. King, but not right here in Birmingham, Alabama, where the man faced death to fight segregation. Why did you all not even put up a flag at all?"

"Shelley, the flag is not up because it's raining. We don't raise the flag when it rains."

Shelley looked out the studio window. There had been a light sprinkle earlier, maybe.

"Mr. Mayor, you telling me you have people put up the flag according to the weather?"

"Now, Shelley, listen. It's not even 9 A.M. yet. Some days we don't get that flag up until . . ."

Shelley saw red. He interrupted the mayor's weak explanation.

"I tell you this, sir. If that American flag is not put up at half-staff to honor the memory of Dr. King, there will be hell to pay!"

And Shelley hung up on the mayor of Birmingham.

Afterward Shelley considered that he may have been a bit abrupt and disrespectful to the city's top elected official. After all, Seibels was nearly an opposite to previous Birmingham city leaders when it came to racial discrimination. Still, it was a sad day in history and the message being sent by City Hall in Shelley's hometown was the wrong one, especially given this city's particular history.

Soon Shelley got a call from a listener that the flag at City Hall was up, flying halfway up the pole.

However, his emotional tirade on WJLD had set in motion events that would again have Shelley on the move, out of Birmingham and back again. The station manager was upset by what he saw as his program director's impertinence for Mayor Seibels. Another announcer was named WJLD's new program director; his first task was to fire the old one, Shelley.

When news got out about Shelley's termination, picketers showed up in front of the studios, carrying signs and chanting, "We want Shelley! We want Shelley!" After a few days, Shelley called them off. He was not so certain he wanted to work for folks like those anyway.

This time he knew that he had lost his job by taking a stand he was certain was right. He was confident yet another door would open for him. One quickly did, and it took him in a most unusual direction.

WITHIN TWO DAYS OF being fired, Shelley got a call from Nashville, Tennessee. Shelby Singleton was one of the more prosperous music promoters and record-label owners in Music City, his success based on an unusual mix of country and R&B acts. His biggest success had come with former Music Row secretary Jeannie C. Riley and her ten-million-selling story song, "Harper Valley PTA." Singleton knew of Shelley from his work with Otis Redding and Phil Walden and he wanted him to help recruit black artists. Still, much of Shelley's work involved booking the country artists. He often had to employ a "white" voice on the telephone to get concert promoters to even talk to him. Many were never aware that they were helping break new ground in Nashville by working with a black booking agent to secure white country talent.

During his time back at WJLD and then in Nashville, Shelley still found time to drive down Highway 280 to Columbus and visit with his children, Sherri and Kip. The visits usually ended up with him arguing with Lucille. Also, Sherri often cried when he left and begged to be able to go live with him. He loved seeing the children, but it usually meant a tearful drive back north from Columbus. Family closeness continued to be just out of reach.

Of course, the beacon of Birmingham beckoned yet again. While he enjoyed being a part of the music industry in Nashville, it was difficult to turn down the offer he received from WENN-AM to come back to town, to be back on the radio and doing his thing for such an appreciative audience. They always were willing to follow him from one spot on the dial to another, and to bide their time while he was off someplace else until he popped up again on the Birmingham airwaves.

There was another factor this time, too. A powerful one. Cy Steiner, after working in radio and TV sales and as an account executive in an ad-

Shelley at control board during broadcast.

vertising agency, had finally realized his dream of starting his own agency. He wanted Shelley to be a partner in the venture. Steiner and Stewart both knew that in Birmingham, even with things slowly changing, it would not be acceptable for a black man to be a business partner with a white man. For the time being, Shelley would be a silent partner in a struggling agency, one that was just trying to get its client list and reputation established. But a partner, nonetheless.

Shelley knew that if he were still living elsewhere it would be difficult for him to bring to the agency table all he could offer. The WENN job offer—although for less money than he was making in Nashville—came at the perfect time. He vowed this would be his last move. Birmingham would be his home from now on. Besides, he barely had enough money to make another jump, even if he had wanted to. Most of what he earned went to child support and he could never get ahead.

A DAY OR TWO after returning to Birmingham, Shelley got a phone call from Al Bell, a former disk jockey in Arkansas who went on to become part-owner of the legendary Stax Records label in Memphis. He told Shelley that he and Isaac Hayes (songwriter, studio musician, "Theme from *Shaft*") had been talking about his return to the airwaves and wanted to do a "Welcome Home Shelley the Playboy" show for him. There was no mention of the event being a benefit. Bell told him such acts as Johnny Taylor, the Staple Singers, the Dramatics, Hayes and his group, and the surviving members of Otis Redding's band, the BarKays, had committed to be there.

WENN was not doing much promotion around his coming back to Birmingham so Shelley agreed, in principle, to the offer. There was one concern, though. He had no idea how he would pay the fees for all those top stars who were coming in for the show. If something happened and the event did not draw as well as expected, Shelley would be ruined. When he tried to discuss his concerns with Bell, the record company exec hung up on him. So did Isaac Hayes when he asked him the same questions. Stax wired Shelley enough money to secure the town's biggest concert venue, Boutwell Auditorium. Then they sent him thousands of handbills to distribute and tack up all over town.

The other personalities on WENN refused to even mention the show. Still, the building was packed and the performances that evening were spectacular. Johnny Taylor did a song he had just recorded, "Who's Making Love," that would soon become a million-seller. Isaac Hayes performed "Soul Man," a song he had written for the duo Sam and Dave that had topped the charts as well.

All night long, though, Shelley was worried about whether they had taken in enough ticket money—even from the sold-out house—to cover the show's expenses, including the fees of the top-line acts that had put on such a powerful show for everyone. Shelley had a good idea of what it cost to book these acts and when he did the math, he knew it was going to be tight.

Pops Staples was the business manager that night and he called everyone into an office backstage at Boutwell after the show was over. Huge stacks of cash money covered a desk. Staples pulled to the side a couple of stacks of bills "to cover travel expenses for the groups," he explained. A couple more stacks were set aside to cover the cost of the sound system, security person-nel, and other incidentals. That left a sizeable pile of greenbacks on the desk, but now Shelley knew for certain that it would not pay for the talent that had performed on his behalf that evening. He felt sick to his stomach.

Johnny Taylor, who already had number-one hit records, had trouble remembering names, so he called everyone "Pete." He put an arm around Shelley's shoulders.

"Aw right, Pete. Tell you what. You can just keep my part."

One by one, the other stars told him the same thing. The remaining money stacked up on the desk—about $24,000—was Shelley's. Tears streamed down his face as he profusely thanked each of them for their generosity.

"Hell, Shelley, you earned it," Hayes told him in his deep bass voice. "I could count the radio personalities on one hand who have done as much good for our people and our music. You earned it. And we probably owe you a hell of a lot more. Now quit crying and take the damn money!"

Then, instead of rushing out for an after-show party somewhere, they bowed their heads as a group and each man said a prayer. Shelley thanked God out loud for the generosity of these artists whose talents he so greatly admired.

And, much more quietly, he thanked Him once again for blessing such an unworthy man with a mother who loved him so much that she continued to support him from beyond that simple grave at Grace Hill.

30

TaKiNg oFF the MaSK

Shelley still did not drop his continual search for family, the quest that so far had left him with failed marriages and no real relationship with his two surviving brothers. David had fled to California after some questionable activities in Birmingham had gone sour. Now, when David visited Alabama and stayed with Shelley, it was obvious that he was leading a lifestyle that was both shady and dangerous. Shelley worried, prayed, and tried to give David brotherly advice, but he knew that it would take a major turnaround to get his brother off the path to self-destruction.

Sam had migrated west as well—walking and hitchhiking the entire way, but Shelley rarely heard from him. He later learned Sam survived by writing poems and selling them to passersby on the street.

Meanwhile, just before Christmas in 1970, his daughter, Sherri, finally got her wish and moved to Birmingham from Columbus to live with her daddy. For the first time, Shelley was a full-time single parent, going to school events, helping with homework, shopping for things he had never even considered buying before.

The next year, Shelley met Doris Richardson and they started dating. She already had two daughters. The relationship moved to the point that Doris moved into Shelley's home in the West End section of town in the summer of 1972. Shelley knew that Sherri needed a female role model, too. But that also meant he went from having one girl in the house to being blessed with four. And Doris soon became pregnant. Their son, Corey, was born in July 1973.

As with many such "his, hers, and ours" families, there was often tension. Shelley felt Doris did not place as much value on education as he

David & Shelley, 1970.

Shelley holding brother Sam hours before he died.

did, and she did not push her girls to excel in school as hard as he did Sherri. On the other hand, Doris accused him of treating her daughters differently from his own child. Still, Shelley was determined to work through their differences, to make things far better for these children than his own upbringing had been.

One day Shelley took a telephone call at the station from his brother, Sam.

"Shurley, David's been shot. Now you and me got to kill his wife," he reported. Then Sam spun a wild tale of domestic violence that now left their gravely wounded brother David shackled to a hospital bed and under police guard. Their brother was near death and under arrest for numerous outstanding warrants.

Shelley dropped everything and flew to Los Angeles. David survived the incident and nobody killed anybody's wife, but his marriage was over. Still, despite Shelley's concern and advice, David several years later ended up in the same prison as Charles Manson and Sirhan Sirhan. Shelley visited him in that awful place, to lend support and to try get an appeal going of David's twenty-year sentence. He was unsuccessful and David eventually died of lung cancer while still incarcerated.

When Shelley visited David, he had also talked with other inmates and saw firsthand how their lack of education—so many of the convicts could not even read or write—had led other men—just like David—to take the wrong path. Everyone he spoke with had wasted what could have been a productive life, often as much out of ignorance as meanness.

Sam also eventually developed lung cancer. By that time, Shelley had the wherewithal to bring him home to Birmingham and provide the medical help he needed if not to survive to at least have a better quality of life in his last days. Sam lost his battle four months after coming back to live with Shelley.

All three of his brothers were gone. Still, Shelley knew he had done Mattie C.'s bidding in trying to help his brothers. He also knew that their dysfunctional upbringing had saddled Sam and David with simply too much baggage for them to tote.

BY THE 1970S, SHELLEY was thinking about moving away from his Shelley the Playboy persona. The name fit the personality he projected on his radio show and it had certainly served him well. Most everyone in the towns where he was on the air—white or black—knew who Shelley the Playboy was and enjoyed his style.

Now, though, more than ever, Shelley wanted to remove that happy-go-lucky mask. There was a very good reason.

He had enjoyed his time in management and business with RedWal and Shelby Singleton. He was already active—but still "silent"—with his partnership with Cy Steiner and the ad agency, learning more every day and using previous relationships with some of the area's top businessmen to help the client list grow. But with all the responsibilities with Doris and the kids, he decided he had to be able to have more control over his income. That meant a move to radio sales. That would also be the only way to advance to a management position and, eventually, station ownership. Only then would he control his destiny. It was time to quit jumping from market to market and to finally settle down. Being Shelley the Playboy, a deejay, would never allow that to happen.

Shelley had made it plainly known that he wanted to apply for the next sales position that became available at WENN. His requests were not acknowledged. He finally cleaned off an unoccupied desk in the station sales area and made it his own, telling ownership that he intended to become a salesman when there was an opening for that position.

Then, in 1976, a very big door swung wide open. John McClendon passed away and some of his radio stations, including WENN, were put up for sale. Station manager Joe Lackey, along with Erskine Faush and Shelley, saw this development as a golden opportunity. They got all their paperwork in order to show how profitable the station was and secured an appointment with A. G. Gaston, by far the wealthiest black businessman in Birmingham. They made a strong case for borrowing money from Gaston's bank so the trio could purchase the station. Gaston seemed duly impressed. The three men left the meeting certain that they would receive the loan and would soon own WENN.

Gaston had been impressed by the numbers. So much so that he immediately approached the McClendon estate and bought WENN himself. For Lackey, Faush, and Stewart, that big door had been slammed shut in their faces.

Shelley and the others were stunned. And even more so when Gaston's first act as owner was to fire Joe Lackey. He told others that he did not want a white man running any of his businesses, including his new radio station.

"Joe, this is not right!" Shelley told Lackey. "We're not going to let him get away with this."

"It's all right, Shelley. I'll be okay. You know he won't keep you folks around if you buck him on this."

But Shelley had already made up his mind. Racial discrimination was wrong, regardless the race that was being discriminated against. One of Shelley's favorite expressions was, "It takes both the white keys and black keys on the piano to play 'The Star-Spangled Banner.'"

He talked to the other employees and most were willing to risk their own jobs by walking out in protest. With Shelley in the lead, they picketed the station for the next seven weeks, opposing the firing of their manager. The demonstration attracted news coverage not just locally but across the nation. Black employees protesting the unfair dismissal of a white boss? And in Birmingham, Alabama, of all places?

Despite the news coverage and the support expressed by his listeners, it was a tough time for Shelley. Doris was expecting their second child and when he walked off the job to picket, Gaston cancelled his hospital insurance. Shelley also knew that Gaston, with his vast business empire, had the assets to endure any protest he and the others might muster. The new owner could run the station at a loss for years to prove a point, and there was no doubt he would do just that.

Then one day Lackey received a phone call from the owner of another station in town, WATV. The station had studios on the top floor of the Cabana Hotel downtown and was playing a mix of adult-contemporary and easy-listening music, but with little success. The owner told Lackey that if he could bring over the whole staff of WENN—at least those who had walked out and were still faithfully picketing the station—he would change to a black-oriented format and hire everyone.

Shelley & co-workers protesting firing of white station manager.

The station, including the transmitter, tower, and studio equipment, was in terrible shape. The offices and studios in the old hotel were decrepit and cramped. Some of the new employees were afraid to ride the rickety old elevator to the top floor, though it was often out of service anyway. The on-air booth was not set up for a live, high-energy radio show. The previous format had come mostly from old reel-to-reel tape automation. There would be no money for promotion and no time to get a campaign together even if there had been. The offer was that they had to start the very next day. Still, everyone agreed this was where they needed to be, with the opportunity to do what they wanted and build the station from the ground up. Plus it would be ultimate rejoinder to Mr. Gaston to take the station and soundly beat WENN in both ratings and billing.

The station engineer spent all night rebuilding, rewiring, and using glue and ingenuity to get the studios and transmitter in as good a shape as he could, ready for Shelley to hit the airwaves the next morning. The

Shelley with Vanessa Williams (above) and Gladys Knight (right).

white engineer was still wiring things together when WATV 900 Gold AM signed on the air.

With the proven line-up and the publicity that had been generated by the protests against Gaston and WENN, the new format was an immediate hit. Folks who had been walking back and forth in front of their former radio station one day were, the very next day, part of a brand new one.

Shelley reveled in the electricity he felt from listeners. He loved the way they responded, on the phones, on the street, in church, anywhere he went. They were listening and reacting to what he said and did on WATV, just as they had ever since he uttered his first words on the air at WBCO in Bessemer.

Like the crowds in Papa Clyde's mirror, like the kids who streamed out their school windows to march for freedom, people still listened to what Shelley said and responded, to him, to his platter parties, to the sponsors for whom he advertised. After all this time, and all the coming and going, he could still turn them out.

With this exciting new situation, Shelley felt even more strongly that it was time to put the Shelley-the-Playboy mask into the drawer once and for all. That persona had served its purpose.

Then, if there had been any doubt about it, he received the strongest message in a while from Mattie C. Not as strong as the punches to his ribcage in that fleabag hotel in St. Louis, but there was no mistaking her message and the way she delivered it to her boy.

31

' TURN DOWN that RADIO '

It was the same old problem with no easy solution. Shelley now had a houseful of mouths to feed and child support payments to his son down in Columbus. Even with the new situation at WATV, he was still subsisting on a disk jockey's salary and what he could make at the platter parties. Doing sales or moving to management was still not an option for a black man.

He still put on one frenetic, entertaining show when he did the dances, but he was feeling more and more out of place in character as Shelley the Playboy. Still, he knew that the thoughtful, reserved Shelley could never get a packed house of young people going the way his alter ego could do. He needed to make money, so he postponed firing "The Playboy."

Then three omens and another door widely opened showed him the way.

On the way to a platter party one night, barreling down a two-lane highway, Shelley was stunned to see a trio of ghostly white horses suddenly appear at the side of the roadway and gallop directly toward him. He slammed on the brakes, praying no one was following too closely behind, and skidded sickeningly toward the animals. He came to a smoky stop close enough to see the wild look in the animals' eyes as they raced on past him and into the piney thicket beside the highway. When he finally caught his breath, Shelley looked toward where the horses had dashed into the woods. The encounter was so sudden and over so quickly, he could not even be sure he had seen them.

Were they real? Spirits? A sign from God and Mattie C. that he needed to do what he knew was right and give up these appearances? He drove on, hands shaking on the wheel.

A few weeks later, Shelley was on the way to another out-of-the-way venue when fatigue overcame him. He had to rise every day at 4:30 or 5 to make his morning show, and then was usually up to midnight or later, helping the kids with homework, talking with Cy Steiner about agency business, and more. He was exhausted and still had an energetic two-hour platter party to do. A nap would not hurt. He eased the car off the highway into a dark churchyard, shielded from the road by honeysuckle. He had been asleep only a few minutes when he heard voices outside the car.

"Hey, they's a drunk nigger done passed out in there."

"Find a rock and we'll bust out the window," a second voice said.

"Yeah, let's pull his damn ass out of there," came a third. "Then we'll beat the shit out of him and show him he better not come out here no more."

Shelley tried to remain as still as he could as he cautiously pulled his .357 Magnum from beneath the driver's seat. He often worked in rough neighborhoods and usually went home with cash money in a sack on the seat beside him. The gun was a necessity.

One of the scruffy white guys was drawing back, about to smash his window with a big rock, when Shelley abruptly sat up and pointed the pistol at him. He had every intention of shooting at them through the window if they were going to carry out their threat.

All three men yelped and tore off through the honeysuckle. Shelley cranked up the car and spewed gravel as he plummeted back out onto the roadway. Again, his hands trembled on the wheel. Was this another sign?

A WEEK LATER SHELLEY told Doris and the children goodbye and headed out for another platter party in the same venue as the one the previous week. As soon as he crawled behind the wheel of the car, he felt an odd sensation surrounding him, as if someone else was inside the automobile with him. He looked around, checked the mirror and the back floorboard, and shook his head hard. There was no one there. He would have to slow down, get more sleep, and stop imagining spirits in the backseat.

As he backed out into the street, he cranked up the radio's volume until it was almost painfully loud. That would keep him awake. But the peculiar atmosphere remained. It made his skin tingle.

He realized the last time he had felt such a strange sensation was the night his momma came to him as he sat in Aunt Mamie's outhouse in Collegeville.

He reached over and turned the radio up even louder and guided the car onto the main street headed south and out of town.

Turn down that radio, Shurley! It was his mother, plain as day even over the throbbing music from the car radio. *I need to talk to you, son.*

Shelley looked around, checked the mirror again. There was still no one in the car with him. Still, Momma had told him to turn down the radio so he did.

Yes, ma'am?

Listen to me, Shurley. I want you to stop going to these clubs and hosting these parties, she told him. *You are better than that. You know already you need to put Shelley the Playboy aside. That is not you and never was. It's time for you to be who you really are.*

Shelley listened to her as he drove right past the turnoff that led to the little town where that night's booking was. He was not even aware he had missed the turn and he kept driving south.

Yes, ma'am.

You know that alcohol has been the cause of so many of your bad decisions, don't you? I've told you to leave that alone. You have to quit it. It was one of the reasons that your daddy was such a mean, shiftless man and it'll ruin you and your family, too, if you let it. You can't do it if you are still The Playboy and you don't quit these dances.

Shelley concentrated on the broken white line down the center of the highway. He had no idea where he was or where he was going. He just knew he needed to keep driving as long as his mother was talking to him.

Yes, ma'am.

Things are already planned out for you, Shurley. You still have some more big things to do. Big things that will help so many people. First, though, you got to do more on the business side. Get yourself into sales at the station. Work hard. Show them what you can do. More doors are going to open. Don't let 'em back you down, son. You got a lot more to accomplish, Shurley. So much more.

When she finally left him, Shelley pulled to the side of the road and wept. Then he checked his watch. He had been driving for almost two hours! The road sign outside his windshield said "Prattville 2 miles." He was a good sixty miles south of where he was supposed to be an hour before.

Shelley did a U-turn and headed back to the platter party. He had never missed a show, or even been late for one. He felt he owed that much to the people who paid him and to those who paid to come see him. The club owners were worriedly waiting for him when he pulled up. He had shared the incident the previous week with them. Most of the crowd was still there, too, hoping he would show up.

"I'm going to get up on the stage now," Shelley told the owners, "And I'll explain."

Once behind the microphone, Shelley told everyone that he was sorry for being late. This, however, would be his last platter party ever. The Playboy was retiring. The crowd was shocked. Most of them had been coming to Shelley the Playboy's platter parties for years. He promised them this one would be the greatest they had ever attended and then he did his very best to back up that promise.

He awoke Doris when he got home that night and told her of his decision. She was worried. How could they get by on just his deejay salary? He told her he knew how much the station's two white salespeople were making and he was confident he could do as well or better. She merely shook her head and went back to sleep. But Shelley knew what had to happen.

He talked again with Joe Lackey the next day about him "carrying a list," getting a group of potential advertisers to call on and trying to sell them commercials on WATV. Lackey just waved his hand dismissively, went to his office, and closed the door.

A few days later, the station owner came to town for a visit and Shelley asked for a brief word with him. He explained to the executive that he had been talking to Lackey about a sales position, in addition to his on-the-air shift. Shelley wanted to make sure the executive knew that he wanted to apply for a sales job when a position came available. Of course, he expected a run-around and was prepared to issue an ultimatum on the subject.

"Hell, why wait?" the owner said. "I think it's a great idea!"

Shelley was stunned. So was Lackey. But just that quickly, Shelley moved into radio sales.

Of course, his list consisted of advertisers that the other two salesmen had not been able to get on the air, or in most cases had not even been able to get an appointment to see. There were still many who would not even consider advertising on a black-formatted station. Shelley's list was, in fact, the businesses the other two salespeople had given up on. Shelley ran his finger up and down the list and circled a few to get started. At the same time, he vowed to sit down across the desk from each and every one of them.

His first call was to a department store called New Ideal. The manager knew Shelley from his childhood days at the shoe store and at Yielding's. He said he would be happy to meet with Shelley and they made an appointment for the next morning, as soon as Shelley was off the air.

Shelley had been selling all his life, whether it was shoes, groceries, or musical acts booked by RedWal or Shelby Singleton. He sold every day on the air, pitching himself, the music, and his sponsors' products and services. He also knew that New Ideal would welcome dollars from blacks who would shop in the store if somebody only invited them to do so.

Shelley left the appointment with a contract for $25,000. People back at WATV were incredulous. Such contracts were rare and this rookie black salesperson had gone out and closed his very first deal for an unheard-of amount.

Soon one of the other long-time white salespeople "retired," apparently because he believed he had been put on the same level as a "Negro deejay."

SHELLEY WAS DRIVEN TO succeed, partly because he needed the income, partly because he wanted to prove something to himself and others, but mostly because his mother had told him to. At one point, Shelley was directly responsible for about eighty percent of the advertising on WATV. He did it with skill, smarts, and about as strong a work ethic as anybody in the town had seen. He kept a small journal with the names of each client on whom he called with exhaustive notes about each visit. He also made certain he visited every viable merchant or ad agency on his list every single week whether they spent thousands of dollars with him or spent nothing at all. It was work, and it put lots of miles on his automobile, but one thing Shelley had learned from Clyde Smith was the value of relationships. He was not there to sell advertising. He was there because he had a real desire to help the business succeed. He could not determine how to do that over the telephone or by dropping by only when he was in the neighborhood. He had to maintain a relationship with the client if their partnership was to be successful.

It was not always easy, of course. He was often kept waiting in a lobby before finally being told that Mr. So-and-so had left for the day. When he started calling on advertising agencies, he soon learned that several of them told the female media buyers that they were to keep their doors open any time "that Negro salesman" came calling, and were to scream for help if he made any suspicious moves toward them. Shelley was under no delusions. He knew that in addition to the usual objections any radio salesman would have to overcome he, as the first black with such a position in Birmingham—and one of the first in the entire South—would have others no one should have had to endure.

But it was what it was. He would simply work harder and smarter to overcome such garbage.

Besides, he was also in the process of walking through that other wide open door: Cy Steiner's advertising agency, where Shelley was a partner, albeit still a very well-concealed one.

Soon after he began selling radio time, Shelley the Playboy was officially retired from the radio, finally and forever. Shelley eventually came off his regular record show as well but still held onto a new talk show he had begun to do. On that program, he expanded on the social commentary that he previously had to slip in between the music, high school roll calls, and platter party promotional announcements.

There was no goodbye party or cake or testimonial dinner for Shelley's more visible alter ego. It was simply over.

It was not easy for him to slip off the mask that had led to so much acclaim and adulation. That identity was the only one most people knew, in Birmingham and the other markets, as well as throughout the music industry. Some of the people he encountered insisted on continuing to use the name when they saw him or talked with him. Shelley politely asked them not to, telling them that fellow had retired and was not coming back. Sometimes he had to tell them less politely, and when he did, they often accused him of being uppity, of thinking he was too good for his old friends, abandoning those who had made him so successful.

Shelley knew, though, that the break had to be quick and final, just like quitting alcohol and giving up the platter parties, even when there was no hope of replacing that income or notoriety.

Why?

Because Mattie C. had told him so.

'a SPOT FOR you at CITY HALL'

Shelley Stewart's role with Cy Steiner's ad agency had become more and more defined, and more and more of a contribution to the company's success. Both men had many valuable contacts within the city's business structure and they were able to mine those veins. Still, they both knew that Shelley's partnership affiliation with Steiner was a taboo that should continue to remain a secret.

Shelley's primary contributions were in the areas of marketing and public relations, especially in businesses interested in attracting black customers. His clients included a rapidly growing local chain of grocery stores and pharmacies, Bruno's, which had started as a single store in the city's Ensley section, owned by a family of Italian immigrants. Another was Parisian department stores, a Jewish-owned business that was also expanding quickly.

To maintain the clandestine nature of his affiliation with Steiner, Shelley created a separate company he called Shelley Stewart and Associates. Behind the scenes, though, he and Cy steered business each other's way, depending on the clients' needs. Steiner paid Stewart as if he was just another vendor, but Shelley often gave the money right back to him as an investment in the agency.

Later, Steiner took on New York ad man Harry Bressler as an associate to expand the agency's reach. Still, Shelley and Cy agreed to not even let Bressler know the true nature of their partnership.

By the time Doris gave birth to their daughter Corlette in March 1976, Shelley and Doris had made their union a formal one, saying their vows at the courthouse in Columbiana, not far from the site of his last dance parties. Their marriage—formal or common-law—was still far from perfect.

That could also be said about the racial atmosphere in Birmingham at that time. The city had come so very far considering its history of bigotry, stifling segregation, and police brutality, but there was still opposition—some subtle, some brutally obvious—to much of the change that was taking place so rapidly in the mid-1970s. As usual, Shelley Stewart was in the middle of it all. First, of course, through his commentaries and observations on his WATV talk show. Nobody would consider running for office, be they white or black, without making an appearance with Shelley. There they had to answer pointedly honest questions, regardless of who they were, what color they were, or for what office they were running.

Secondly was Shelley's work with a science professor and academic dean at Miles College, Dr. Richard Arrington, the son of a sharecropper. Arrington became one of the early clients of Shelley Stewart and Associates, though not necessarily an enthusiastic one. He had been elected to the city council in 1971 before as only the second black member of that body and during the 1970s gained considerable influence in Birmingham's black community through the Alabama Democratic Conference and, beginning in 1977, with a new black political organization called the Jefferson County Citizens' Coalition. At some point, he and his group hoped to back a candidate who could become Birmingham's first black mayor. Such a success in this particular city would send the strongest message possible that things really had changed in "Bombingham."

Talk had already begun that Arrington himself might someday be the best choice to run. Not everyone agreed. Many in the black business and religious communities did not even feel that the time was right to run a black candidate. Also, the white mayor who had been elected in 1975 was David Vann, a moderate who had served on the city council with Arrington. Vann, an attorney and former law clerk for U.S. Supreme Court Justice Hugo Black, had been one of the original negotiators when the Children's March forced an end to Bull Connor's tactics and the city's racist statutes. When he was elected mayor, Vann continued his progressive ways and was quite popular with the black establishment, including Arrington and his organization.

The dynamics of the campaign quickly changed in June 1979 due to a tragic event.

A white police officer, responding to a robbery call, shot to death an unarmed black woman. In the resulting fallout, Vann was caught on a slippery tightrope between blacks and progressive whites on the one hand and police organizations and conservative whites on the other. Suddenly there was an opening for Arrington.

There would be others in the race but Shelley was convinced that Arrington could beat them all.

"But Shelley, I don't have enough money to run," Arrington told him. "You know I would need Mr. Gaston and some of the others to contribute and they are in David's camp. Larry Langford's running, too, and he might get enough black votes to throw it Vann's way." Langford was a young, black former TV news reporter. "Besides that, very few whites and a bunch of blacks don't even know who Dick Arrington is."

"Dick, if not now, when?" Shelley asked him. "I can make that money go a long way, you know. People will know who you are and what you stand for by election day. I'll make sure of that."

Shelley and others finally convinced Arrington to take the risk. All were aware that if he lost, it would be seen as a repudiation of the changed atmosphere in Birmingham and an indication that a qualified black man still could not get elected mayor there.

SHELLEY WENT TO WORK. Arrington had scraped together a little less than $19,000. Word was that Vann had four times that much in his war chest and could tap Gaston and others for more if he needed it. Still, Arrington was savvy enough to know that he could only win if there was a massive black turnout on primary day. White voters outnumbered blacks, but the white vote would probably be split between the moderates for Vann and, on the conservative side, another white lawyer named Frank Parsons, who nonetheless also promised even-handedness toward all races.

Shelley was perfectly prepared for turning out the vote. After all, that was what he had been doing for years between Temptations songs and commercials on the radio.

Working mostly in the background, Shelley did what he had been doing all along and helped deliver an unprecedented black voter turnout in the October general election. There would be a runoff, but Arrington was the top candidate with 33 percent of the vote. Parsons finished second with 17 percent, and Vann was a distant fourth; the incumbent mayor did not carry a single black box.

However, Shelley and Arrington knew that if the white vote consolidated in the runoff for a single candidate, Parsons, it would be difficult for the black candidate to win. They would not only need another historic black turnout but also a significant number of white votes as well.

A few days after the first election, Shelley was taking his usual stroll through downtown, meeting and talking with people. That morning he happened by the headquarters of Frank Parsons. The men knew each other well and when Shelley waved to Parsons, the lawyer motioned for him to come inside.

"Hey, Shelley!" he shouted. "Listen, I know I can count on you to help me win this thing, right?" Shelley had kept his involvement with Arrington's campaign as quiet as he could.

"Well, I don't know, Frank."

"Look, you know I got a spot for you at City Hall when I win. I need folks like you in my administration. If I win, of course."

As the two men talked, Shelley took note of some familiar faces in the office. They were former advisors to none other than Eugene "Bull" Connor. Vann and his predecessor had effectively purged City Hall of anyone associated with Connor. Now, it appeared that those same characters had wheedled their way back into the good graces of a candidate who had a good chance of getting elected.

Without committing to anything, Shelley reminded Parsons that he was welcome to come on the talk show at WATV and they tentatively set a day. Then he took his leave.

Shelley made his way discreetly to Arrington headquarters. "We just won the election!" Shelley told workers there. He told them who he had just seen at the Parsons headquarters and how they could use that information to help elect the city's first black mayor in two weeks.

When Parsons appeared on Shelley's talk show, the candidate repeated his intention to continue improving race relations and equal opportunity. In the course of the interview, though, Shelley brought up the name of one of the key Connor operatives he had seen participating with the Parsons campaign staff. Parsons bit hard. He praised the man and assured the listeners that the man would be a key member of his staff when he was elected.

A few days later, at a candidates' forum at a community college in a mostly black area, Shelley made certain that someone in the audience asked Parsons about his choice of aides. Again the Republican proudly said the man would be one of his trusted staff members. When reminded that the man had been a member of Bull Connor's staff, Parsons realized what had just happened and offered a stammering explanation.

Film of the forum on the TV stations included that exchange. The *Birmingham News* ran a story in which the reporter specifically mentioned that Bull Connor's dark shadow had now been cast across the Parsons campaign. Later, both the *News* and the *Birmingham Post-Herald* endorsed Arrington's candidacy.

Voter turnout was almost 70 percent, an unprecedented response for a mayoral election runoff. Richard Arrington became Birmingham's first black mayor by a winning margin of only 2.2 percent. He again received almost all the black vote but also got about 15 percent of the white vote. Even so, if blacks had not registered and gone to the polls that day, the historic symbolism of electing a black mayor would likely have been postponed for years.

Shelley was elated, first that his city had come far enough to elect a black man to its highest office. That was quite a journey from the brutal, racist city Birmingham had been. He was also proud that he had proven once again that he could turn out people for something that truly mattered.

There was still a nagging thought in his head, though. Most of the votes had been cast along racial lines. Someday blacks would have to be willing to vote *against an unworthy* black man, and more than a token few percent of whites would have to be willing to vote *for a worthy* black man.

Only then would real progress have been made. Hearts and minds—of all races—still needed some work before they were all truly changed.

President Carter & Shelley at White House.

33

a VISIT with the GOVERNOR

In 1988, Shelley Stewart realized another long-held dream. With his success as a salesman and talk show host at WATV, and as a move to keep him in the fold, he was given stock in the company that owned the station. Then, when the opportunity came up, he and Erskine Faush formed Birmingham-Ebony Broadcasting and purchased the station outright.

Shelley Stewart, the former homeless boy who had to scavenge for food in dumpsters, was now a radio station owner.

Other opportunities came his way as well. He managed a local singing group, the Dynamic Soul Machine, who recorded for Stax Records. He was appointed president of the Birmingham Parks and Recreation Board.

Throughout this time, his affiliation with Steiner-Bressler Advertising was still secret, hidden behind Shelley Stewart and Associates. He and Cy still talked about making his partnership common knowledge but both agreed the time was not yet right.

A tragic event forced the issue. In 1992, Steiner, who had been suffering from debilitating depression, took his own life.

After Steiner's death, Shelley shared the true nature of his involvement with the firm with a few key members of its management team. Together, Shelley and the agency's creative director, John Zimmerman, bought out Harry Bressler. New ownership papers showed Shelley and Zimmerman as owners. That pairing would last for most of a decade before Zimmerman exited to pursue other interests.

The partnership, never formalized beyond a handshake between a white man and a black man, was now official.

Another goal had been reached. Shelley Stewart, who had once sacked groceries at Yielding's and rode the bus to Bessemer to work for free on WBCO, was now the owner of a major advertising and public relations agency with billings that soon approached $75 million a year and employed seventy-five people. Satellite offices were opened in Chicago and in Greenville, South Carolina.

Still, at Shelley's request, they kept his connection quiet for a bit longer. He was still hesitant, worried about how it might affect the agency's business. It was a big company now, and many, many people depended on its billings for their income and future. There was also a concern about how the people who worked there might accept this bolt out of the blue.

However, when the agency staff found out, they were thrilled. With everything positive to that point, Shelley finally concluded it was time to see how some of the agency's clients would accept racially integrated ownership of the company.

They decided to announce Shelley's partnership to one of the companies the agency had represented for a long time, Parisian department stores. It came at a meeting with the chain's top executive, Donald Hess. He was delighted, congratulating Shelley heartily and telling him how much he looked forward to continuing to work with him. Ronnie Bruno, the chief executive of the Bruno's grocery/pharmacy chain, was equally enthusiastic. He said he saw this announcement as a positive business breakthrough.

As Shelley shared the news with other clients and members of the community, reaction was almost universally positive. He began to wonder if they should have let the cat out of the bag sooner. Maybe not. Times had changed for the better in Birmingham slowly and relatively recently. Still, Shelley was relieved at the response.

A name change for the agency was inevitable. Most ad agencies carry a long list of last names of its partners, much like law firms and accountant groups. Shelley wanted something different, something that would connote creativity and be global in its impact. After considering many suggestions, they settled on o2 Ideas. Oxygen, after all, is one of the basic elements of life. And Shelley wanted the agency to stand for new ideas and unfettered creativity.

There was something else unusual about o2. Visitors were (and still are) greeted as often with hugs as with handshakes.

o2 Ideas flourished (and continues to do so), adding clients worldwide and doing work not only for Birmingham firms, but also for international companies that are household names, such as Verizon Wireless, Home Depot, Honda, and Books-a-Million. Shelley also proudly welcomed his daughter, Corlette, to o2 in 2003.

DESPITE ALL THE SUCCESS, Shelley vowed not to lose touch with where he came from. He made it a point to visit the alleyways and street corners where he spent so much time with fans and friends, visiting with people who kept him grounded and told him what real folks were doing and thinking. While he might eat lunch one day with a company executive in one of the top-floor private clubs in a downtown building, the next day he would enjoy soul food in any one of a number of restaurants much closer to the ground.

He also spent a great deal of time studying and learning more about prisons and what had led the inmates there to get so crossways with society that they had ended up behind bars. That visit to the California prison to see David on his deathbed had sparked something in Shelley's mind. Someday, he decided, he would do something to try to prevent all those lives from being wasted.

One day in 1992, Shelley received a visit from George Wallace Jr., the son of the former Alabama governor. He brought an invitation from his father for Shelley to come visit him.

Shelley hesitated. He had received similar invitations from Wallace in the past, including during the governor's final term in office. People were telling him that Wallace had changed, that he wanted to make amends for his inflammatory defiance of integration. Indeed, in his last election, Wallace had carried the black vote in Alabama.

But Shelley was certain that the governor's words and actions had led to people being hurt and killed. That was why he had declined any invitation to speak with Wallace. He had even turned down an invite that came with a gubernatorial proclamation of appreciation and another that arrived with flowers and a get-well card when Shelley was hospitalized with a back problem.

However, the younger Wallace was so sincere that he convinced Shelley

Shelley & George Wallace.

that his father really did want to meet him and speak with him. Shelley accepted.

The former governor was in very poor health. He had been in a wheelchair since an assassination attempt while running for president in 1972. It was clear that Wallace was a very sick man and wanted to get some things said before he passed on.

"Shelley, I want you to know that I was convinced I was doing the right thing back then," Wallace said, his voice raspy and almost incoherent. "I had strong black preachers telling me I was right about segregation and I had strong white preachers telling me the same thing. Now, if I had it to do again, maybe I'd do something different. Then, I thought I was doing the right thing. I just want you to know that."

He went on to tell Shelley that he admired him for what he had done to stand up for his people. And, almost too tired to speak any more, the former fiery politician said that he was truly sorry and asked Shelley to forgive him if his actions had hurt him in any way.

Shelley had to write much of his response on a note pad because Wallace's hearing was failing.

"Governor, I can forgive, and I will, but I cannot forget the harm you caused so many black folks. Anything else is between you and God."

The governor accepted Shelley's words graciously. Wallace died six years later.

ABOUT THIS TIME, SHELLEY decided he wanted to remodel the house he and his brothers had built in Shelby County and move his family down there. Aunt Emily had passed away in the early 1990s and at that time the deed, as Shelley had set up, made him the owner of the property. The place—still pretty much a shack without most of the modern conveniences, the way Emily preferred—was vacant. Doris informed him she had no interest in moving out to the middle of nowhere but he could go ahead and fix the place up as a get-away.

Several contractors looked the place over and recommended razing the shack and starting over. But Shelley had another idea. He asked an architect to draw up plans that would encompass the shanty as part of the new structure. He wanted to keep the house he and his brothers had worked so hard to construct.

He finally got plans he liked and a contractor who could do the work for less than a fortune. Still, there was one feature he insisted on keeping in the plans, no matter what it did to the construction budget—a blue stained-glass window with a big cross embedded in it, looking down on the home's living room. It was a monument to Mattie C., who still looked down on him every day.

By the early 2000s, and as WATV and o2 Ideas continued successfully, many had begun to forget what had happened in Birmingham in the stormy 1960s. Even Shelley, who was busy working and dealing with continuing family issues.

There were reminders, though. He still talked about the issues on his radio show, just as he always had done, and he made sure everyone knew the fight for human rights was not yet over. When he went downtown and ate at the restaurants near the old black business district, Shelley could look out on Kelly Ingram Park, an area designated by the city as "the Civil Rights District." There were monuments there now to the people who had led the charge in the early 1960s. The impressive Birmingham Civil Rights Institute had opened nearby. Sixteenth Street Baptist Church still stood tall and regal, reminding everyone of its pivotal role as well as of the tragic bombing there.

It irked Shelley that this area was called the "Civil Rights District" because the Movement had been active from Tuscaloosa to Gadsden, from north and south, from "Dynamite Hill" to Rosedale. He understood it was all about marketing, and that was the reason for the decision to focus on this area where the Children's March had made so much difference in only a few days, and where the precious little girls had died across the street at the church.

STILL, THERE WERE DAYS when the pressure of business and other distractions took him away from those days and what had happened outside the window of Shelley's Record Mart.

Then, one day in the spring of 2001, his telephone rang, and before he hung up, September 1963 was once again foremost in his thoughts. Shelley

Stewart looked out his office window for a while, contemplating the import of what he had just been asked to do.

The man on the other end of the phone line had offered him the opportunity to help lance a very old and festering wound.

34

Testifying

Martin Luther King often said that he considered himself to be a "drum major for justice." That was why the Southern Christian Leadership Conference, an organization founded by Dr. King, named their top honor the Drum Major Award. The award has gone to the likes of Hank Aaron, Bill Cosby, Oprah Winfrey, Rosa Parks, the Tuskegee Airmen, and Arthur Ashe. The list of honorees in 1992 included Harry Belafonte, Maya Angelou, U.S. Representative John Lewis, and professional basketball coach Lenny Wilkens. Also honored was Shelley Stewart, radio personality and advertising executive.

That was only an example of the prestigious recognition that would come his way over the next two decades. He was also named to the Black Hall of Fame and as one of the Outstanding People of the World. He was named a "Living Legend" in Hollywood by Warner Bros. Records, was inducted into the Smithsonian Institution as a "Pioneer of Radio," and received the "Footstep to Freedom" award from the 16th Street Foundation. In 2008, Shelley became the first African American inducted into the Alabama Broadcasters Association Hall of Fame. In 2013, he was awarded the Community Service Award by the National Association of Black Journalists.

Among Shelley's proudest accolades, though, were two from educational institutions: honorary doctoral degrees from Miles College and Faith College. The young man who did not have the "family background" to qualify for a college scholarship could now legitimately introduce himself as *Doctor* Shelley Stewart.

Shelley always considered the awards and honors to be nothing more than recognition for him doing what his mother and others told him to do, using his God-given talents to tell the truth. Mattie C. had told him to do his best to do the right thing. His first-grade teacher had told him he could do anything he wanted to do, if he learned to read and worked hard. Papa Clyde Smith taught him that love had no color, that people were people, good and bad, and that he could use his gifts to help bring good people together to accomplish great things. The plaques and certificates and degrees that were now coming Shelley's way were simply acknowledgment that he had done what he had been taught to do.

THEN, IN APRIL OF 2001, Shelley had the opportunity to use his talent to help right a wrong that had occurred almost thirty-eight years before. The terrible bomb blast at the Sixteenth Street Baptist Church on that Sunday morning in September 1963 claimed the lives of four young girls and horrified not only the city of Birmingham but the whole world.

The City of Birmingham offered an award of $52,000 for information leading to the arrest and conviction of whoever did this terrible thing. Governor George Wallace added $5,000 on behalf of the state of Alabama.

But no one was convicted of the crime for years afterward, even though there was considerable evidence immediately after the bombing implicating four Ku Klux Klan members. One, "Dynamite Bob" Chambliss—so named because of his familiarity and presumed use of the explosive against those who fought for human rights—was arrested three weeks after the bombing. However, investigators determined there was not enough evidence to charge him and he was released after paying a $100 fine for possession of explosives.

When he was elected in 1970, Alabama Attorney General Bill Baxley had vowed to solve the case. In 1977, using newly uncovered FBI evidence—evidence that had never been revealed to prosecutors, some say by direct order of FBI Director J. Edgar Hoover—he won a conviction of Chambliss in a Birmingham courtroom. "Dynamite Bob" died in prison in 1985 while serving a life sentence for the crime.

Many assumed the other three would soon be indicted and tried. That was not the case. One of the men died in 1984 without ever being brought to trial, and it would be another twenty years before the other two were brought to justice.

In 2001, U.S. Attorney Doug Jones was finally able to get an indictment against Thomas Blanton, a Klansman who had openly advocated church bombing as a way of keeping "niggers" in their place. A fourth suspect, Bobby Frank Cherry, was indicted at the same time but was ordered held for psychiatric evaluation and his trial was postponed. He would later face a jury and was found guilty.

When Doug Jones addressed the jury on the opening day of the Blanton trial, he promised that they would hear testimony from a number of people who would tie the Klansman to the crime. That included a man who, on a Saturday night two weeks before the bombing, frightened away from Sixteenth Street Baptist Church Thomas Blanton and three other white men. That witness would tell the court that three of the men remained in a car but one of the men was outside, on the sidewalk near a stairwell of the church. He carried a bag big enough to hold a dozen or so sticks of dynamite. That was likely what made up the deadly time-bomb that was placed near that same spot two weeks later. The men raced away when they realized the witness had seen them.

This compelling witness was black Civil Defense volunteer James Lay. Lay had also been one of the first on the scene after the blast and helped pull the bodies of the children from the rubble. His accounts before the grand jury had been gripping and emotional, and they were a key element of the state's case against Thomas Blanton.

There was a problem, however, and the prosecutor was aware of it at the time of his opening remarks to the jury. A few weeks before the trial started, James Lay had suffered a serious stroke. He was in very poor condition and likely would not be able to speak loudly or plainly enough for the jury to understand or hear him. The full impact of what the man saw before the explosion and the terrible things he witnessed that awful morning would have certainly been lost.

Jones had a plan, though, on how he might be able to get Lay's absorbing eyewitness account in front of the jury. He had the transcript of the testimony given before the grand jury that had helped get the indictments in the first place. Now he just had to get them admitted as testimony in the Blanton proceedings without having to call Lay to the stand.

As the dramatic trial progressed, Jones spoke with Blanton's defense attorney and suggested to him that they allow someone else to read the transcript aloud in court. The defense attorney was willing. He knew the danger of appearing to be badgering a sympathetic witness on cross-examination. Mr. Lay was not only a recent stroke victim but he was considered a hero for chasing away the would-be bombers but also for his brave actions on that Sunday morning. It was not unusual for terrorists to have a second bomb ready to go off as soon as rescuers and onlookers arrived at the scene of the initial blast. Still, Lay had plunged into the wreckage to try to help those who were injured.

Now Jones had another quandary. He needed to find someone who could do justice to the powerful testimony that so far only existed on paper, someone who could instill in the words the color they needed to convey what Lay had beheld. While searching a list of other Civil Defense volunteers who might be able to do it, a very familiar name suddenly jumped off the page at the prosecutor.

It was the name of a sergeant in the group: Shelley Stewart.

Perfect! But would Mr. Stewart, a big executive in his own advertising and marketing agency, be willing to do something controversial, something that might bounce back and hurt him and his business? There were many in the community who felt the trial was merely opening old wounds, bringing negative attention on Birmingham thirty-eight years after the fact.

Shelley, of course, was more than willing to help. He, a father of girls, still cried sometimes when he passed the church and remembered the tragedy that had taken place there. He rehearsed briefly with Jones and his team, but they knew already he was the man to do this job.

From the stand that day, Shelley read James Lay's words in his powerful, deep voice, first describing what James Lay saw the Sunday evening when, it was assumed, the Klan members were attempting to place a bomb at the church. He emphasized the certainty with which Lay felt the man carrying the black bag that night was Thomas Blanton.

Still, the most compelling part of Shelley's "performance" was Lay's recollections of what he saw when he arrived about the same time as the first ambulance at the church the morning of the bombing. He talked of digging through the rubble, of feeling something soft and still warm, and of uncovering the first little girl's body. At times, Shelley's voice was so quiet people in the courtroom had to lean forward to hear. Other times, he thundered, conveying Lay's anger as he pulled those precious children from the splinters and busted masonry that had so recently been a house of God.

The horrible details caused many in the courtroom that day to shed tears. Observers noted that Blanton himself, seated at the defendant's table, seemed shaken by what he heard.

Of course, there were other witnesses and evidence introduced, but most agreed Lay's testimony, as delivered by Shelley Stewart, was a key element in the trial. Jones, an experienced prosecutor and trial lawyer, was quoted as saying it was one of the most amazing things he had ever witnessed in a courtroom.

Blanton was found guilty and sentenced to life in prison. James Lay passed away shortly after the trial.

35

COMPLETING the CIRCLE

By the time he entered his seventies, Shelley Stewart could have slowed down, started taking it easy and enjoying the fruits of all his hard work. No one would have thought less of him for doing so.

His company was successful. His legacy was secure. He had been recognized far and wide for his accomplishments against unbelievable odds. (As one pundit put it, "Horatio Alger would have given up in 1939 had he been saddled with Shelley's upbringing.") He carried on an exhausting speaking schedule that took him to schools, churches, civic groups, and other venues.

There had certainly been disappointments and frustrations. He had never enjoyed the family relationships he craved so desperately. He had not been able to free his brothers, Sam and David, from the demons that haunted them from birth. Even in the 2000s, he still saw racial prejudice—from both sides—that broke his heart. He also saw statistics and heard heartbreaking stories about school dropouts and how many of them went on to serve time in prison, especially among young black men and women and lower-income whites.

He decided to talk with Mattie C. about what they might do about solving some of this. One afternoon, as he did almost weekly, he got in his car and drove down what was now Martin Luther King Boulevard to Grace Hill Cemetery. His mother's presence was stronger there, it seemed.

Shelley was standing there by her grave, enjoying the peacefulness of the place, when an older gentleman walked up beside him.

"Are you Shelley Stewart?" the man asked.

"Yes, sir, I am."

The man explained he was on the maintenance committee for the cemetery.

"I don't know how to tell you this, Mr. Stewart, but your mother is not buried here. She's over yonder."

The man pointed to a spot a hundred feet away. Shelley was suddenly too dizzy to notice.

Since he was old enough to walk this far, and then when he learned to drive, he had been coming to Grace Hill, sitting here next to this grave, talking with his mother. And she had talked back to him. How was it possible? How had he been coming to the wrong grave for over sixty years? And why had nobody told him before now?

He somehow thanked the man and walked over to the weed-covered spot of sand the gentleman had indicated. He knelt in the dirt, not caring about getting the knees of his expensive suit pants dirty, and angrily pulled and snatched at the cocklebur and Johnson grass and snaky honeysuckle.

You know I'm not here, Shelley. I'm not over there, either. Her voice was clear as the blue sky above and the songs of the mockingbirds in the bushes alongside the graveyard. *I'm with you. I've always been with you. And with Jerome and Sam and David, too.*

That was when Shelley had the most profound thought: he could not mourn someone who never died. And Mattie C. Stewart had never died. Just as she promised him, she had never left him.

He watered the weeds on his mother's newfound grave with a stream of tears. He knew he would continue to come to this place, just to feel closer to her. But now he fully understood that his mother had been, was, and always would be wherever he was.

Shelley also knew what he had to do. In 2007, he founded the Mattie C. Stewart Foundation. The organization would work with educators, community leaders, and other interested groups to reduce school dropout rates and encourage young people to graduate. He based the mission on what Mamie Foster, his teacher way back at Union Baptist Church School had told him: "If you learn to read, you can be anything you want to be."

Shelley penned an article for *AdAge*, the primary trade publication for the advertising business, in which he said, "It takes us all—rich and poor, black and white, haves and have-nots—to unite and improve the quality and quantity of education in this country. Without it, we are all at risk."

The foundation created a documentary film, *Inside Out*, in which prison inmates tell their powerful stories and urge kids not to drop out and make the same mistakes they did. They were the same stories Shelley heard over and over when he visited his brother in the California prison.

One of the organization's primary visuals is a bus—half school bus and half prison transport bus—an image that came to Shelley as a revelation one day when he saw a bus load of prisoners leaving for a day's work on the prison farm. Facts stream across the foundation's web site: dropouts are six times more likely than high school grads to commit a crime and go to jail; 75 percent of America's prison inmates are high school dropouts; more than 80 percent of prison inmates are functionally illiterate. There is also a countdown clock that recycles every twenty-six seconds, illustrating that a student drops out of school on average that often.

In January 2013, Shelley's daughter, Sherri, became executive director of the Foundation. She had worked with Shelley previously for years at WATV and then for its owners after Shelley sold his interest in the station.

"The meteoric rise in the impact of the Mattie C. Stewart Foundation has been amazing to observe. It is humbling to not only serve in this organization named after my grandmother, but to also see how her legacy lives on through America's children, whose lives are being saved by the Foundation's message," Sherri Stewart said in a press release.

Shelley believes that each of the tragic events in his own life ultimately led to something triumphant. He knows—and shares with the many groups to whom he speaks—that he could have given up. He might well have ended up as so many have (including his own brothers), a victim of circumstances, had it not been for one insatiable trait: reading. That and the constant guidance of his mother.

As O2 IDEAS CONTINUED to prosper in the 2000s, and as its total number of employees approached one hundred, it became clear that the company needed much more office space. They had simply outgrown their home on Birmingham's Southside. Shelley also wanted room for the Foundation somewhere in the same space as the agency.

However, he was still reluctant to move. The current office location was in two buildings, one of them a historic structure (built in 1892, it was the first gas-lit house in the city). It was just over the hill from Rosedale. It was also not far from the route Shelley had taken the day he, a six-year-old child, decided to leave Aunt Emily's place on foot and go looking for Bubba.

However, in the old locations people were literally on top of each other or constantly running between buildings. Shelley knew a space more conducive to creativity and a positive work environment was needed. The search began but nothing seemed to quite meet the company's needs.

Then one day in the midst of a busy morning, Shelley's telephone rang. It was the real estate agent who was assisting in the hunt.

"Mr. Stewart, I've got another space to show you," he said, but did not sound all that enthusiastic.

"Tell me about it then. But I don't know if I can look at anything today. Or tomorrow."

"Well, it's a whole floor, 25,000 square feet, nice, newer building."

Shelley had deliberately not restricted his search to any particular area of town. He just wanted space that would meet their unique needs. Still, he had to ask before he told the agent that he was simply too busy to take a look. "Where is it located?"

"It's off Lakeshore, where the old Edgewood Lake used to be."

There was nothing but a slight hum on the telephone line for a full fifteen seconds.

"Edgewood Lake?"

"Yes, sir."

"How soon could you meet me there?"

When Shelley hung up the telephone, he sat there for a moment, a smile on his lips and a tear rolling down each cheek.

"Momma, this could be it. The circle might finally be complete."

～

Shelley's last radio broadcast, 2002.

Shelley and Doris Stewart with Lou Rawls.

Top, as commencement speaker at Jacksonville State University; bottom, with James Bevel and Oscars for Mighty Times, The Children's March.

Rosa Parks & Shelley, 1997.